3

(· L

8. 6.97

D1429060

SPECIAL RELATIONSHIPS

Special Relationships
America in Peace and War

by

Sir John Wheeler-Bennett
G.C.V.O., C.M.G., O.B.E., F.B.A

© Sir John W. Wheeler-Bennett 1975

All rights reserved. No part of this publication may be reproduced or transmitted, in any form or by any means, without permission.

SBN 333 18401 7

First published 1975 by
MACMILLAN LONDON LIMITED
4 Little Essex Street London WC2R 3LF
and Basingstoke
Associated companies in New York Dublin
Melbourne Johannesburg and Delhi

Printed in Great Britain by
WILLMER BROTHERS LIMITED
Birkenhead

For
RUTH
with my devoted love
JOHN

The Author

Contents

List of Illustrations

Introduction

THE previous volume of my recollections, *Knaves, Fools and Heroes*, gave some account of my life and experiences in Europe during the years between the wars.

The present volume tells of my discovery of America as a young man in the early twenties and of the special relationships which I formed there, both in my love for the country and in my personal romance. It also deals with my more mature years, my war service in the United States and in Britain. It begins in the Age of Affluence in America before the Great Depression of the thirties; it concludes on the threshold of the Nuclear Age into which we were ushered by that blinding flash which pierced the skies above Los Alamos, New Mexico, in July 1945.

There is adventure in this narrative and also reflections and memories, both grave and gay. I offer it with all humility and with the warning that my life in the period between the beginning of the Nuclear Age and that of our world today, which Peter Drucker has called the Age of Discontinuity – the one being a corollary of the other – will, I hope, be the subject of a third volume.

My loving thanks are due to my wife Ruth, who has listened to the reading of the M.S., and has proved my most discerning, trenchant and constructive critic. I am also deeply grateful to those of my friends who have helped me in many ways, either by reading the typescript, in whole or in part, and giving me the benefit of their criticism, or by aiding me in establishing facts, dates and quotations. These include Sir Isaiah Berlin, the late Sir James Butler, Lord Caccia, Professor Francis Carsten, Martha Brestead and Jack Greenway, Lord Inchyra, the late Philip Kaiser, Mr Harold Macmillan, Aubrey and Constance Morgan, Anthony Nicholls, and my charming niece Sara Risher.

I owe, and acknowledge with thanks, the title of Chapter 4, 'Muffled Mission', to the suggestion of Professor Arthur M. Schlesinger, Jr.

The London Library, the Library of the Royal Institute of International Affairs and the research department of the Imperial War

INTRODUCTION

Museum have provided once again their kind, patient and efficient services.

I am once more indebted to Mrs Sybil Cook for her pertinacity, patience and success in deciphering and transcribing my execrable handwriting, and to my friend Rex Allen, who has most kindly read and corrected the proofs.

As always, I offer my sincerest thanks to my editors at the house of Macmillan, Alan Maclean and Richard Garnett, to whose wise suggestions and kind encouragement I am much beholden.

Garsington Manor,   J. W. W.-B.
Oxford,
June 1975

On Discovering 'God's Own Country'

MY association with Canada and the United States goes back for over a hundred years. On a day in July 1863 my great-grandmother, an elderly widow with one daughter, stood on the sidewalk of the main street of Culpeper, Virginia, and watched the return of the Confederate Army from the holocaust of Gettysburg. A nation had died on that stricken field among the rolling farmlands of Pennsylvania, and when, on the third day of the battle, Pickett's Virginian veterans touched, but could not hold, Cemetery Ridge, the forces of the Confederacy lost the power to attain victory. Now the Army of Northern Virginia had begun its long, tragic, bloody retreat southwards to the defence of Richmond and eventual surrender at Appomattox.

It did not need a great strategist to recognise that the future held nothing but ultimate defeat. Although the Army of Northern Virginia fought gallantly to the end, something had gone out of them at Gettysburg, something irreplaceable. Ruby Anne Hill knew that never again would these beloved soldiers return to Culpeper in a soldierly formation. When the last files of the rearguard, the Third Corps, commanded by her kinsman Ambrose Powell Hill, resplendent in the glory of his auburn hair and beard and his red battle-shirt, had disappeared into the dusty shadows, she had taken a momentous decision. She knew that it would not be long before the Army of the Potomac would follow Lee's retreating grey forces. She did not wish to live in occupied territory; she would not take the oath to the Union. She was a loyal Confederate; she believed in the right of a sovereign state to secede from the Union.

She was also a woman of courage and determination. Accompanied by her daughter she took what little gold she had and passed through the Federal lines, entered the hostile North, and, traversing fanatically abolitionist New England, came at last to the Maritime Provinces of what was not yet the Dominion of Canada. There she found asylum in a tiny village called Economy, hard by the provincial town of Truro, Nova Scotia. The old lady did not long survive this remarkable anabasis, but her daughter, my grandmother, soon married a young local attorney named Alexander McNutt, who came of good Scottish stock and irreproachable United Empire Loyalist ancestry. The U.E.L. is a kind of male equivalent of the Colonial Dames in America and represents those families who refused to accept United States citizenship and wishing to remain subjects of the British Crown, migrated from the rebellious American colonies to the loyal Canadian provinces.

The United States Congress and certain of the State legislatures were not ungenerous in compensating these emigrant Tory families, some of whom were shrewd enough to acquire recompense from the British Government also. Such a one was my grandfather's maternal ancestor, Colonel Roger Morris, who, having fought with the Royal American Regiment, went to live in Nova Scotia. His financial astuteness belies the look of adenoidal arrogant stupidity which appears in his portrait by Benjamin West in my possession.

In due course my grandmother bore two daughters, the younger of whom became my mother. The old lady remained an 'unreconstructed' Confederate to the end of her long life (she lived to be ninety-two), and never ceased to abominate the crimes of 'that Mr Lincoln', as she always referred to him who had robbed her of her Virginian birthright. She never returned to the United States and was outraged by the fact that my mother and father spent part of their honeymoon in the eastern states.

My mother, on the other hand, had no interest in what is still referred to in the South as 'the War'. She never mentioned it to me, even in explanation of my grandmother's diatribes, and it was by pure 'happenstance' that I acquired my personal interest in American history, which led me to my love for that country. I had heard my father speak with enthusiasm of both Canada and the United States, in both of which he had travelled extensively and had wide commercial associations, but this made no greater impression on me at the time than his equally eloquently expressed dislike of the European continent. It was not until much later that I discovered what lay behind and beneath these prejudices.

In the summer of the Year of Grace 1911 King George V was crowned with due solemnity and much public celebration. This great event was the occasion for a big house-party at my parents' Kentish home. Every room was filled with visitors from all parts of the Empire and from the United States, and so great was their number that some of them had to be boarded out with friends and in the local country hotels. My father had also invited a large number of friends and neighbours to view the procession from a stand built out from his offices on London Bridge, and thither the whole party was transported from Bromley Station in a special train.

One of my mother's friends who had come from America for the occasion gave her a copy of a highly successful novel just published, a story of the American Civil War by Miss Mary Johnston, entitled *The Long Roll*. It was a long book and my mother was not particularly interested in it but she read parts of it aloud to me and far-reaching effects upon my life began. At nine years old I had barely heard of the great American struggle but I became immediately fired with its magnificent gallantry and its poignant tragedy. I borrowed the book for myself and read it greedily, not once or twice, but half a dozen times, till I was word perfect and had completely identified myself with the Confederate cause. The Confederacy as a whole and the Army of Northern Virginia in particular became my hobby and have remained so for the rest of my life.

From this early experience derived not only my lifetime avocation but in due course my deep affection and admiration for the United States and for its fundamental greatness and virtue. It provided me with a second country, where I have always felt as happy and as at home as in my own. More important than all, however, it gave me in later years a wife to whom I cannot be too grateful and whose abiding love and deep understanding – in Francis Bacon's phrase – 'redoubleth joys and cutteth griefs in halves'.

In his autobiography, John Buchan, who was a friend of mine from an early date until his untimely death in February 1940 as Governor-General of Canada, wrote of his love for America in a passage which represents to me the epitome of my own feelings:

> I came first into the United States by way of Canada, a good way to enter, for English eyes are already habituated to the shagginess of the landscape and can begin to realize its beauties. My first reflection was that no one had told me how lovely the country was. I mean *lovely*, not vast and magnificent. I am not thinking of the Grand Canyon and the Yosemite and the Pacific coast, but of the ordinary rural landscape. There is much of the land which I have not seen, but in the east and the south and the north-west I have collected a gallery of delectable pictures. I think of the farms which are clearings in the Vermont and New Hampshire hills, the flowery summer meadows, the lush cow-pastures with an occasional stump to remind one that it is old forest land, the quiet lakes and the singing streams, the friendly accessible mountains; the little country towns of Massachusetts and Connecticut with their village greens and elms and two-

century-old churches and court-houses; the secret glens of the Adirondacks and the mountain meadows of the Blue Ridge; the long-settled champaign of Maryland and Pennsylvania; Virginian manors more old-English perhaps than anything we have at home; the exquisite links with the past like much of Boston and Charleston and all of Annapolis; the sun-burnt aromatic ranges of Montana and Wyoming; the Pacific shores where from snow mountains fishable streams descend through some of the noblest timber on earth to an enchanted sea.[1]

There are two main obstacles which occlude a complete understanding of America by Britons, or even, in many cases, by Americans themselves. The first is a failure to recognise the fact that the United States is a continent composed of a variety of regions, as different from one another as European states, save in language – and even that varies locally. To ask what America thinks on such and such a subject is as fruitless as to enquire what Europe thinks under similar circumstances – and this was brought home to me with great emphasis during the Second World War.

Ignorance of each other has always been a barrier between the two countries. When my father told his English friends that he was about to wed a Canadian girl of Virginia stock, one of them remarked quite seriously to another: 'I can't understand how he can marry a black woman.' This may have been excusable in the eighties of the last century, but as late as the forties of the twentieth I have been asked in California, 'What rights have these Lords over you in England?' I longed to answer 'only that of "*droit de seigneur*",' but refrained.

Similarly, when I first came to know the States, I found a basic nescience, amounting in some cases to hostility and suspicion and in others to contempt, between one region and another. For example, those living north and south of the Mason and Dixon line frequently entertained a warped and distorted impression of one another. Many Northerners believed that the South was largely populated by an effete and decadent aristocracy, living on its impoverished acres amid the faded dreams and vanished glories of its past; a type of which the apotheosis is the character of Ashley in *Gone with the Wind*. Equally the South, in my young days, was apt to regard its Northern brethren as 'town-dwellers' and mercantilists, lacking in breeding and obsessed by lust for the 'Almighty Dollar'.

Both sides were wrong, of course, but errors of judgement and bias are long lived. I remember a number of 'raised eyebrows' – as my father had experienced some sixty years before me – even among my

[1] *Memory Hold-the-door* (London, 1940) p. 262.

more enlightened Northern friends, when I announced my engagement to a Southerner – until they met her, of course, when she triumphed everywhere. On the other hand, Ruth, who has on her mother's side an impeccable Virginian lineage dating from the Harrisons of 'Berkley' which includes a signer of the Declaration of Independence, the author of the Bill of Rights and two Presidents of the United States (not to mention a more shadowy claim to descent from Pocohontas!), has confessed that she spent much of her childhood concealing from her friends and schoolmates in Virginia the fact that her dead father had been born in Pennsylvania!

Even within the North and South themselves there are divisions. Bostonians hold themselves aloof from New Yorkers and it was not uncommon for them to travel to England and France before making contact with the great commercial capital of their own country, let alone the states of the Middle West. There is the story of the lady who was visiting friends in Boston. What state, they asked, did she come from? 'Iowa,' she replied. 'My dear,' said her hostess warmly, 'how I love your Western way of speaking. Here in Boston we always speak of that place as Ohio.' *Se non è vero, è molto ben trovato.*

In the South there is a profound difference between, say, Virginia and North Carolina, on the one hand, and the states of the Deep South, Alabama, Mississippi and Georgia on the other. California and the South West, Arizona and New Mexico, by reason of their common Spanish origin, differ profoundly from the civilisations of the Eastern seaboard, and between lies the great expanse of the Middle West, with its rich farmlands and great cities, different from both the coast-lands and suspicious of both; independent, individual and perhaps more basically 'American' than anywhere else.

There was a moment during the War when Aubrey Morgan and I were summoned from New York to the British Embassy in Washington 'to explain America' to the new Ambassador, Lord Halifax. We lunched *à quatre* with him and Charles Peake, his Personal Assistant, essentially a European, and developed this theory of a continent composed of regions. Aubrey, like many Welshmen, can speak with tongues of men and of angels, his affection for America is as great as mine and his knowledge considerably greater. On this occasion he was in excellent voice, limpid and lapidary. Under his graceful yet vigorous prose the pageant and romance of America were unrolled before his audience. I, myself, was spellbound but I was even more fascinated by the look of utter bewilderment which gradually crept across the faces of his other two listeners. When Aubrey finally checked, perhaps a trifle breathless, there was a silence, then Lord Halifax remarked: 'Thank you, Mr Morgan. How very interesting.' Neither Aubrey nor I was ever asked to expound on any subject on any other occasion during Lord Halifax's embassage.

The harshness of these lines of regional delineation has I think (hopefully) been blurred to some degree. A new generation, better travelled and consequently less biased, has grown up since the Second World War, but the old prejudices die hard and cannot yet be totally ignored.

The other great difficulty in the way of complete Anglo-American understanding is that great deception 'our common heritage of culture and language'. It produces too great a familiarity, too easy an acceptance, and a consequent disregard of sensitivities. The superficial similarities are misleading since they mask far more deep-seated differences of personality. American hypersensitiveness, coupled with their not infrequent habit of sharp criticism of others, are matched by British bland indifference and by our maddening *superbia Britannorum*. The warmth and naïveté of the American character encounters, too often disastrously, the more frigid sophistication of the British, failing to penetrate behind the façade; while Englishmen, schooled in restraint and understatement, recoil from the American addiction to hyperbole and superlatives.

Like my friend John Buchan, I too first entered the United States by way of Canada. It was the Fall of 1923 and I was lucky enough to be able to follow that gorgeous autumnal season from the fleeting, breathtaking blaze of colour on the Gatineau River, through the brilliance of New England and finally to the soft lingering golden hues of Virginia. The beauties of that period of the year on the North American continent are bewitching and bewildering in their diversity, just as the spring, beginning in the south with camellias and azaleas in great banks of varying tints, moves northwards on faery feet, amid clouds of dogwood, Judas trees and wistaria. These, to my mind, are the two most gracious American seasons of the year, its birth and death. The hey-day of summer is too sultry; the grip of winter too perishing.

I had very few contacts but I did not really need them. At that time there was still a bounteous hospitality and a warmth of welcome for the visiting Englishman and, in any case, I wanted to get the feel of the country. I wandered down the Eastern seaboard from Maine to Charleston, passing through Boston, New York, Philadelphia and Washington. I was part-traveller, part-sightseer and revelled in it all, enjoying the strange yet familiar differences, but always with a curious sense of *déjà vu*. From the first time I set foot in the country I felt that I *belonged*. It has never been a foreign country to me, and though I have been infuriated from time to time by its public behaviour – as I certainly have also with that of Britain – it was the anger born of love and disappointment, rather than of hostility, contempt or fear.

On this first visit I had two fixed ambitions. These were my 'salad days' when I still believed in the possibility of attaining international peace and in the successful future of the League of Nations. Woodrow Wilson was my hero and I had been shocked at the rejection of his policies by the United States Senate and by the American people. I was then too immature to assess him with an historical perspective; my enthusiasm blinded me to the facts of his own part in his own failure. I only knew that I wanted to meet him and to pay my own small tribute to what he had tried to do.

At Geneva, at the sessions of the League Assembly, I had met a few Americans who had dedicated themselves to the cause of the League and become international civil servants in its secretariat. Through their introductions I was granted a brief audience with President Wilson in Washington at his home on S. Street. He was already a failing man, for although he had recovered his mental faculties after his massive stroke and prolonged illness in 1920, he seemed to me desperately frail – a death's-head awaiting the final summons – which came in February 1924.

It was obvious that he tired easily, but he was able to discourse clearly and succinctly on the birth of the League at the Paris Peace Conference and he paid noble tributes to the major contributions of General Smuts and Lord Robert Cecil. Conversely he was pithy on the subject of Senator Cabot Lodge, who had led the opposition to the Covenant in the Senate.

In retrospect it is almost impossible to recreate for those who did not witness it the amazing impact which Woodrow Wilson had made on Europe when he first arrived there in the middle of December 1918. Whatever reservations the European statesman – and especially Clemenceau – might have had about the President's 'New Diplomacy' as represented in the Fourteen Points, whatever might have been the chilling effect of his own pedantic personality upon those individual leaders with whom he came in contact, to the *peoples* of Europe, war-weary and longing for peace, he represented little short of the Second Coming. Here was the new saviour of mankind who came 'with healing in his wings' to make real the promises of 'a war to end war' and of a 'world safe for democracy'. In Paris, in Rome and in London Wilson was received with tumultuous enthusiasm, bordering in some instances on hysteria. In the recently reborn state of Poland students exchanged hand-clasps, with 'Wilson' as their mutual fraternal greeting.

I remember vividly being taken by my father to Guildhall in the last week of that December to see the President receive the Freedom of the City of London, a rare honour to be bestowed on a foreigner. The audience was a distinguished one, the flower of Britain's leadership, including Lloyd George, Arthur Balfour, Bonar Law and Winston Churchill, together with a hard core of tough, unemotional, speech-calloused City Fathers. Wilson's entry was a personal triumph, he was received with loud applause which continued unstemmed, despite the lack of evidence of any great appreciation on his long, pedagogic countenance. His speech, with its tribute to the prowess and achievement of Britain, was delivered in a cold, emotionless voice, yet it evoked a standing ovation.

At that moment of his hey-day many a greater man might have been excused for accepting with self-confidence the belief that, whatever difficulties he might encounter with the national leaders with whom he was about to grapple at the conference-table, his hold upon the peoples of the world was sufficiently strong to command ultimate success for his policies. If necessary, he would appeal to the peoples over the heads of their leaders.

This halcyon honeymoon period was short-lived. Wilson's godhead withered and perished in the climate of ideas at the Paris Peace Conference and at the hands of his political enemies at home. In the inevitable clash between the New Diplomacy and the Old, compromises proved inevitable if any peace settlement were to be reached at all, compromises which would ruin his record and his reputation at home and abroad. And there were also failures to compromise, adamant obstinacy but for which something might have been saved from the wreck, his defeat at the hands of the Senate.

In less than two years physical prostration and political discomfiture had reduced this great and sad man from the high eminence of world arbiter to the semi-helpless prisoner of a wheel-chair; a tragic figure who in his bitterness had cast off his friends – House, Tumulty, Lansing – all of whom had given him affection, devotion and loyalty throughout his public life. In many ways it had been a heart-rending experience to see this sadness of decline, but I would not have willingly forgone it.

My second ambition was to meet Miss Mary Johnston, and this presented more difficult problems of transport. She lived in Warm Springs, Virginia, a part of the state not easily accessible by rail, and in the mountainous region of the west in Bath County, on the lower slopes of the Alleghenies. Even today it is not really very easy of access, but half a century ago the roads were uncertain and many of them unpaved. I went by train to Charlottesville, and there visited briefly the University of Virginia. Though I had no inkling as to how great a part Mr Jefferson's University would play in my life, nor of what happiness I was to find there, I recognised it immediately for what it is, namely the most beautiful man-made thing in the United States, an opinion I was later to have authoritatively confirmed by Kenneth Clark.

Of my life at The University (as it is always called in Virginia) I shall write later in this book, but I can never forget the witchery of beauty, the spell of the peace of soul, which caught and enthralled me for ever when I first stood on the Lawn in the late fall of 1923.

In Charlottesville I hired a car and a talkative driver, a 'red-neck', poor white from the mountains, who drove me in an ancient model-T Ford with some dash and verve, and with a running commentary of pungent anecdote and local scandal, across the Blue Ridge and into the Alleghenies to Warm Springs. Miss Mary Johnston lived in a house of some pretension to style, with a *porte-cochère*, some fine trees of box-wood, and magnificent views over the mountains. It was called Three Hills and was really an elegant boarding-house where carefully approved 'P.G.s' lived almost as members of the family. Her two sisters ran this side of the business and a curiously secluded brother drove an ancient car and did odd jobs. A suite of rooms was set apart for Miss Mary, to whom all the rest of the family deferred as 'the gifted one' and who was never to be involved in or trammelled by the circumstances of mere day-to-day life. Guests might come and go and never see her, for she ate alone or sometimes with some specially favoured companion.

This household was typical of such establishments throughout the South. The Civil War and the Reconstruction had impoverished the gentlefolk of the Confederacy. The people of the seceding states had given their all to the new nation which they hoped to create and become paupers in terms of currency, without servants and dependent upon barter as a means of subsistence. The men who had served the Confederacy were disenfranchised. A civilisation of elegance and gracious living had crumbled. Nevertheless the women of the South, more especially the widows and spinsters, never lost their proud spirit, never lowered their standards. It became essential, and therefore fashionable, for ladies of aristocratic families to take in lodgers and this tradition persisted well into my lifetime. Miss Mary and her sisters had been descendants of the distinguished Confederate commander, General Joseph E. Johnston, and they lived in an aura of the past, quite incomprehensible to some of their Northern boarders but perfectly understandable to me who had made a study of the social conditions in the post-bellum South. My appreciation of the past, and the fact that I had written explaining the great influence which her two Civil War books had had on me, established an empathy between Miss Mary and myself. She was then fifty-three years old, small, dignified, even elegant, with very blue eyes and a charming smile. She had written twenty-two novels of which the three best known were To Have and to Hold, By Order of the Company and Audrey, all dealing with colonial Virginia before the American Revolution. She was not generally considered such a great writer as Ellen Glasgow, with whom she has sometimes been compared – but in my opinion she was sufficiently mordacious to hold the attention of her readers – which Miss Glasgow never achieved. Miss Mary was a confessed idealist, even verging in her later works on the mystical, and her characterisation was sometimes stilted and artificial, but no one could touch her ability to recreate atmosphere. Her two Civil War novels The Long Roll and Cease Firing were constructed with minute attention to military detail and historical fact. Between them they constitute a narrative that has been weighed in the balance and found to be true history by some of the greatest authorities on the subject, and certainly I have never found a flaw in the pure gold of their precision.

I found her an enchanting person and we would spend hours together – to the unveiled surprise of her sisters – talking of 'The War' and of her books on it and of the circumstances in which she had written them. She admitted frankly that she had introduced a melodramatic love story to add a popular interest and had laid the pathos on pretty thickly. We became close friends and I often visited her thereafter. I saw her on her death-bed in Richmond in 1936 and in her will she left me part of her Civil War library. On this first occasion of our meeting she wrote a charming inscription in my original copy of The Long Roll, and added a verse of 'Dixie' on the fly-leaf.

*

With my return to New York my first visit to the United States was concluded. I had yet, however, to survive my introduction to the Atlantic Ocean. British shipping losses had been cruelly heavy at the hands of the U-boats during the First World War and in compensation, the flower of the German ocean-going passenger fleet was handed over under the Reparation Clauses of the Treaty of Versailles. To the Cunard Line went the Hamburg-Amerika's pride, the *Imperator*, to be renamed the *Berengaria*, and to the White Star her consort the *Bismarck*, which was rechristened the *Majestic*. It was on this latter vessel that I had taken passage and scarcely had we cleared Sandy Hook than we ran into an early winter storm of major proportions. There were no stabilisers in those days, and though she was really an excellent sea boat, the *Majestic* rolled to an absolutely terrifying degree.

The storm increased as we ploughed our way eastwards and the words 'England, home and beauty' seemed wonderfully remote. Finally, in about mid-Atlantic we were struck by an especially evil spasm, were it typhoon, tornado or cyclone, just about dinner-time. I had passed a miserable first few days but was just beginning to feel human again, and, with due care and precaution, I reached the grill-room on the upper deck. I ordered a plain (a *very* plain) fillet of sole and a bottle of champagne and had just been served when the thing happened. There was a roar so loud that it sounded like an explosion and then the ship began to tilt to starboard and she went on and on tilting, until I was convinced she would never regain equilibrium. Meantime everything had lost its moorings. Tables and chairs, diners and stewards, mingled in an unhappy heap in what in any smaller ship would have been the scuppers, to the accompaniment of a rending crash of broken glass and crockery. I fetched up against some sort of metal grille-balustrade, clutching my bottle of champagne to my bosom and feeling rather dazed. And then I saw it coming. Have you ever been charged by a grand piano? If so, you will recognise the characteristics of a rogue elephant at its most destructive. The great instrument had broken loose from the rods which normally secured it and it seemed to be careering directly towards me. There was no way of getting out of its way but at the last moment its direction was diverted by a collision with a table, which it smashed to matchwood, and it went straight through the metal grille-work and down the stairs. Actually it hurt nobody but I imagine it could have been regarded as a 'write-off'. I did fall a victim to the bass-cello which came galumphing in its wake but this was only minor damage compared with what might have been.

All this time – and it seemed an eternity though it was probably only about five or ten minutes – the ship hung at an angle with heavy seas pounding on her port beam. Then slowly – oh how very slowly – she began to right herself and, though she perceptibly listed to starboard for the remainder of the voyage, our sense of confidence returned. I was afterwards told that the outer hull of the *Majestic* had cracked down the side, and we certainly limped into Southampton nearly forty-eight hours behind schedule.

CHAPTER TWO

Young Man in Manhattan

I returned to America in the following summer and thus began a series of annual visits. Even when closely occupied in Germany, I always found time to spend at least a couple of months in the United States each year. Until I left Germany for good and in some haste at the end of June 1934, these trips were necessarily brief. Thereafter, until the Second World War interrupted the rhythm of my life, I made a second home for myself in Charlottesville, though I frequently visited further afield.

My earlier visits developed a regular pattern. I would arrive in New York where I would see my friends and then go up to Boston and Cambridge, then down to Washington and as far south as Charleston and then to Chicago and the Middle West. Occasionally I would go as far as Arizona and California.

In New York my first and greatest friend was Hamilton Fish Armstrong, for fifty years the editor of *Foreign Affairs*, that formidable quarterly organ of the Council on Foreign Relations. The Council and Chatham House had a common origin in the informal meetings of experts and young assistants who had been members of the British and American delegations at the Peace Conference of Paris. The two organisations have developed along very different lines but a close alliance has always existed between them. This was the basis of my introduction to Ham, who remained among my closest friends for over fifty years, and with whose widow Christa I am happy to continue this relationship. He was one of those rare relics of the old, aristocratic New York way of life before the First World War, an anomaly of elegance and wit and humour that in a strange way bridged the gap between the serene and gracious world of Edith Wharton and the turbulent universe of Scott Fitzgerald. He was shrewd and fastidious, a man of the highest principles and the greatest integrity. It was impossible to conceive of Ham doing a shady or an unkind act. He was the most lovable of men, a true friend, an honest enemy and a man capable of righteous wrath to a superb degree. He was no Puritan and the greatest fun to be with, yet he was essentially 'a good man' in the best possible sense of the word. In fair weather and in foul there was no truer nor more

23

courageous friend of Britain in the whole United States, and there were to be moments when his friendship was to be of the greatest value.

At this, our initial meeting, Ham did me the first of a long series of favours and kindnesses. He sent me to the Chatham Hotel, on the corner of East 48th Street and Park Avenue, where I remained a steady client until it was pulled down, as being in the path of progress, in the years of rebuilding in mid-town New York after the Second World War.

The second favour was more difficult. I am a political animal. I like the world of politics and statesmanship and, though I have never been tempted to seek a parliamentary career, I have always been deeply interested in the machinery of democratic institutions. The Party National Convention in the United States, at which the presidential candidates are nominated, is unique in such processes, and it fascinates me, just as a small child is held in delight by a great circus. 'The smell of the grease-paint, the roar of the crowd', the brass bands playing the campaign-songs of the rival candidates for nomination, the ovations – some organised, some spontaneous – which greet the appearance of some 'favoured son' (Franklin Roosevelt's famous 'Happy Warrior' speech in which he proposed the name of Al Smith in 1924, was followed by a ninety-minute demonstration!), the rotund and otiose rhetoric of much of the oratory. All these things enthral me and never have I been more grateful than when Ham presented me with a ticket for the National Democratic Convention of 1924 then being held in the old Madison Square Garden.

This was the convention to beat all conventions. Normally these gatherings last at most for a week, but on this occasion the delegates sat, sweating in the humid heat of a New York summer, for two everlasting weeks, while the embattled forces of Governor Alfred E. Smith and Woodrow Wilson's son-in-law William McAdoo, stubbornly locked horns in a desperate battle, which involved over 100 ballots. Smith, a Roman Catholic, was the darling of the people, partly because of his easy, spicy personality and partly because he stood for the repeal of Prohibition. He commanded the powerful backing of the bosses of Tammany Hall; his theme song 'The Side-Walks of New York' was sung again and again by voices growing ever hoarser and coarser. Over against him was McAdoo, a former Secretary of the Treasury, representing the Puritan wing of the Democratic Party, anti-Catholic, anti-Semitic and Prohibitionist.

Neither candidate could muster the necessary majority to secure nomination and neither would concede. 103 times did the moist and weary delegates answer the roll-call, which began (shall I ever forget it?) with a high nasal voice which chanted the never changing cry: 'Alabama gives twenty-four votes to Underwood.' (Oscar Underwood, it should be explained, was 'a favoured son' of his state who refused to release his votes to either side.) At length, when sheer exhaustion had sapped the stamina of even the most zealous campaign-manager a compromise was effected and on the 103rd ballot the Convention nominated a great gentleman, John W. Davies, a jurist of high standing who had served as Ambassador to the Court of St James. He was a man of great charm, handsome appearance and high principles – and he was soundly beaten in the following November by the Republican candidate, Calvin Coolidge.

Some sixteen years later, in June of 1940 – a critical moment in Britain's history and in that of Anglo-American relations – I was lucky enough to gain admission to the Republican convention at Philadelphia. This time it was through the good offices of Alice Roosevelt Longworth ('Mrs L.'), who at the splendid age of ninety remains a very dear friend whose affection I value deeply. This was the dramatic occasion when the galleries stampeded the delegates into nominating a dark horse, Wendell Wilkie, over the more orthodox claims of Robert Taft and Thomas Dewey. It was a turbulent and euphoric occasion at which many pundits were confounded and the new young men had their way, but here again I was witnessing the choice of a loser, for President Roosevelt was returned with a comfortable majority for a third term.

There is nothing dull about American politics.

I have known New York from its *Great Gatsby* days of the twenties to the concrete and glass jungle which it has become in the seventies. I still love it, find it stimulating and exhilarating, experiencing a thrill each time I first set foot on Fifth Avenue. But, alas, I cannot but deplore its present condition, when litter crowds the gutters and danger stalks in broad daylight.

When I first knew it, it seemed to me the most romantic city in the world and the most friendly. There was a charm and excitement which I can only describe as a sort of 'blue champagne'; every hour was a delight. Apart from the pleasure of seeing one's friends, many of whom still lived in their family brownstone houses, there were so many nice things to see and do. Youth and beauty still gathered at the Plaza, and one could ride in a hansom cab – long after they had disappeared from the streets of London – round the winding avenues of Central Park and stop to listen to a band-concert on the Mall. Entertainment abounded, from the Ziegfeld Follies at the Amsterdam Theatre on 42nd Street to the old Metropolitan Opera House on 57th Street, with its Diamond Horse Shoe. The food was excellent, whether one frequented Delmonico's, Sherry's, or the Brevoort or the more exotic delights of Chinatown, Greenwich Village or Harlem, and if one wanted night-life El Morocco and the Stork Club were in their glory.

There were splendid book-shops, both modern and second-hand, and, for the ladies, excellent *couturiers*. One danced on the St Regis Roof Garden and always had the address of a reliable bootlegger and a respectable speakeasy. Nicholas Murray (Miraculous) Butler ruled in glory at Columbia University and all was well with the world, demonstrated by the fact that an ordinary citizen could walk all over the city in perfect safety at any hour of the twenty-four.

Much of this has changed, perhaps most of all the conditions described in this last sentence, yet New York retains something of its fascination for me, if only because I never experience such entertaining adventures as when I am there. Once on a cold and frosty morning – and nowhere can it be colder than in New York – I was walking from the Chatham westwards towards Fifth Avenue. The pavements were slippery and the steps which led down to them from houses and shops were even more so. Suddenly, to my surprise, I found a little man literally sitting in my outstretched arms. He had slipped on a top step, 'taken off', as it were, into space and I had instinctively caught him as he was falling. The whole thing resembled a comic travesty of an apache act. My new friend was in no whit embarrassed and completely in command of the situation. While I still held him, he raised his hat with impeccable aplomb and announced: 'I'm Mr Goldberg.' The social amenities having been observed, I deposited him on his feet and he disappeared as mysteriously as he had arrived. This has never happened to me in London.

On a different level – as they say today in our classless world – I was waiting for my wife in the hall of one of New York's more exclusive ladies' clubs, where she had been lunching with a friend. An old lady approached the hall-porter and, to my unspeakable delight, told him: 'When my guest arrives, please tell him I'm in the men's room.' Her meaning was clear to all except myself, namely that she was awaiting her guest in the room in which gentlemen might be received. The ways of a tongue not entirely one's own are fraught with pitfalls.

Finally, on yet another level, only recently I was in an all-night

Lexington Avenue coffee-shop early on a Sunday morning trying to get some breakfast before leaving for Kennedy airport. It was the sort of place where porters and bell-boys and the like were the usual clientèle, but it was the only place open at that hour and its 'coffee-and-Danish' were excellent. On my doctors' orders I now take a good deal of medicine during the day and, as I counted out my morning pill intake, which is quite voluminous, I became aware of the riveted interest of my next-door neighbour, a truck-driver of gigantic size who, in Damon Runyon's immortal phrase, gave the impression that he habitually 'chewed nails and spat rust' but was, unexpectedly enough, drinking a glass of milk. Moreover, beneath his gorilla-like appearance there clearly lurked a kind heart. Having watched me absorb my galaxy of potions with something akin to horror, he said in an awed voice: 'Gawd, brother, you *are* hooked! Shouldn't you see a head-shrinker?' This was indeed the milk of human kindness.

Curiously enough some years before – indeed before the Second World War – I had had a similar experience in Paris. At that time my current treatment consisted of a series of white powders which had to be taken in a glass of water several times a day. On one occasion I performed this feat in the lounge of the Hotel Wagram and was vastly amused to hear one of two American ladies at the next table say to the other in a hushed yet audibly scandalised whisper: 'Dope, my dear, I can tell by his eyes.' Medical treatment has its hazards to one's reputation.

Before the Second World War New York had a wonderful selection of four morning papers: the weighty *Times* and *Herald-Tribune* and the more popular *Daily News* and *Mirror*; in the evening one had the choice of the *Telegram* or the *New-York-American*, one of William Randolph Hearst's great chain. Later, of course, the *Post* was added to these. There were also excellent local journals like the *Brooklyn Eagle*. Today only the *New York Times*, the *News* and *Post* remain – a sad decimation. I was lucky enough to know the *Times* in the last days of that truly remarkable man Adolph Ochs, a veritable giant among newspaper proprietors. His daughter Iphigen married Arthur Sulzberger and their son Punch is now the third of the dynasty to preside over this great organ. They were always very kind to me and I used to stay with them at White Plains, New York, at weekends. But the exciting and, I may add, exacting experience was to be asked to lunch with the editorial board when either Adolph Ochs or his son-in-law was in the chair. Around the table sat some of the best brains in American journalism, including the editor Jimmie James, and the literary editor F. P. Adams. Fred Birchal the foreign expert would be there and generally a correspondent or two who were home on leave from their posts abroad. The talk was splendid and any visitor was quizzed with a shrewd background knowledge that kept one on one's toes. As my books became known in the United States and I myself was recognised as someone who knew something about Germany in particular and Europe in general, I was a fairly regular guest and was able to exchange my news for the views of my hosts on what was going on in the United States and also on what they were thinking of Europe. It was sometimes gruelling but always rewarding, and I never came away from these meetings without having learned a very great deal.

As a result of my regular visits to New York I found myself gradually accepted into its club-life. As a member of Brooks's in London I had reciprocal facilities with the Knickerbocker, which was always welcoming and which still has the best Saturday buffet luncheon in New York. Ham Armstrong put me up for the Century, where one met the *literati*, artists and journalists and the pleasantly mixable intellectuals. There is nothing exactly comparable to it among London Clubs save perhaps the Beefsteak. Eventually I was elected to the Brook, which has the best food, the most comfortable accommodation and the best service in New York and where one may be certain of finding as conservative a climate of ideas as the Century is liberal. Such was my gradual growth of experience in New York as an annual visitor.

The worlds of Boston and Cambridge, Mass., though near neighbours, and in some ways closely affiliated, are yet strangely disparate. This is probably even truer today than when I first knew them. The Boston that one knew best was that stately circle of Beacon Street, with its elegant house-fronts and glowing lilac glass windows, and Mount Vernon Street, Louisburg Square and Commonwealth Avenue. If one was lucky one was invited to lunch at the Somerset Club, that impeccable palladium of tradition and convention, the very epitome of Bostonian Brahminism. Here one could admire the superb collection of American silver bequeathed by Daniel Webster, of the same beauty as that presented by Mr Henry Stimson to Philipps-Andover Academy.

Whether or not Paul Revere did, in fact, make his legendary ride 'to give the alarm to every Middlesex village and farm' is less important than his unquestionable mastership as a silversmith, and he had many contemporary competitors of great ability. The simplicity and purity of their early silver is an aspect of a past culture of which Americans must be proud.

There was also the Tavern Club, the atmosphere of which was more relaxed than that of the Somerset and where one met one's more Bohemian friends; writers, artists, journalists and the like, and even some members of the Harvard faculty. It was very much akin to the Century in New York, though perhaps a little gayer. Always a student of social history and customs, I greatly enjoyed having a foot in both camps, finding most congenial company in each.

One of my happiest recollections is of being taken to meet a very old lady who, as a very young lady, had married Mr Wirt Dexter, a man much older than herself and the attorney for (I think) the Central Illinois Railroad. They then lived in Chicago where Mr Dexter was a power in the local Republican organisation and, in the historic year of 1860, he was a staunch supporter of Governor Seward of New York for nomination as the party's presidential candidate. The Convention met in Chicago and it was soon clear that Seward did not have sufficient support. Sitting in what used in my youth to be called a *boudoir* in a 'grandmother' winged chair and periodically refreshing herself with a sip of neat whisky, Mrs Dexter described to me the subsequent scene. Her husband had been furious and she recounted with considerable authority his bitter remark: 'They won't have the Governor (Seward) but I'll make them take that gorilla from Springfield.' A party caucus was called in their drawing-room that evening and the historic decision taken to nominate Abraham Lincoln for the presidency.

So is history made, or at least recounted. For what degree of accuracy Mrs Dexter's memory could muster at the age of near-ninety I am not prepared to vouch, but this is what she certainly said. For good measure she added a vivid and dramatic account of General Philip Sheridan's making his headquarters in her house on Prairie Avenue and directing the operations to counter the disastrous fire which swept and ravaged the city of Chicago in the winter of 1871, when widow O'Leary's cow inconsiderately kicked over the lamp and set the barn ablaze. Mrs Dexter recalled the General's standing on her roof and pointing out which city blocks must be dynamited to create lanes too broad for the flames to cross. 'I sent him up champagne and mulled wine,' she said, 'for it was a bitter night. I think he drank both.'

She told both stories in a frail old voice but with no hesitation. The events seemed to be clear and vigorous in her memory. She had lived an active and exciting life and in her reminiscences could contrast the primitive and robust society of Chicago in the sixties and seventies of the last century, with the more orthodox and conventional Bostonian way of life in the twenties and thirties of this one. Her conversation always reminded me of a novel by Louis Bromfield.

One was also conscious of that very different Boston which lay towards the South. The Irish quarter seethed with gaiety and politics and such controversial but highly entertaining figures as Mayor Curley – immortalised in John Connor's splendid story *The Last Hurrah*. Curley once ran for re-election as mayor from gaol, where he had landed on some sort of a charge of irregularity. He won. I repeat, American politics are never dull.

Mrs Dexter's daughter had married a McCormick of Chicago and she was always very kind to me. Through her and other friends I grew to know the North Shore district: Myopia, with its famous hunt club, and the little seaside townships such as Magnolia, where she had a charming house, and Pride's Crossing, where I had the good fortune to have an afternoon with Colonel Edward House, President Wilson's 'Texas Talleyrand', who had played so vitally important a part in the history of the First World War and its sequel. With some diffidence, but irresistibly impelled, I ventured upon the delicate subject of his breach with the President. Colonel House was courteously disposed and gave me the same answer that he had given to others. It was a mystery, he said, to which he did not hold the key. He admitted that it had been a source of great sadness to him, sadness amounting to grief, that a man whom he had admired so greatly, with whom he had worked so closely, for whom he had entertained so sincere an affection, should have terminated the amicable partnership, for no reason that he, the Colonel, could ever fathom, with the curt dismissal: 'Good-bye, House.'

It is the insoluble, the incomprehensible mysteries of history, the problems for which the answers can never be found in the back of the book, that make it so worthwhile a study. This is one of them, the disappearance from the scene of this charming, grey, unassuming little man, who had ranked and negotiated with the crowned heads and statesmen of the world.

With Harvard University, my connection was with the schools of history, government and international law. I was lucky in that the vintage of professors in these fields was unusually rich and I formed lasting friendships among them. There were the grand old men of their day, such as Sydney Fay, the historian of the First World War, and Archibald Cary Coolidge, who had been identified with Ham Armstrong in founding *Foreign Affairs*. Then there were the younger men who have become elder statesmen in their turn: William L. Langer, William Yandell Elliot and Joachim Friedrich among the historians and also, much later, of course, a young and brilliant scholar called Henry Kissinger, who was destined for greater things than all the others. Then there was Manley O. Hudson, of the Law School, who subsequently became a judge of the Permanent Court of International Justice, and Bruce Hopper in Government, of whom more later.

At first I sat at the feet of these pundits. I attended their lectures and was hospitably entertained by them in their houses, or at the Faculty Club, of which I was usually made a temporary member. Then, as my own reputation became established, I would be accorded the honour of addressing their classes and seminar sessions and of this I was, not unnaturally, extremely proud. They were great historians of their time and their generous acceptance of me as a 'brother brush' touched me not a little.

Perhaps my best friend of all in these eclectic circles was Bruce Hopper, who, hailing from Montana, described himself as 'a cowboy with a brain'. He and his wife Effie made me free of their delightful old house on Brattle Street, where I nearly always stayed, and showed me every possible kindness. Bruce was a remarkable chap. He was a good historian, a Russian expert, who had written a book called *Pan-Sovietism*, which was percipient beyond his time, and acknowledged as a remarkable piece of writing. Thereafter, however, his Muse dried up and, as far as I know, he never produced another major work, though he embarked on several projects. He was, nevertheless, a born teacher. Never have I seen undergraduates so enthralled by a magisterial discourse such as his. He was at once authoritative, frivolous, stimulating and outrageously funny. It was always a delight to talk to his classes because they were so well prepared, so appreciative and so keen to learn. 'No one,' said one of his students to me, 'could ever forget a word he had said. We thought he was the greatest.'

Bruce Hopper's magnanimity – and that of Harvard – were put to the test in an incident not entirely creditable to myself. The Widener Library at Harvard, one of the most famous university libraries in the country, had (and still has) been most generous in their dealings with me, even allowing me the liberty of the stacks, a privilege rarely granted to outsiders. On my return to England after a visit there I found that my researches required reference to a book published in America, but not apparently in any British library. I sent out an S.O.S. to the Widener and eventually, after much deliberation, for it was against their rules, if not their inclinations, to make loans of this kind outside the country, the authorities made a special exception, and agreed to send the book to me for the shortest possible period, but only under the personal guarantee of a member of the faculty – Bruce Hopper.

In due course the book arrived by registered post at A14 Albany, beautifully packed and seemingly impregnable. It was a Saturday morning and I was about to leave for the country by car, in company with my bulldog, an animal who gave and elicited the greatest affection and whose fierce demeanour concealed the greatest cowardice. He went everywhere with me and snored loudly on the back seat of the car. I drove to Chatham House in St James's Square and paused there for a moment to pick up some papers. When I returned the worst had happened. I had placed the book on the front seat beside me for safety and during my absence that infernal bulldog had climbed from the back seat into the front – a thing he had never done before – and had ravaged the precious volume with delighted mastication. Perhaps the most maddening thing of all was that he looked so damned pleased with himself about it, rolling that roguish eye as only a bulldog can who has performed some mischievous feat and thoroughly enjoyed it.

I spent a terrible week-end. The book had not been destroyed beyond use, nor even beyond repair, but it was covered in toothmarks, soaked with saliva and obviously entirely unreturnable. I was devastated, but eventually decided to 'come clean' and confess the worst to the Widener and to Bruce Hopper. In mitigation I pledged 'my life, my fortune and my sacred honour' to replace the book, by hook or by crook. And so I was able eventually to do, though it cost me a great deal in advertising and in purchase, but I had the satisfaction of sending to the Widener a copy in better condition than that which they had originally lent me, even before it received the attention of my dog. My relations with the Library and with Bruce Hopper resumed their usual warmth; I was even reconciled with my bulldog. The original of the book, still showing the effects of having been chewed some forty years ago, now reposes in the library of St Antony's College, Oxford.

In mid-September 1936 Harvard celebrated its three-hundredth anniversary with much pomp and ceremony and in vile weather. I was among the delegates from other universities and learned bodies, and for three days we were entertained sumptuously and all possible means were employed to make up for the weather. The high-point of the ceremonies was the academic procession, followed by an address in an open amphitheatre by President Roosevelt. Sheets of rain drenched us as we assembled and were deftly corralled by an efficient corps of well drilled young marshals drawn, I gathered, from the more recent alumni, and in sodden silence we made what soon became a very unstately procession.

We were supposed to be arranged in the order of the foundation of the institution which we were representing and I had been told that there had been some back-stairs jockeying for position among the delegates from Oxford, Cambridge and Paris as to who should have pride of place at the head of the procession. When, however, we moved off we were led by a rather depressed little man in bowler-hat who represented the University of Cairo, of unquestionably the greatest age of all present.

Ham Armstrong and I were at the extreme end of the cortège, representing respectively the Council on Foreign Relations and the Royal Institute of International Affairs, and an unimpressive academic appearance we made, he with a rather shabby Princeton B.A. hood and I, with no degree at all, wearing a graduate's gown over morning dress ! However we had great fun, especially in evading the glare of the lynx-eyed marshals, who disapproved of levity on the march. Arrived at the amphitheatre we seemed to lose all sort of order and I found myself sitting next to, and sharing an umbrella with, a formidable lady professor from some mid-Western University, who remarked sardonically : 'There'll be a packet of funerals after this business.'

It was on this occasion that President Roosevelt made a fine oration on freedom of speech and education, seeming to fix a minatory frown upon the delegates from Italy and Germany who were just in front of him. But the thunder was stolen, as it were, just before he began to speak by a remark apparently made by President Angell of Yale, which though obviously intended to be an aside, was picked up by the public address system and resounded throughout the auditorium : 'This is what Franklin Roosevelt calls "soaking the rich".'

I would like to record, as a tribute to the efficiency of Harvard's emergency organisation, that when later we gathered indoors, drenched and dripping, to shed our dampened finery, we each found in our place a large tot of Medford rum, which probably did a lot to change the odds on the prognostication of my lady from the Middle West.

Bruce Hopper's travels in Europe and Asia had brought him into contact with circumstances and personalities, with the result that he

B

spoke from his own experience rather than from the ivory tower of pure scholarship. Perhaps understandably he was not too warmly appreciated by his colleagues. Well ahead of most of the intellectuals in foreseeing the inevitably disastrous results of Appeasement, he taught accordingly, and of this I had a particularly interesting example.

In the course of Mr Joseph Kennedy's disastrous period as United States Ambassador to the Court of St James, I was invited one evening to dine informally at the American Embassy (then in Rutland Gate). We were a small party, not more than ten, as I recall, and the three eldest Kennedy sons sat in a row on the far side of the table to myself. The Ambassador was not forthcoming as a host but Mrs Kennedy was charming and warm and outgiving. She was and is a great lady. 'I'll tell you about these boys,' said the Ambassador to me in his rasping nasal voice, as if they weren't there at all. 'There's young Joe, he's going to be President of the United States; and there's Jack, he's going to be a university president; and there's Bobby (tapping his nose in a cunning manner) he's the lawyer.' No bad prophecy in its way, but happily we could not tell at that moment that all three sons would die violent deaths; one in action against the enemy and two of them by an assassin's bullet.

This incident, apart from its immediate interest, made little impression on me. Indeed I had entirely forgotten it until, on returning to America in October 1938 after the Munich crisis, I addressed Bruce Hopper's class on what it had been like to be in Europe, and particularly in England, at this time. I must in all modesty admit that they were an enthralled audience, and when at the end of my talk I whipped on my gas-mask, which I had brought along as a 'prop', I received an ovation. A most pleasing, open countenanced, blue-eyed young man came up to me afterwards and introduced himself as Jack Kennedy, reminding me that we had 'met at his parents' house in London'. Could he, he said, come and talk to me. I was very glad to assent and a date was made at the Hoppers' house for the following afternoon.

Meantime Bruce had had a bright idea. Would I, he asked, supervise Jack's thesis for his master's degree? I was already attached to the Law School of the University of Virginia and was holding a weekly seminar; moreover, apart from a very pleasant first impression, I knew nothing of the young man's capacity, so I played for time and said I would wait until after our talk before giving a definite answer. The following afternoon we walked for two hours along the banks of the river Charles, at the conclusion of which I had decided that here was a highly exceptional young man who surely merited all the help that I could give him.

In the next few weeks I travelled periodically from Charlottesville to Cambridge, and despite the journey and the climate, I much enjoyed my association with this attractive boy who was to be the young Knight of Camelot. It was not all easy going. Jack had chosen as his subject the reasons which lay behind Britain's policy of appeasement, culminating in her complicity in the Munich Agreement. He had done some research at the London School of Economics and had drawn widely on the views of his father, who was an arch-appeaser and an extreme admirer of Neville Chamberlain. Not unnaturally the boy had arrived at a definitely prejudiced point of view and it fell to my lot, without trying too hard to prejudice him in the opposite direction, at least to expound the other side.

'Old Joe' did not altogether approve of my association with his son and would telephone him at frequent intervals to ask 'what's that Limey been telling you?' But Jack had a reasoning and a balanced mind; everything was grist to his mill, but he formed his own opinions. His view was not by any means that of his father; otherwise it could not have been alleged (however ludicrously) that I had ghosted his book *Why England Slept*, under which title his thesis was ultimately published. Every word was his own and I never even saw the final version. I did however greatly appreciate the tribute he paid me in the introduction and the charmingly inscribed copy with which he presented me.

This was in 1940 and twenty-two years later it brought its own sequel. In January 1962 Ruth and I were staying with David and Cissie Harlech at the British Embassy in Washington and one morning the Ambassador announced that the President of the United States wished to see me. Jack Kennedy and I had kept up a desultory correspondence over the years, especially during his period in the Senate, and I had written to congratulate him warmly on his election to the presidency, to which he replied as warmly, but I certainly had had neither expectation nor desire to see him in the White House simply because of our earlier association. However I was of course delighted to be asked and before going I bought a copy of the second edition of *Why England Slept* which had just been published. Anxiously turning to the introduction I found that the same tribute still remained.

On entering the Oval Room I was delighted to find that, whereas years and experience had matured him, President Kennedy was still at heart that delightful, open-minded young man I had met in Bruce

Hopper's government class. We talked for a while on international affairs and then I produced my new copy of his book, saying with some mischief that it was unusual to have a second edition published twenty years after the first. It was a stroke of luck not accorded to all authors. He grinned his boyish smile and took the book. As he wrote in it, sitting in his rocking-chair, he looked up over his spectacles and grinned again. 'We've both come quite a long way since the first edition, haven't we?' he said. This was undeniably endearing. An incidental fact is that the handwriting of the two inscriptions would seem to be that of two totally different people.

The President said one other thing which gave me a sense of warmth and pleasure. 'During those walks we used to take by the Charles River,' he reminded me, 'you used to tell me that in writing modern history you should be fair and objective up to a point, but sooner or later the time would come when you had to take a stand and then you had to come down off the wall with both feet. One shouldn't try to straddle, you said, you shouldn't be mealy-mouthed. I think you might like to know that I've always remembered that as a principle.' I may well have mixed my metaphors to that extent but it is pleasing to think that my message had got across, and it was very nice of him to tell me so. I mourned him personally at his tragic death.

CHAPTER THREE

Cave-dwellers, New Dealers and Others

When I first knew Washington it still enjoyed the agreeably small-town atmosphere that had survived from the previous century. Society was restricted; everyone knew everybody else. Georgetown was still lived in by people who had done so for a long time and the top of Massachusetts Avenue, by the Naval Observatory and the great Glover estate, was considered as being almost in the country. People speculated on why the Cathedral had been built 'so far out'. Was it really true, one was asked, that the British intended to build a new embassy 'out in the sticks'? The British Embassy, at that time, was an ugly but comfortable yellow-brick building on Connecticut Avenue and the State Department was still housed in that delightful wedding-cake edifice next door to the White House, at the corner of Jackson Square and Pennsylvania Avenue, which it shared with the Departments of War and the Navy.

All this was changed and swept away when Franklin Roosevelt introduced the New Deal in 1933, creating innumerable extra-governmental agencies and filling them with temporary civil servants and university professors. The result of this was a tremendous boost in real estate. Washington became a 'boom town' almost over-night and the city was filled with a society of new men of whom most of the old style 'cave-dwellers' profoundly disapproved. It was then that the term 'egg-head' became current as a semi-pejorative term.

But this was all in the future when I made my début. Mr Coolidge was in the White House and the British Ambassador was Sir Esmé Howard (later Lord Howard of Penrith), a dignified, refined and cultured man and a successful diplomat of the old school. He had married Princess Isabella Giustiniani-Bandini, a charming and delightful hostess. The Howards were highly popular in Washington and along the Eastern seaboard, but I rather doubt whether the Ambassador was a familiar figure in the Middle West.

By far the most influential Britisher in Washington was Bill (later Sir Willmott) Lewis, who was correspondent of *The Times* there for twenty-eight years. Bill was a character, if ever there was one. He had been an actor in some distant past and a whiff of the Lyceum still clung to him. A fishy eye, a tall, commanding figure, and a bass voice which could rumble and reverberate so that even his simplest remark took on a special profundity and which could sink dramatically to a penetrating sibilant whisper, all combined to make of him a personality of tremendous panache. And so he was, for his knowledge of the country as a whole and of Washington in particular was prodigious and successive members of the Embassy staff constantly imbibed from his sardonic wit and sagacity. Americans treated him with the greatest veneration and regarded him as the repository of all wisdom. Many of them believed that he was the head of the British Secret Service in America, an impression he made no effort to destroy. Senators and hostesses sought his counsel and he loved every minute of it.

Even incumbents of the White House found Bill awesome. An eyewitness records that he once addressed Herbert Hoover thus: 'As you gaze, Mr President, into the future, as you peer down the grey vista of the years, do you not apprehend, sir, that the problems of the United States are problems not only of growth [and here the great voice sank to its mighty whisper] but of decay?' So powerful a question might well bewilder and disturb the greatest of politicians; the fact remains that shortly thereafter President Hoover made a speech in which he emphasised that the problems of the United States were those of growth only – not of decay.

When I first knew Bill he was married to Ethel, a scion (or is it scioness?) of that great Washington newspaper dynasty of Noyes. She was a splendid person, somewhat formidable of mien but with a heart of gold. I was exceedingly fond of both of them and they were benignity itself to me. I was constantly in their house on New Hampshire Avenue, where one met everyone of any interest at all in Washington, and they once gave a party for me on a four-masted schooner moored in mid-stream on the Potomac. It was a wonderful party and the feature which remains most vividly in my memory is the opening conversational gambit of the lady who was sitting on the other side of me. She was the daughter of a former member of President Wilson's cabinet and it was clear from the first that she had sought refreshment from the *vin du pays* – in this case, mint juleps. Without further preliminary she turned to me and said in a Southern voice and with no sense of confidentiality: 'If Ah let down mah hair it comes right below mah fanny.' After that conversation was very easy.

Among the other kindnesses which Bill Lewis bestowed on me was to arrange for me to be received by President Coolidge. I was then writing a book, which, a year or two later, appeared entitled

Disarmament and Security. It dealt with these two vexed subjects from the Treaty of Versailles until the opening of the General Disarmament Conference in 1931. At that moment I was researching into the reasons for the failure of the Geneva Naval Disarmament Conference of 1927, which, far from alleviating rivalry in naval armaments, had closed with the relations between Great Britain and the United States considerably acerbated. Each side blamed the other, the Americans claiming parity in cruisers with the British, and the British refusing to concede it. Nor was the position improved by a monster disarmament campaign on the part of the League of Nations Union coupled with a trenchant attack on the Conservative Government. I was in New York when this offensive was launched in London on 21 October 1927 (Trafalgar Day) and had been deeply impressed with the unfortunate effect which it had had on the average American, who at once took it as a confirmation of his distrust of the British Government. It was also regarded as an additional cause of congratulation to American statesmanship on having avoided a repetition of that policy of renunciation which it had adopted at the Washington Conference of 1922. At that conference an American building programme, which would have reached parity with Great Britain had it been carried out, melted like snow before the bland charm of Lord Balfour's smile.

In my career as an historian I have always found it best to go to the top man for information and in this case it happened to be the President of the United States, on whose initiative the conference had been called. Bill Lewis 'worked the oracle' for me and I was duly received. Mr Coolidge has gone down to history as the most silent of presidents and I cannot say that I charmed him into verbosity. But he *did* talk – wisely and with considerable detachment. As a result of what he told me, I myself was able to see the issue in a greater perspective than I had, perhaps, previously. In any case he was most kind and courteous and I was impressed by his slightness of build and his shrewd New England sense of humour. He certainly said more than three words to me, and his smile, though frosty, was in his eyes as well as on his lips.

History will, I believe, eventually award a higher place to Calvin Coolidge among the Presidents of the United States than he has hitherto received. He succeeded to the Presidency at precisely the psychological moment when his austere personality was exactly what was needed. He was the 'Mr Clean' of his day. He brought to the White House a whiff of those New England puritan virtues calculated to disperse the murk and pollution which had become attached to the Harding Administration. By his calm unemotional appearance, small and grey and somewhat wizened; by his reputation for uncommunicative monosyllables, he restored to the high office of Chief Executive a dignity and integrity of which the florid, facile amiability of Warren Gamaliel Harding had robbed it. It should be remembered that though the Harding cabinet had contained some 'rotten apples' from which its unsavoury reputation derived, it had also numbered such distinguished names as Charles Evan Hughes, Herbert Hoover and Dwight Davis. These Mr Coolidge retained, replacing the undesirables by men of equal standing and high repute.

In foreign policy Coolidge pursued the line consistently followed by the Republican Party since 1920, namely that, though it had repudiated the League of Nations, it was definitely desirous that the United States, under its guidance, should welcome a wary association with her fellow nations through 'peace by conference'. This had achieved a certain success in the Washington Naval Disarmament Conference of 1922 and also in taking a share in the launching of the Dawes plan in 1924. Mr Coolidge had hoped to achieve an international *coup* by bringing the United States into the World Court on her own terms, but this was doomed to disappointment when only five of the six American reservations were accepted by the other powers and the Coolidge Administration would not abandon the remaining one. Equally abortive was the attempt to reach an Anglo-American agreement for further naval disarmament at the Geneva Conference of 1927. This hopeful barque foundered on the technical hazard presented by the inability of the British and American delegates to agree on whether the problem should be considered on the basis of numbers or of total tonnage.

It was not, therefore, until 1928, the last year of his presidency, that President Coolidge achieved a crowning success with the negotiation of the Kellogg–Briand Pact, which, though it was hailed at the time with euphoric enthusiasm, proved, as I have described in *Knaves, Fools and Heroes,* but a papiermâché achievement.

Though his hopes in foreign policy had not been crowned with success, Mr Coolidge's intensions had been admirable, if conservative, and the same quality of conservatism characterised his conduct of internal affairs. He was responsible for little important legislation, but what there was of it was in tune with the prevailing mores of an affluent and established society. He believed in reducing taxes, in practising economy and in granting aid to private business. Like most of his fellow countrymen he appeared confident that such a state of affairs would continue indefinitely. In effect, however, he was the last President of the age of False Security; the last President who could boast in his autobiography that he was in bed by ten o'clock each night; the last President who refused to have a telephone on his office table.

It was in 1929 that Claud Cockburn came into my life. He arrived in Washington from Printing House Square as an assistant to Bill Lewis, lean, cadaverous and untidy, a couple of years younger than myself. We took to each other at once and I have always retained my liking for him throughout the years. For, though we belong at extreme opposite poles politically, he a Communist and I a Tory, our friendship was founded on a common sense of humour, perhaps the soundest foundation of all. We found the same things funny and I enjoyed his basic sense of irreverent disregard for many of the things which I held in respect. He too never resented my criticisms of his own tenets of belief. Moreover, in the general battle against Appeasement we were ranged on the same side, though under different banners, and at the time of Munich he was courageous.

Claud did not last long – a bare three years – in his job with *The Times*, which already at that period was inclined to Appeasement. He was altogether too extreme in his politics for them both idealogically and politically, but his arrival in Washington was not without an historical precedent. He was a descendant of that Admiral Sir George Cockburn who in 1814 had burned both the Executive Mansion (thereafter called the White House because of the repainting necessitated by the effects of the fire) and the Capitol, and had sent Dolly Madison scurrying for safety with the original of the Declaration of Independence in her hand-bag. So far as is known no other member of the family had since visited Washington until Claud's arrival, at which moment the dome of the Capitol burst into flames !

Claud had a brilliant mind and was a first-class journalist, but he was erratic and clearly not intended by God to be a conventional newspaper man. There was something of a virtuoso about him and he was, and remains, an original. In 1932, having left *The Times*, he returned to England and the following year founded a fearsome periodical called *The Week*, mimeographed on buff paper in brown type, which for the next ten years held its place in history. Thirty years before *Private Eye* it employed the same shock tactics, with the great difference that it was devoted entirely to politics and international affairs. It was vitriolic and even venomous. It attacked *The Times*, the *Observer*, the Foreign Office and especially the Foreign

Secretary, Lord Halifax, and the Astor family; it created the phrase 'The Cliveden Set' with devastating effect. It was certainly fearless, though I never could fathom what Claud's sources of information were. Perhaps he evolved them out of his own inner consciousness, but the conclusions at which he arrived frequently hit the nail very squarely on the head. There were, however, many occasions when I felt that Claud was over-playing his hand by over-statement. Though I agreed with his non-appeasement policy I considered his arguments sometimes unbalanced and therefore less effective than they should have been.

Like many of his other friends, I was alarmed to think where his quixotic one-man crusade might lead him. Because we liked him we tried to reason with him, as he has recorded in his autobiography:

> 'If you go on like this,' said Mr John Wheeler-Bennett, then head [sic] of the Royal Institute of International Affairs at Chatham House, 'you will soon, I should think, be either quite famous or in gaol.'
>
> 'Lots of people,' I said, 'have been both.'
>
> 'That,' he said, turning upon me his luminous smile, and beaming as though an awkward question had now been satisfactorily resolved, 'is so.'[1]

My prophecy failed of being a bull's eye but can fairly be described as an 'inner'. Claud never did actually go to gaol, though he came jolly near it once or twice, and, if he did not become 'quite famous', he at least achieved considerable notoriety.

The New Deal, with which Franklin Roosevelt successfully combatted the effects of the Great Depression, was also a major social revolution. Its short-term results were little less than miraculous, for, in the course of the First Hundred Days, he convinced a distressed and disheartened American people that the only thing they had to fear was fear itself and set them again to work with fresh courage for the re-establishment of the economic system. The long-term results may, however, be more debatable in the minds of historians.

Of all the alphabetical agencies created by President Roosevelt at that time and staffed with 'new men' drawn for the most part from academic backgrounds, the National Reconstruction Administration (N.R.A.), established by Act of Congress in 1933, was, perhaps, the best known. It was one of the most comprehensive and elaborately

[1] *In Time of Trouble* (London, 1956) p. 230.

executed pieces of legislation in American economic history. Briefly, it gave the President authority for a two-year period to promulgate codes of fair competition for industries in order to achieve economic recovery, and although it was originally intended to apply only to those industries concerned in interstate commerce, the Agency eventually extended its code-making powers to include nearly every industry in the country, including morticians.

I was, of course, deeply interested in this new political phenomenon in Washington and set myself to master the working of the N.R.A., its principles and its machinery. Among the moving spirits was the strong-minded, deeply devoted Mary Romsey, who had long been addicted to social work. With her she had brought her brother, a handsome man of some forty years, whom I had met during my brief contact with the Meadowbrook, Long Island, polo-playing set. His name was Averell Harriman and this was virtually his début in public life.

Between them he and his sister were of the greatest help to me. They supplied me with seemingly inexhaustible piles of documentary material, talked to me themselves and arranged an array of interviews, including to my intense pleasure, one with the Director of N.R.A., General Hugh ('Iron-pants') Johnson. This was the man who had established and successfully directed the unpopular system of the Draft during the First World War, and his appointment to deal with contumacious industrialists was a brave one. For though his courage was beyond dispute, tact was not among the General's salient qualities.

The hour which he set for our appointment, after long and seemingly fruitless negotiations with his fiercely protective secretary 'Rosie', was late in the evening, and he was a very tired man. I realised at once that it would not be a lengthy interview and that I should be lucky if I got a coherent answer to one major question. So I picked the one subject which was uppermost at the moment, Henry Ford's open defiance of the N.R.A. What, I asked, was the General going to do about it? The General looked at me with a newly kindled interest. It was clearly a question to which he enjoyed addressing himself. His face grew purple with emotion and he said, in a voice which sounded like steel filings being drawn over sandpaper, 'I'll tell ya something, brother, I'm going to break that bastard up – right up.'

In this he actually failed for, although the rest of the automobile industry toed the line, Mr Ford pursued his independent way.

When I returned to London I found a letter from Emil de Nagy, who had briefly held the portfolio of foreign affairs in a fleeting Hungarian Cabinet. We had first met in Geneva and later in Budapest and he now wrote to say that he had heard I was in America and would I come and talk to the Foreign Affairs Committee of the Hungarian Parliament on what he called 'The American Revolution'. Primed as I was on the N.R.A., and never averse to visiting the lovely city of Budapest, I accepted his invitation. I prepared a lecture of about forty-five minutes, and had it translated into both German and Magyar, for my audience might well not fully understand English and I wanted to avoid the awful ordeal of an interpreter reading out two translations of my remarks which would have lengthened the proceedings to two hours and a quarter!

Armed with my stack of 'bumph' I reached Budapest in comfort and found that I was the guest of the Committee in a luxurious suite in the Hungaria Hotel overlooking the Danube. All went well. The translations had been distributed and my audience appeared to follow me with understanding and interest. When it was over I answered a few questions through an interpreter and then, according to custom, the member of the Committee most senior in service rose to move a vote of thanks. In this case it was an ancient lady, the Countess Apponyi, whose husband, a descendant of the great Hungarian statesman, had been active in Hungarian politics during the turbulent period following the First World War. She was also very much a person in her own right, but neither her eyesight nor her hearing were what they had been, and now in a quavering old voice she said, 'Thank you so much, dear friend, for coming here tonight to tell us all these terrible things about *Australia*.'

There was a stunned silence and then a thunderous burst of applause and some laughter, which I hoped was intended to make me feel that the rest of my audience had at least understood which country I was talking about. But it was a bad moment. Incidentally, when I re-examined the translations afterwards I found to my relief that nowhere was the name 'Australia' mentioned!

I first met Ted Roosevelt, Jr, the late President Theodore Roosevelt's eldest son, by chance at a dinner at the Century, and was invited to spend a week-end at Oyster Bay. Ted was rugged in appearance and in intellect. He was essentially tough-minded and rough-hewn and as such a born leader of men. But he was capable of great gentleness and kindness, and though his temper would flare up in argument it would subside with equal suddenness, and thereafter he would pay meticulous consideration to his opponent's point of view. He had the great irresistible grin of his father and his roar of laughter would fill a room or send birds flying startled from their tree-tops.

Ted was a wonderful chap, with all his father's drive and a secret ambition to excel or at least equal his father's record. Unfortunately he rarely succeeded in bringing this dream to pass. He explored the Amazon, with never quite the showmanship of his father; he campaigned as Republican candidate for the governorship of the state of New York but was not elected. Only in his military career did he outdo the President. He attained the rank of brigadier-general as compared with his father's colonelcy and he led his troops into action in wars, in comparison with which the Spanish-American conflict was the merest skirmish. He died a soldier's death, than which nothing could have given him greater pleasure, in his truck in Normandy on 12 July 1944. The order for his promotion to major-general lay on General Eisenhower's desk awaiting signature at the moment of his death.

When not consumed by ancestor-worship or in competition with his father, Ted was a man of many interests. He was among the founders of the American Legion, a national leader in the Boy Scout Movement and a successful publisher. He attained great success both as Governor-General of the Philippines and Governor of Puerto Rico, America's only two colonial possessions. Above all he was one of the nicest people in the world, with a rambunctious sense of humour and a capacity for friendship manifested in a heart 'like all outdoors'.

I often stayed with him and his charming wife Eleanor (and she was most particular in pronouncing it 'Eleanor' to distinguish it from President Franklin Roosevelt's wife, 'Eleanor') and their two younger sons, Cornelius and Quentin. They had a delightful old rambling house on the water-front at Oyster Bay and later the rather more dignified Old Orchard in the grounds of Sagamore Hill. This was the President's hideous, self-designed but fascinating residence, where in my time, the President's widow, Ted's mother, still lived. She was indeed a formidable *grande dame* and Eleanor was frankly afraid of her. When a summons to Sunday supper would come down from 'the Big House', she would dispatch Ted and me to the ordeal and remain behind at Old Orchard. Ted would subside in stature to that of a little boy on these occasions, but they were really not an ordeal at all. The old lady loved an audience and once one could get her to 'reminisce', she would do so in a salty, uninhibited manner which I found riveting. She had a tongue like a 'branding-iron', as her son said – and she was immensely entertaining. 'I used to enjoy observing the vagaries of society, my dear,' I remember she once said to me, 'but now I prefer to watch the antics of the barn-yard. They're less complicated.'

Week-ends with Ted and Eleanor could be as active or inactive as you wished. I recall many Sunday mornings stretched out on the shore in the hot sun and soft breeze off the Sound talking with one or another of the family at intervals – for as a unit they never stayed still for a moment. A favourite pastime was the swapping and capping of quotations with Ted, who shared my love of poetry and could quote by the yard Kipling, Macaulay, Browning, Tennyson, Longfellow, Rupert Brooke and John Greenleaf Whittier. It was great fun and excellent intellectual gymnastic exercise.

All sorts of entertaining people arrived for lunch. Norman Thomas, the veteran Socialist leader who ran as a presidential candidate on no fewer than six occasions, and Charles and Anne Lindbergh. There was Joe Alsop, already a power in the Washington press, who was a cousin of Ted's and usually ended by having a splendid row with young Quentin, and Mary Roberts Rinehart, the authoress of detective stories and the delightful Tish novels. I especially remember a wet autumn afternoon when we settled down in the music room and Richard Rodgers played at our request all our favourite songs from his productions with Oscar Hammerstein and Lorenz Hart, singing them with a verve and gusto which seemed to delight him.

One week-end stands out in my memory. In August 1937 Keith Officer and I were alone with Ted at Oyster Bay, Eleanor and Quentin being in China at the time. Suddenly we heard on the radio that aerial warfare between Japan and China was in full blast and that both sides had dropped bombs on the Shanghai International Settlement. Ted was beside himself. His wife and son were right there at that moment. He burned up the wires between Oyster Bay and Shanghai and eventually established a connection. Eleanor told him that she and Quentin, like true Roosevelts, were thoroughly enjoying the excitement and adventure, and held the telephone out of the window so that Ted could hear the bomb-bursts and anti-aircraft fire. Had he been there he would have been equally enthusiastic but under the circumstances he issued imperative commands for immediate evacuation, and backed it up with a peremptory cable: 'HEREAFTER YOU STAY HOME'.

But more effulgent than all others of that family was Ted's half-sister Alice, the only child of the President's first marriage. In her youth she had been something of a tartar, and she was the apple of her father's eye. She married Nicholas Longworth, the Speaker of the House of Representatives, in the first wedding to be held in the White House and has ever since been the reigning queen of Washington even at the age of ninety. She has the swift percipient reflexes of a bird and a spontaneity of intellect, blinding in its brilliance. Acrid in her criticisms, she is impartial in her castigation. She was devastating in her comments on her Democratic cousin Franklin and his wife and equally destructive of her fellow Republicans. She blasted Thomas Dewey's electoral hopes in two successive campaigns, first by describing him as 'the Little Man on the Wedding-Cake' and then with the warning that 'a soufflé never rises twice'.

Alice had a deep reverence for her father's memory and had a multitude of good stories about him with which she would regale me, two of which concerned the death of the American Ambassador in London, Mr Whitelaw Reid, in 1912. The British Government, as a pleasing gesture, sent the Ambassador's body back to the United States in a warship and the Republican Party seized upon the event as an opportunity to heal the breach between President Taft and ex-President Roosevelt, both of whom were invited to be pall-bearers of honour at the funeral. On hearing the news of the Ambassador's death, Alice had said something to her father about his having died in harness, whereupon Theodore Roosevelt had corrected her with a snorted remark: 'Nonsense, my dear child, nothing of the sort; the trappings of a circus horse!'

However he accepted the office of pall-bearer and took Alice along with him. Her eagle-eye did not miss the fact that at the end of the ceremony, President Taft rose and, with his aides, left the church ahead of the coffin. In answer to her question as to whether this wasn't rather odd, her father replied: 'Not odd at all, my dear, merely one political corpse preceding another. Rather an interesting sight.'

There were those who feared Alice Longworth, but I confess that I have been in love with her since I first met her nearly fifty years ago and she has always been the one person I most want to see whenever I am in Washington, for I revel in her wit and humour and mischievous gossip. Over the years she has shown me every kindness, not least in accepting Ruth into the intimacy of our friendship. For many years after our marriage, Alice would give a delicious dinner party for us, at which she and I would have a formal exchange of tiny gifts. She remains one of the great joys of my life.

The stories about Alice ('Mrs L.' as she is widely known in

Washington) are legion. During the war I was lunching with her alone and was extolling the great qualities of our then Ambassador, Philip Kerr, Marquess of Lothian. There was, I said, only one thing about him which I found hard to understand: his renunciation of the Roman Catholic Church for that of Christian Science. It was very strange. 'Not strange at all, my dear,' said Alice, without a moment's hesitation. 'Merely a matter of swapping Blessed Virgins in midstream.'

It was about this time that I had the unusual experience of reading my own obituary.

I sailed from Southampton in the *Queen Mary* on 16 March 1936 and almost at once began to feel very ill indeed. The ship's doctor, the redoubtable Dr Maguire, diagnosed it as a severe streptococcic infection, for which there were then few treatments. The ship was not very full and I was therefore able to have the care of both the nurses from the sick-bay, who looked after me with every attention and kindness; I needed all the skill they could give me, for I had a pretty rough time. However by the time we reached New York I was on the recovery list, though still extremely weak. I was carried off the ship on a stretcher. Having cabled to a friend to meet me, I languidly handed him my keys and as soon as he cleared my baggage through that ordeal of officialdom, the U.S. Customs Service (who on this occasion, I must admit, were extremely helpful and solicitous), I was driven away to the Chatham Hotel.

That night the friend who had been good enough to meet me went to a party which he regaled with the saga of my arrival, concluding with: 'Poor old John, he looks like death.' Now there also happened to be there my old friend Dorothy Thompson, whose fame as a journalist was, at that time, world-wide, and for whom I had affection and a deep respect for her fearless denunciation of the Nazis. We had met originally in Berlin during those last sad days of the Weimar Republic when she obtained her famous interview with Adolf Hitler. Dorothy had a column three days a week in the *Herald-Tribune* and in her next contribution she referred to me as 'the late' and went on to say what a loss my death had been and what a nice chap I was. I was greatly touched and flattered to read it – but, of course, I wasn't dead at all.

By that time, I was feeling a good deal better, so, resisting the temptation to quote Mark Twain's remark that the rumour was grossly exaggerated, I wrote and thanked Dorothy for her 'piece', but pointed out that its basic premise was inaccurate. She recanted most charmingly in her next column, whereupon I telegraphed her that she had conferred upon me the only attribute I was ever likely to share with the Almighty in that I had been raised from the dead on the third day!

I have a copy of Dorothy's book *Let the Record Speak*, which appeared shortly thereafter, with an inscription: 'To John Wheeler-Bennett, in pleasure that he lives.'

The whole incident had caused some perturbation among my friends in America and especially in Charlottesville, where I was delighted to hear that Ruth, to whom I was not yet married, was deeply concerned. The newspapermen called my aged mother on the telephone in London in the middle of the night and asked if she could confirm or deny my death, but she replied tartly that if I had died she would certainly have learnt of it long before the press.

The infection had a prolonged 'hang-over' that kept me listless and debilitated, and I had another collapse in May during a visit to Canada. At length a decision was taken for me which had a far-reaching effect on my life.

I was staying during that autumn in Washington with Sir Ronald and Lady Lindsay at the new embassy which Lutyens had built at the north-west end of Massachusetts Avenue amid much criticism from 'the locals'. Ronnie Lindsay was one of the nicest people and a remarkably shrewd observer of men and events in Washington, as he had been in Constantinople and in Berlin. His wife Elizabeth, who was a Hoyt from Long Island, was a woman full of courage and character, and she had a certain fierceness which rather frightened me, although I knew it masked a very real sense of kindness. She said to me. After Memphis, the land changes quite abruptly and I shall and south. You must go West. In fact you must go to stay with my old friend Isabella Greenway King at Tucson in Arizona. I will arrange it all. You just get yourself there.'

One did not disobey or argue with Elizabeth Lindsay, especially when she spoke in that minatory tone, and I at once put my plans in train. I had an elderly Packard and a black driver called Joe, whom I had taken on at Charleston, South Carolina, and we all headed west. It was a fascinating drive and it opened up new areas of the country to me. After Memphis, the land changes quite abruptly and I shall never forget crossing the Mississippi River in the early morning, with the white mists still lying on the water and the black soil of the cotton-fields looming up on either side of the road. We drove by way of Little Rock, Arkansas, and then across Oklahoma and New Mexico, eventually arriving about a week later at Tucson, where I found myself greeted and welcomed by one of the most enchanting women I have ever known.

Isabella King was originally from Kentucky – her father being a Selmes and her mother a Flandrau. From her earliest childhood she was beautiful and when her mother took her to Paris at the age of sixteen she caused a sensation. Attended by her black 'mammy', clad in ample skirts and headscarf, she went to sketch in the Luxembourg Gardens. Here she at once found herself the centre of a crowd of students lost in admiration of her charms and her unusual chaperone, and when the time came for luncheon, they first danced around her, and then escorted her in a body to the Hotel Meurice, in the rue de Rivoli, blocking the streets as they went. As a result Mrs Selmes was called upon by a representative of the Prefect of Police, who politely requested her to persuade her daughter to choose some other site than the Luxembourg Gardens for the exercise of her artistic propensities, so that her admirers should not disrupt the traffic of Paris.

Subsequently Isabella married a Scotsman, Robert Munro Ferguson, brother of that Lord Novar who had been Governor-General of Australia, and secondly, after his death, the splendidly dashing and soldierly figure, Colonel John Greenway, who shared with Theodore Roosevelt the glories of the charge up San Juan Hill. She married thirdly Harry O. King.

Both Isabella's first and second husbands were close friends of Theodore Roosevelt, and a girlhood friend of hers was Eleanor, one of whose bridesmaids she was at the latter's marriage to her cousin, Franklin.

When the bride and bridegroom left for their honeymoon, they delegated to their bridesmaids the duty of acknowledging many of their last-minute wedding-presents. Isabella did her share, but her letters somewhat puzzled their recipients by reason of the fact that, beginning, 'Franklin and I are so grateful for your lovely (whatever it was) which we shall always use,' they concluded: 'Yours affectionately, Isabella Selmes.'

Delightfully vague though she seemed, it was very soon apparent that she was not only a shrewd businesswoman but a brilliant amateur architect and she personally planned and directed the building of the Arizona Inn at Tucson. This project originated in an enterprise of hers after the First World War when Arizona, with its clear dry climate, became a haven for those veterans who had suffered tuberculosis and the pulmonary effects of poison gas. Isabella Greenway discovered that they had no therapeutic facilities and supplied this deficiency by setting them to work making furniture to her own enchanting design. So enthusiastic was the response that the supply tended to overrun the immediate demand, whereupon she met the situation with characteristic practicability and imagination, establishing the Arizona Inn, partly as an adventure of her own and partly to absorb the rising flood of furniture. In both objectives she was highly successful and the Inn has been frequently acclaimed one of the most attractive, nay, paradisal, hostelries in the world. Moreover Isabella was an able politician and served one and a half terms as Congresswoman from Arizona in the House of Representatives at Washington.

With her physical beauty and elegance of manner which proclaimed her a great lady, was combined an inner beauty which radiated an essential goodness and serenity of spirit. With her and with her son Jack and her daughter Martha, I (and, later, Ruth also) formed a deep and abiding friendship, which has resulted in kindnesses which we can never repay.

Such was the person whom I now met for the first time, whom I revisited again and again both in New York and in Arizona, and under whose hospitable roof-tree in Tucson, Ruth and I are still welcomed each winter. I was cosseted and cherished and made one of the family and in these enrapturing conditions – and also thanks in some measure to the wonderful climate of Arizona – I soon recovered my health and returned to Virginia where I was to spend much of the latter days of peace.

I came to the South by way of the Confederacy. From my earliest visit in 1923, I was fascinated by this amazing episode in American history and felt impelled to study it. At first I did so sporadically, for my visits were mere annual intervals in my European activities. I went to Charleston, South Carolina, to visit, as it were, the cradle of secession and fell at once under the enchantment of one of the most beautiful cities in America, with its galaxy of graceful houses, the unique setting of the Battery and the glory of its magnificent gardens which gave some idea of what *ante-bellum* elegance really meant. Of these, Middleton Place (to my mind the most beautiful of all) now belongs to a much loved godson of mine, Charles Pringle Duell, a direct descendant of the original owner, who received his grant from Charles II.

I passed on to Montgomery, Alabama, to see the State Capitol where Jefferson Davis was first inaugurated as Provisional President of the Confederate States, on which occasion William Yancey coined the immortal phrase: 'The man and the hour have met.' I traversed the route of Sherman's historic progress 'from Atlanta to the sea', riding part of the way through the beauteous woods of Georgia, exquisite in their wild apple-blossom and wistaria. I eventually arrived at the city of Savannah, with its architectural delights in both the grace of its houses and the design of the city in a charming series of squares. In the opposite direction to the westward I visited Vicksburg on the Mississippi River, the only city in the United States where the national flag does not fly on 4 July, because it was on that date in 1863 that General Grant received its surrender. And finally in 1935, after my second journey to Russia, which I have described in *Knaves, Fools and Heroes* I came back to Charlottesville, to the peace of the University, the charm of the community and the comely attractions of the countryside – rolling farm-lands, pastures and behind them the azure loveliness of the Blue Ridge Mountains.

It was then that I made several important decisions. I had to finish my book on the Brest-Litovsk Treaty, *The Forgotten Peace*, but after that I had visions of writing on the Army of Northern Virginia, fired as I was by the strategic genius of Lee and 'Stonewall' Jackson, of Jeb Stuart and A. P. Hill and Longstreet.

I had read every memoir and historical study from Henderson's *Stonewall Jackson* downwards and also many historical novels, and felt myself to be pretty well equipped, as regards the written word, but I lacked local colour and local knowledge. I needed to study the terrain over which these famous soldiers had displayed their military talents. Forthwith I betook myself to Richmond, the State capital, because I had been told that the editor of the evening paper there, the *Richmond News-Leader*, was the greatest living expert on my subject.

Through the kindness of the Bryan family, grandees of Richmond, who owned the paper, I met its editor Douglas Southall Freeman, one of the most outstanding American historians and biographers of the Civil War period. Douglas Freeman was what you might call odd. He had been a Baptist lay-reader in his youth and had retained something of the austerity of his upbringing; he had later become a journalist and had risen to the top of his profession, but, over and above his calling, he had made himself a meticulous student and scholar of his period. His detailed knowledge of the Army of Northern Virginia was fantastic. I was rather proud of the fact that I knew the 'top brass' of that Army down to and including major-generals, but Freeman could tell you the names of brigade and regimental commanders, and the order of their succession, a particularly difficult achievement because of the very heavy casualties among these cadres of officers.

He would rise at four in the morning and work in his office on his pet subject before the daily routine of an evening daily newspaper office began, but he always found time to talk to me when I called on him at a more reasonable hour! We became fast friends and he was good enough to give up his precious week-ends to conducting me over the battlefields. We rattled along in his outrageous old motor-car, which he drove with the dash and verve of a cavalryman, and later tramped from Winchester to Cross Keys and Port Republic. We followed Jackson's Valley Campaign, through the tangled country of the Seven Days' battles before Richmond, the almost jungle fighting of Chancellorsville and the bloody massacres of Fredericksburg and the Wilderness, and finally to the ramparts of Petersburg and the last scene of Appomattox. We sat together in St Paul's Church at Richmond in the pew where President Davis received the fatal message from General Lee that the Confederate capital must be evacuated and together we roamed through the White House of the Confederacy, where Davis presided for the four years' history of his infant nation.

In some ways it was like working with Lewis Namier, for Douglas Freeman would tolerate no slovenly scholarship, no sentimental preference, no biased excuses. His knowledge was so prodigious that, though he was but in his middle age, it was as though he had lived in full maturity through the whole period which we were studying.

Though I would not have forgone one hour of these incredible expeditions, the experience that I gained eventually convinced me of my own inadequacy. When Douglas Freeman produced his great biography R. E. Lee, whose four magnificent volumes I reviewed for the New York Times, I considered that any contribution which I might make to the study of the Army of Northern Virginia would be but feeble and superfluous, and I transferred my researches to the less furrowed field of a political history of the Confederacy.

It was consoling to discover that I was not alone in my disappointment. John Buchan's biographer records that he had long entertained an ambition to write a life of Lee but when he had made the tour of the Seven Days' battlefields with Freeman and read his book, he, like myself, bowed his head before a master and abandoned the project.[1]

These forays with Douglas Freeman extended over some years, and during them I made my headquarters at the Farmington Country

[1] Janet Adam Smith, John Buchan (London, 1965) p. 247.

Club, a fine example of Jeffersonian architecture, set in beautiful park-land surroundings. I even persuaded my mother to come over and visit the land of her ancestors and she took very kindly to it and its denizens to her.

I also resumed my equestrian interests. My circle of friends embraced all sorts and conditions of men from University professors – including my oldest friend in Virginia, Robert Kent Gooch – and students to professional men such as lawyers and architects and doctors, and from landed gentry and farmers to the fox-hunting circle of the hunt-club, to which I was elected a member. Among these last was a tall, skinny, leathery, raw-boned old chap, who might well have been a veteran of Jackson's Army of the Valley. Norris Watson had a capacity for bourbon whisky and innocent exaggeration of which I have never met the equal. No one had galloped so fast, jumped so high or mastered such headstrong mounts as he had, and it was pure joy to listen to him piling Pelion upon Ossa, without a hesitation or a blush.

Through him I acquired a really splendid horse, Red Match, a son of Gallant Fox, the Kentucky Derby winner of 1930. Red, despite his aristocratic ancestry, was no race horse, but he was beautifully put together and a first-class hunter, having been trained to jump by a previous owner. He carried me well and gave me great pleasure.

It was now that I took a further major decision. On a spring evening in 1935, my mother and I were sitting on the terrace of the country club watching the glow of the setting sun on the Blue Ridge, a pleasure which for me never palls. There passed us a group of young faculty members from the University together with their belles, among whom was one who was obviously 'Queen of the May' and surrounded by admirers. Petite, blue-eyed, golden-haired, with a wonderful complexion, she had a smile and a laugh which warmed the heart and sent the blood coursing through one's veins.

I was aware that my heart had turned a somersault. I sat bolt upright and said to my mother: 'That is the girl I am going to marry.' And she, being wise in the ways of the world, replied: 'You might do a great deal worse, my dear,' and that was all she did say.

This was my first sight of my future wife, though for one reason or another we didn't get married till ten years later. It was not an easy conquest. Ruth did not undergo the same immediate reaction on meeting me. In fact she rather disliked me, and when I told her of some of my experiences in Germany, including the complicated circumstances of my sudden departure just before the Night of the Long Knives, she frankly disbelieved me, thinking me 'the biggest liar in seven counties'. It was not until she had met other friends of mine who corroborated my stories, some of which got into the press, that the credibility gap began to diminish. It finally closed altogether and despite all obstacles, we were married in 1945 under circumstances which I shall relate in their place.

Life in Virginia was for me a delight, and it remains so. I rented several houses, three in all, between 1936 and 1939. This earned me the friendly nickname of 'The Cuckoo', for I was always seeking a pleasant place. My favourite was a charming estate in the country, called Spring Hill, dating from the early nineteenth century. Virginians, when they like you, take you to their hearts, and especially if you are an Englishman, for the great majority are of English or Scotch-Irish stock, and justifiably proud of their lineage. Indeed genealogy is a strong suit with them and perhaps the most devastating comment I have ever heard was of a Richmond lady who, when asked who somebody's mother was, replied: 'His mother, my dear? I didn't know he went back so far.'

But they were wonderful to me, and I look back on those years before the Second World War and on my associations afterwards with the University as the happiest of my life. In a curious way it was an antidote to the hideous prospect which I found building up in Europe when I returned there each summer. I would come back to Virginia filled with premonitions of disaster, which were all too well founded, to find the balm and peace of a community, which, though intelligent and informed on world affairs, were yet not oppressed by the ever increasingly propinquitous proximity of war.

Friends came to stay with me who brought with them a breath of starker reality, Keith Officer from Washington, Paul Scheffer from New York, whom I had first known in Moscow in 1929, Heinrich Brüning from Harvard, and Bruce Lockhart from England, who mingled happily with my local friends but marvelled at their detachment. The variety or notoriety of my guests, plus the fact that members of the Embassy staff often came to me from Washington for week-ends, caused me to be suspected, like Bill Lewis, of being a highly placed official in British Intelligence, and I became known facetiously as 'operator 269'.

Once in 1937 I had an unexpected visit from Karl Goerdeler, who had been a member of Brüning's cabinet, and was now an acknowledged leader in the German Resistance movement. He was being kept very much 'under wraps' by the State Department on the express orders of Sumner Welles, but he slipped away to Charlottesville to spend the night with me. We sat late talking and he told me *inter alia* of his hopes that the overthrow of Hitler would result in the restoration of the monarchy, at any rate in Prussia, and possibly the reconstitution of the German Empire on a more liberal, constitutional basis. This was exactly the idea that Brüning had broached to President von Hindenburg in 1932 with such negative results. He nearly scared the wits out of me, however, by having a heart attack during the night. Though it proved to be only a minor one, I had visions of his dying on my hands. He wasn't supposed to be there anyway and I could foresee exceedingly unpleasant consequences ahead. I shot him back to Washington by car with all possible speed, where he arrived, to my great relief, still living and with his absence undetected.

On another occasion, unexpectedly enough, I found myself entertaining Earl Browder, the chairman of the American Communist Party. He had been invited to speak at the Institute of Public Affairs, an admirable foundation held under the auspices of the University of Virginia in the early summer of each year to provide public lectures by eminent persons, and subsequent discussions. Its fame was nationwide and it attracted speakers of every creed, colour and political complexion.

Earl Browder had been invited, but there was a marked local disinclination to give him hospitality, so I did. He proved a most entertaining, intelligent, cultured and considerate guest and, despite our polarised political credos, we got on very well together. He had a delightful sense of humour and a pretty wit in dealing with hostile questioners after his lecture. A somewhat pompous lady, who was obviously convinced that all communists were foreign agents, arose in her place and asked: 'Would the speaker be prepared to tell us when he came to this country?' To which Earl Browder, in his silkiest tones, replied: 'Certainly, Madam, my family came to this colony as indentured labour before the Revolution, so I think that perhaps I might say that I come from the "First Families of Virginia".' There was an almost audible sound of what Mr Punch used to call: 'collapse of stout party'.

One of the many joys of living in Virginia at that time (for alas it is barely possible to find them today) was the personalities of one's black servants, with their protective affection and their wonderful use of language. I had a delightful old cook, who liked to speak of me as 'my little lamb' to all and sundry. I entered the house one morning after riding to hear her concluding a conversation on the telephone: 'Ah'm real sorry but mah little lamb has just stepped out.' Subsequent enquiry disclosed that the call was from the British Embassy! It took me quite a long time to live that one down.

She was a peerless cook but she had one maddening failing; she had absolutely no sense of time. Delicious meals would appear sometimes nearly an hour late, by which time one's guests had absorbed so many cocktails or high-balls that they were incapable of tasting – let alone appreciating – the most Lucullan of repasts. In desperation I bought the cook an alarm-clock and showed her how to set it to warn her when to begin cooking dinner. She nodded silently but did not object. My next party was the same as those which had gone before. A befuddled company sat down to an admirable dinner served over an hour late. The following morning I admonished her and asked her why she hadn't used the alarm-clock. 'Oh,' said she, 'I fro ol' clock out de winder. He make dinner so late.' After that I surrendered to *force majeure.*

Her most pleasing mishandling of the English language was her question whether she should 'uncrack the nuts' for dessert – an excellent and highly expressive phrase.

At Spring Hill the king-pin was Andrew, a man of magnificent physique, considerable intelligence and great devotion. One turned to Andrew to solve every problem from a leaking pipe to the trickier question of how to evict a skunk, which had taken up residence under the porch steps, without too great a disaster to all concerned. He was never at a loss, and never was his ingenuity more powerfully displayed than at an outdoor supper party which I gave in honour of that eminent historian, Professor William E. Dodd, whom I had known well when he was President Roosevelt's first ambassador to Berlin at the beginning of the Nazi régime. A buffet supper was to be eaten at small tables dotted about the lawn. The day was fine and all things seemed propitious until, late in the afternoon, one of those storms which suddenly afflict Virginia in the summer, came upon us with the full blast of thunder and lightning and 'a rushing mighty wind'.

It didn't last long, but it left a trail of havoc in its wake. The electricity was off, affecting both the lighting and the refrigerators; the telephone was out of order, isolating us from the outside world and, perhaps worst of all, two large trees had fallen across the private road by which, in some three hours' time, my guests were due to arrive.

In an agony of spirit I called aloud for Andrew, and that splendid person assumed instant and complete control of the situation. He despatched messengers to the telephone and electricity companies and from his own friends and relations living nearby he mobilised a powerful labour force, who, armed with cross-saws and axes disposed of the fallen trees as if by magic. When my first guests arrived the road was clear, the refrigerator was again in action and we were 'back on the air'. They found the whole scene one of great calm and beauty with each table lit by candles protected by those tall glass hurricane-shades which are a feature of southern out-of-doors entertaining.

Apart from the fact that one of the guests became mentally deranged during the evening and had to be taken away, it was a highly successful party.

Beside being a general factotum and a *deus ex machina*, Andrew was also a pillar of the local Baptist church and a regular attendant at Sunday services. He was a peaceful, amiable soul and I was therefore not a little surprised when he arrived one Monday morning with one side of his face raw and swollen. In answer to my enquiry he replied, rather startlingly: 'A gen'lman hit me with a half-brick in church, suh.' It seemed that religious fervour could scarcely reach greater heights. Had not the early Christian Fathers come to blows on mere liturgical issues?

In most southern towns the week-end in the black district is a period of euphoric and hysterical excitement. There is a good deal of liquor about and sometimes the razors are out and there is what is euphemistically termed 'a cutting'; sometimes they cut too deeply. My mother-in-law had an excellent cook, who was lovely to look at, kind-hearted and devoted. Great was our sorrow when in a moment of excessive emotion one Saturday night she severed her lover's jugular vein and was, alas, convicted on a charge of manslaughter. We all mourned her loss, not only because she was a good cook, but because we were all genuinely fond of her.

Time passed with relentless pace and every time I returned to Europe I became more convinced that war was inevitable and imminent. Germany's unilateral declaration of rearmament, her re-militarisation of the Rhineland and her annexation of Austria, though they went unchallenged by Britain and France, yet brought us that much closer to the point when a halt to lawless gangsterism and intimidation must be called. Many thought that the breaking-point would come if Czechoslovakia were threatened; few anticipated that Poland would provide the ultimate *casus belli*.

In Europe I pursued my travels in foreign countries, as I have already described in *Knaves, Fools and Heroes*; in Virginia I completed my book, *The Forgotten Peace*, and strove to maintain my faith in human nature which was so sorely tried on the other side of the Atlantic.

Greatly to my pleasure I received one day in the late spring of 1938, a call from the Dean and Assistant Dean of the University Law School (the latter my old friend, Hardy Dillard, being today a judge of the World Court at The Hague). They suggested that in the coming fall semester which began in September, I should give a seminar on international law and affairs, with the status of a 'lecturer extraordinary' in these subjects. I accepted with delight, feeling that, though my qualifications in international law might be a little sketchy, I could get by in this, my first, adventure into academic life on my knowledge of international affairs.

I arrived back from Europe at the conclusion of the Czech crisis nearly a month after the university semester had started but primed with first-hand experience. The ensuing weeks were of the greatest value to me, for I was forced to collate and analyse my own thoughts and my students seemed to find it of interest also. They were a brilliant lot and as I write I can see them again as they sat around in my drawing-room, for our sessions were very informal and supplemented by beer and sandwiches, and with all of them I established the happiest of relations. There were about a dozen, hand-picked by the law faculty. They included Louis Auchincloss, now one of America's outstanding novelists, Tony Bliss, who became a power in the administration of the Metropolitan Opera, Marshall Field, heir to the great Chicago fortune, Larry Houston, later deputy director of the C.I.A., three others who distinguished themselves in the State Department and Franklin Roosevelt, Jr, son of the President of the United States.

It was a moment of climax in all our lives for I was now convinced that we should have war in Europe within a year, and that sooner or later the United States would become involved. I set myself to awaken the minds of these young men to the problems and responsibilities which they would be called upon to face. It was not without success, as their papers and our discussions showed, and for me it had one particularly interesting by-product.

Towards the end of January 1939 young Franklin Roosevelt came to me with an invitation to spend the week-end of the President's birthday (30 January) at the White House. I was, of course, honoured, and welcomed the opportunity of meeting on intimate terms one of the greatest men of his age. Frank duly drove me up to Washington on the Saturday afternoon at a lawless speed which earned us pursuit by a posse of state troopers, who, unable to overtake us, hung on our tail until somewhat to their surprise we turned into the gates of the Executive Mansion.

I found that I had been allocated the Lincoln Room, which, though of historical interest, has the drawback of being exactly below the roof of the main portico where a light burns all night and under which a marine sentry marches to and fro on guard the whole twenty-four hours, with the concomitant stamp of military boots as he turns at either end of his beat. I was also mildly disturbed at the thought of what my belligerently un-Reconstructed Confederate grandmother would think if she knew I was sleeping in Mr Lincoln's bed and half-expected her ghost to appear and anathematise me accordingly.

There were one or two other house-guests and we had all brought some form of birthday gift, mostly books. (At young Franklin's advice I had brought a copy of *Hindenburg*.) Perhaps the least appropriate was that of Hendrik Van Loon, the eminent author and journalist, who proudly presented the President with a book entitled *The Man who Killed Lincoln*! Mr Roosevelt laughed aloud, throwing back his head with that characteristic gesture, and, quick as a flash came his response: 'Thank you, my dear Hendrik, very thoughtful of you – and we're going to the theatre this evening too.'

And go we did to see a performance of *Outward Bound* at the National Theatre. I was driving in the car immediately behind the President and was fascinated by the security precautions. In those days automobiles still had running-boards and on these stood plain clothes F.B.I. and Secret Service men, with their hands in the pockets of their jackets in which were significant bulges. We entered by the back door of the theatre, which was easier for the ramp for the President's chair, and before going in I chanced to look up and saw that on every cross-landing of every fire-escape within sight was a uniformed policeman with a sub-machine-gun.

I had never before entered a theatre box in the wake of a Head of State and seen the whole audience rise in acclamation. It is a heady experience, and one which makes you think. One begins to understand how mere human beings who had not been brought up to this sort of thing from childhood, as has a sovereign, may become obsessed by delusions of grandeur.

After the performance, which was a good one, we all drove back to the White House where the cast and a number of friends of the family and some political supporters had supper at small tables. I was table-mate amongst others with Senator Alben Barkley of Kentucky, who later became President Truman's Vice-President, and a member of the cast, Morgan Farley, who was really to me the more interesting of the two. I had seen him in Chicago some years before playing the lead in *L'Aiglon*, being the first man to do so, since, following the tradition which Rostand had established with Sarah Bernhardt, the part of the Duc de Reichstadt was always played by a woman. I had seen that splendid actress Marie Löhr in the rôle but, not unnaturally, it is far more convincing in the hands of a man. All this I found great interest in discussing with Morgan Farley, who, from being at first shy and reserved, blossomed forth in a wealth of theatrical gossip which was highly entertaining. As I remember it Senator Barkley was not interested in our conversation.

The following morning (Sunday) I had an hour's talk with the President in the Oval Room before lunch. It was in every way a memorable experience. Franklin Roosevelt was incontestably one of the great figures of this century and it was not really difficult to understand why. He had infinite charm, the manners of an aristocrat, that is to say an amalgam of courtesy and ruthlessness, and a great deal of pragmatic common sense. He was highly imaginative and had a complete flexibility of mind, which enabled him to adopt or jettison matters of principle with the greatest facility. He was not domineering or dominant in conversation; indeed he was a good listener and quick to take a point. To me he was exceedingly kind on a number of occasions.

At this particular time he wanted to talk about Munich and its consequences, telling me that his son had told him of my seminar sessions and of the interest they had stimulated. I told him all I knew, of my conversations with Beneš and with Jan Masaryk and of the fruitless mission of Neill Malcolm and myself to General Syrový in Prague after Munich, which I have described in *Knaves, Fools and Heroes*. He asked me what I thought would happen now and I remember saying that in my opinion, if Hitler would make the Munich Agreement the keystone of his future foreign policy, he could very easily establish a political and economic hegemony over all central and south-eastern Europe without major opposition from Britain or France. But, I added, I would not exclude the possibility of his being unable to do this because his personal and national ambition inclined him towards the East and that if he embarked on another project of territorial aggrandisement, the Western Powers might feel reluctantly compelled to call a halt.

The President said that my views were shared by his ambassadors in Paris (Bill Bullitt) and in Poland (Tony Biddle) but that Joe

Kennedy in London was an enthusiastic supporter and admirer of Neville Chamberlain's policies. On the whole the State Department, in the persons of Cordell Hull and Sumner Welles, shared the view of Bullitt, Biddle (and incidentally myself). He did not say in so many words that he expected war but it seemed to me very apparent from his questions that this possibility was much in his mind. He did say that he had disclosed his own feelings in recalling his ambassador (Hugh Wilson) from Berlin as a protest against the Jewish pogroms of the previous November.

The President also asked me whether I thought there would be a conspiracy to overthrow Hitler. I replied that I should believe in this when it was a *fait accompli*, and added that it was essentially a matter for the Germans themselves; any outside assistance was to be avoided, but that on the other hand any conspiracies should be encouraged but without any commitments as to the future. (This remained my view throughout the war.)

What impressed me about the President throughout my visit was that at no moment was one embarrassed by the fact that he was a cripple. One was aware of it, of course, but he handled himself with such skill and aplomb that the whole thing passed off without distress.

That evening, after the traditional Sunday supper, at which Mrs Roosevelt presided over her chafing dish, there was a movie in the East Wing. It was *Drums along the Mohawk*, the film of Walter Edmonds' novel, out of which the British do not come so well. The President had put me beside him and after about the third occasion on which the peaceful residents of the Mohawk Valley had been massacred by the brutal red-coats and their barbarous Indian allies, he leaned over and said: 'Perhaps I shouldn't have asked you tonight after all!'

Within six weeks of our conversation Hitler had disclosed his hand in dismembering the remnant of the Czechoslovak state on 16 March 1939, thereby tearing up the Munich Agreement, and shortly thereafter the storm signals were hoisted over the Free City of Danzig as a warning to Poland. It was now no longer a question of 'if' there should be a war but of 'when' war would come.

It was in this fateful summer of 1939 that there occurred a vital and unique event in Anglo-American relations, the visit of King George VI and Queen Elizabeth to North America. It not only strengthened immeasurably the sympathies between the two countries but also laid the foundations of a very sincere friendship between the King and the President, which was to bear abundant fruit.

Of this I have written in *King George VI, His Life and Reign*, but my own personal association with the royal visit was the garden-party at the British Embassy on 8 June. It was an affair of the greatest sensitiveness and it caused Ronnie and Elizabeth Lindsay many a headache. The Embassy garden was not then as large as it is now, the addition made by Lord Lothian extending it to Massachusetts Avenue. There was little room for entertaining and earnest discussion ensued as to how many and who should be invited. Should the guests include all the Senate and all the House of Representatives? Who should be asked to take tea with Their Majesties on the terrace? Above all who could be left out? These were not the only problems. For example, could the Senator from Boondocks have two extra tickets for his wife's brother-in-law and his wife? Could the Congressman from Suburbia come in a seer-sucker suit? These and many other conundrums were wrestled with manfully by the Ambassador, his wife and his staff, with varying success. But at last the great day arrived.

I had been whistled up from Charlottesville to act as a sort of extra-equerry. The idea was that the King and Queen should separate and make a circle, meeting again on the terrace for tea. Along the route of each were various individuals who had been selected for personal presentation and it was the job of those in attendance to recognise them and bring them forward. At the bottom of the garden a marquee had been erected, in which were iced tea and coffee and also sandwiches and cakes, but strict injunctions had been issued that these were not to be touched until after the Sovereigns had completed their respective rounds and had reached the terrace.

It was the hottest day I have ever known and I suffered gravely in my morning dress. I was attached to Queen Elizabeth's party and all went famously, as we stopped here and there for momentary introductions. The Queen was superb. Seemingly cool and unruffled, she radiated charm, and the guests succumbed to it in swathes. Her smile alone sent them into transports and her few words delighted them. She was so utterly unlike anything they had expected; queenly but human, regal but sympathetic. She was a revelation.

But then we reached the marquee. In that oppressive heat the orders about refreshments were set at nought. We had just reached the entrance when an unfortunate man came out carrying two glasses of iced tea. Before him he beheld the Queen of England and, like a peccant schoolboy caught at the jam-jar, his nerve forsook him.

'My God, the Queen,' he ejaculated, and dropped both glasses! The Queen laughed delightedly and passed on her triumphant way.

This was a fitting close to my last summer of peace in Virginia. A few weeks later I had returned to England and received my orders for my war-time station. I sailed from Southampton in the *Normandie* on 23 August 1939, on what proved to be her final voyage.

CHAPTER FOUR

Muffled Mission

I had been in Richmond on 21 April 1939, to address the Virginia Political and Social Academy on Hitler's latest malfeasance in tearing up the Munich agreement, when I read in Douglas Freeman's *News-Leader* that the Marquess of Lothian had been appointed to succeed Sir Ronald Lindsay as British Ambassador in Washington when he retired in the following August. My first reaction was one of shocked surprise. I had known, liked and admired Lothian as Philip Kerr for a number of years and had found him a brilliant and sympathetic personality. Rich in intellect, distinguished of mien and bearing, and remarkably handsome, he had a most enjoyable sense of humour and, on occasion, of frivolity. At the time of his appointment to Washington he was fifty-seven years old. His career had had two remarkable intellectual 'flowerings', first as a member of Lord Milner's 'Kindergarten', which had done so much to bring good government, prosperity and reconciliation to South Africa after the Boer War, and secondly as Private Secretary to Mr Lloyd George during and after the Peace Conference of Paris. I had met him at Chatham House, at All Souls' and at Lady Astor's, and had always been impressed by the clarity of his intellect. I did not, however, always agree with his views especially on Germany. Finally our relations suffered an almost total severance, when in 1935 and again two years later, he visited the Reich, where he was received by Hitler, Hess and Ribbentrop, and on his return publicly defended Germany's rearming and the remilitarising of the Rhineland.

As his biographer has written: 'The pity was that Lothian, whose human contacts with the English-speaking peoples were so fruitful knew so little at first hand of conditions in Central Europe and altogether failed to comprehend the mentality of Hitler and his crew.'[1] This was not for the want of warning. While I had favoured making concessions to Weimar Germany (even to the egregious von Papen), I did not believe in doing so to the Nazi régime, and I had said so to Philip Lothian on a number of occasions. With others I had pleaded with him not to compromise himself as an eminent figure in

[1] Sir James Butler, *Lord Lothian* (London, 1960) p. 217.

C

British public life by going to see Hitler, and I did my best to deter him from making his various pro-German *démarches* on his return from his visits, but all to no avail. He openly congratulated Neville Chamberlain on 'the marvellous job' he had done at Munich and it was at this moment that our relations became so strained that, rather than risk a permanent rupture, we agreed an indefinite 'moratorium' on meeting.

Such was the position when I read of Philip Lothian's appointment, nor had it changed when, shortly after my return to England later in the summer, I found myself sitting in the room of Sir Robert Vansittart (Diplomatic Adviser to the Foreign Secretary) in the Foreign Office on 20 July. I told him that I thought Lothian's appointment was a disaster. He could have no possible appeal to the American public and would be suspect in official circles. He was a 'milord', a renegade Roman Catholic and a practising Christian Scientist; his views on Germany were those of the 'Cliveden Set' and he had returned from his two visits to Germany seemingly all too favourably impressed. More recently still he had espoused the cause of Clarence Streit, the apostle of Federal Union between Britain and the United States, a proposal which found little support on either side of the Atlantic. Americans would think he had been chosen to sell Appeasement to the American people.

'Van' heard me out without interruption, leaning back in his chair, as was his wont, and placing the long finger-tips of one hand against those of the other, then, in his deep majestic tones, he pronounced his own judgement. 'It is indeed a disastrous appointment,' he said. 'Not the first to have been made by this Government. But you had better overcome your aversion to it as, in the event of war, he will certainly ask for you to join him.'

How wrong we both were in our assessment of the new ambassador, history was to show. Lothian underwent a complete metamorphosis in the months which followed and 'Van', characteristically admitting an error of judgement, writes in his memoirs that 'he [Lothian] spoke with early authority on the United States, where he became the greatest of all our Ambassadors'.[1]

This is high praise indeed, perhaps even a shade exaggerated. The Washington embassy is one of the rare British diplomatic posts other than Paris to which non-career men are sometimes appointed. Whereas in the course of this century there has been a brilliant galaxy of career ambassadors, of whom in my experience the most outstanding have been my friends Ronald Lindsay, Roger Makins

[1] Lord Vansittart, *The Mist Procession* (London, 1958) p. 255.

(Lord Sherfield), Harold Caccia and Patrick Dean; there have also been at least as many non-professionals who have represented the Sovereign with great wisdom, insight and dexterity. Among the most remarkable of these were Lord Bryce, the historian (who was a bit before my time); Philip Lothian (whom I had the honour to serve personally); Oliver Franks (under whom I could have served but did not, though I should like to have done so); and, for the specific purpose for which he was appointed, David Ormsby-Gore (Lord Harlech). Lord Halifax also had what one might call a 'late blooming' success.

In one respect, however, 'Van' had been accurately prophetic in his remarks that July afternoon. In a few weeks' time, when the war-clouds were gathering over Europe, Philip Lothian did ask me to call upon him, and invited me to join him in Washington. I eagerly accepted for it marked the healing of a breach which I had greatly regretted.

We talked for some hours and as the old intimacy returned we were able to broach the sensitive subject of Germany. Philip admitted frankly that, up to Hitler's occupation of Prague, with its flagrant flouting of the Munich Agreement, he had believed it to be possible that Germany was only concerned with treaty revision and regaining the status of a great power. It had now become clear to him that Hitler was a political gangster who would stop at nothing, and who was determined to beat down all resistance to his will.

I have always believed that Philip's myopic attitude towards the early manifestation of the Nazi menace was occasioned by the part he had played in drafting the Treaty of Versailles. At the famous Fontainebleau meeting of March 1919 he had tried to persuade Lloyd George to mitigate the severity of the draft terms of peace to be offered to the Germans and was in some measure successful. Like General Smuts, however, he had developed a guilt-complex about the Treaty and it had disastrously affected his foresight and judgement.

All this, however, was now mercifully over and he never again wavered in his determination that National Socialism and all its evils must be destroyed. We talked of our future relationship in Washington. I was to be his Personal Assistant, responsible only to him and with direct access. He did not wish me to be based permanently in Washington but to travel widely. 'I want you to be my eyes and ears,' he told me. 'Between us we know a great many people in America and we can use them to make further contacts.

You will have to lecture too. They're an ear-hungry people; they love listening.'

And thus began a new association during the all too brief term of his embassage, an experience which ranks among the most memorable of my life, for in the course of those fifteen months, from his arrival in August 1939 to his tragic death in December 1940, I witnessed Philip Lothian's 'Third Flowering', a period of unqualified success.

I sailed in the *Normandie* from Southampton on 23 August 1939, having just returned from my visit to the Kaiser at Doorn, of which I have written in *Knaves, Fools and Heroes*. It was not a pleasant voyage. We were a very mixed bag. War was now accepted as inevitable and there were those, both British and French, who were leaving their countries 'while the going was good' in order to escape the massive bombing which everyone expected would immediately follow the opening of hostilities. There were some embusqués of military age who were deliberately avoiding their 'call-up' into the armed services when mobilisation was declared. There were refugees, German and Czech and others, who, for racial or political reasons, were very understandably anxious to put as great a distance between themselves and Europe as possible.

The atmosphere was one of near hysteria, assisted to some extent by the fact that we were blacked out at night. More than once it was bruited that war had actually been declared, and on several occasions there were moments of panic when rumours ran through the ship like wild-fire that a U-boat had been sighted on one bow or the other, passengers jostling one another in their rush for life-jackets.

Given the circumstances, I suppose that much of this instability was natural enough, but it did not make for 'happy travelling'. I was full of trepidation as to what might happen if something serious really occurred, for the alarm and despondency could only have degenerated into the most appalling panic. I was much relieved when we landed in New York on the twenty-eighth. The *Normandie* never put to sea again and from my office window I saw her burn at her pier in the Hudson River in February 1942.

I spent two days seeing my friends, 'Ham' Armstrong, Dorothy Thompson and others, and catching up on the development of the climate of ideas since I left America in July. I found there was a marked tendency to believe that, even at this late hour and despite all our declarations to the contrary, Britain, under pressure from France, would 'do another Munich' and abandon the Poles as the

Czechs had been abandoned. Truly 'the evil that men do lives after them'.

I also saw Paul Scheffer. Since our first meeting in Moscow in 1929 we had become good friends. Paul had been through an extremely difficult time. After seven years in Russia he had been sent by the *Berliner Tageblatt* as correspondent to Washington and to London, and had eventually been appointed editor of the paper. Throughout this whole period he had done his best, and an intrepid 'best' it was, to maintain both the high standards of the *Tageblatt*, which for many years had been among the most respected newspapers in Germany, and also the integrity of his own principles, which were those of a Conservative Liberal, a German Whig, if there is such a thing.

While he controlled the paper's policy his courageous editorials were evasive enough to pass the Nazi censorship and yet convey his real feelings to those who cared to read between the lines. As the situation in Germany worsened and the grip of the regime tightened, Paul abandoned the editor's chair and returned as correspondent in New York, whence he did not hesitate to report the rising tide of American opinion against National Socialist Germany.

More than once since 1933 I had tried to persuade him to come out boldly as an anti-Nazi and join the group of distinguished German exiles living in the United States. His many friends there – and indeed his reputation as an international journalist – could ensure him a livelihood. I now made a further attempt to get him to change his mind in the event of war. I begged him to resign from the *Tageblatt*. To give advice of this nature is easy enough when one's own country is not directly concerned. Paul could not bring himself to do what I asked. Though he hated the Nazis and his civilised and fastidious temperament was outraged by their brutish methods, he remained a patriotic German. If war came – and as we talked we both knew that it was now only only a matter of hours – he could not abandon his country. I respected his views but disagreed with his decision. We parted friends.

The sequel occurred some two and a half years later. We had not met during the interim but between the Japanese attack on Pearl Harbor on 7/8 December 1941 and the German declaration of war on the United States on 11 December, I again sought out Paul and made final appeal to him to make a public renunciation of the Axis and all its works. I added a new argument. It was known that the Gestapo were well aware of his fundamental anti-Nazi proclivities. If he allowed himself to be interned with other German diplomats and journalists and eventually exchanged for their American counter-parts in Germany, he would be arrested on his arrival on German soil and the best he could hope for was a prolonged period in a concentration camp. He was much more likely to be shot outright as a traitor. He could do much more for Germany by staying in America and perhaps helping to influence the peace-terms.

This time I felt that I had made some impression, not particularly because I had emphasised the threat to his personal safety but because I had opened up a new vista. Like many enlightened persons at this time Paul was well aware that the entry of America into the war, however reluctantly, spelled ultimate defeat for Germany. He might be able to serve her still. At any rate he promised that he would 'think about it'.

Unfortunately there was no time for cogitation. He was arrested the following day and interned at White Sulphur Springs pending repatriation. I am happy to say, however, that a fall in the bath-tub just before their departure for Germany resulting in a broken hip, prevented his inclusion in the official party, and later, through the influence of General 'Wild Bill' Donovan and other of his American friends, he was paroled for the duration of the war and became a consultant to the General's intelligence organisation.

We renewed our friendship after the war and it continued until his death in February 1963.

In the meantime I left New York for Charlottesville to await the actual declaration of war and to say good-bye to Ruth. I stayed at Spring Hill, as the guest of its owners and I like to think that my last days of peace and of the happiness of my old life in Virginia were ending in these pleasant surroundings. On Sunday, 3 September, I stood on the verandah in the early morning sunshine, looking out toward the untrammelled peace and grandeur of the Blue Ridge, and listened on the radio to the voice of Mr Chamberlain announcing that a state of war existed between Britain and Germany. That evening I left on the first step of my 'muffled mission'.

I had decided to make a swing through the Middle West, visiting friends in Chicago, Kansas, and other cities, to see if I could assay the general opinion of this vital heartland of America. I talked with newspaper proprietors, such as Col. Robert McCormick of the *Chicago Tribune*, and Col. Frank Knox of the *Chicago Daily News*, the one as firmly anti-British as the other was pro; with university professors and businessmen, with men of intelligence and experience like my cousin Ross Hill and with a host of fellow travellers in dining- and smoking-cars on the railway.

The result of my observation was all too easy to obtain and all too clear to read. The predominant desire of every American I talked to was an unqualified determination to keep out of war by all possible means, and woe betide those who might be foolhardy enough to try to make her do otherwise. Their attitude to England varied. The shame of Munich still lingered and it was useless to argue that, though we might deserve their scorn, there had been no sign at the time of the least vestige of support from America if we had gone to war in support of Czechoslovakia. On the whole, the inherent isolationism of the Middle West made for an anti-British feeling, partly traditional and dating from the earliest days of their statehood, partly because they distrusted the anglophile Eastern seaboard, and partly because of an unpleasant nagging impression that the British were 'too clever by half'. All these elements combined to produce a pretty hidebound mental attitude.

The report on my findings which I presented to the Ambassador on my return to Washington was the first of a series written over the ensuing fifteen months. They were always highly confidential, often trenchant and somewhat racy in style but they did furnish a fairly comprehensive picture of the development of American opinion, and of men and events during this period. As a record for history they would have had their value and it was for this reason that I was greatly distressed to discover, when, some twenty years later, I had occasion to examine the Lothian Papers in the Scottish Record Office that they had disappeared. The file remains, 'Letters from John Wheeler-Bennett', together with the reference in the card index, but it is as bare as Old Mother Hubbard's cupboard. I hasten to absolve the Scottish Record Office of any vestige of responsibility, but the disappearance of my reports would suggest that at some moment, perhaps even before they left Washington after his death, Philip Lothian's papers were 'purged'. I have no idea by whom.

The climate of ideas which I had found in the Middle West was prevalent throughout the country. The American people as a whole were determined to keep out of the war at all costs. They were united in condemnation of Hitler and his policies (a poll taken by *Fortune* at this time showed only one per cent as pro-German), but they were wary of the British. Even our best friends were critical of the failure of Britain and France to take any diversionary action on the Western Front, which might have brought encouragement and even relief to the Poles in their gallant if futile resistance to the overwhelming superiority of the Wehrmacht. The ensuing six months of the Phoney War did little to convince Americans that the Allies were really in earnest.

Moreover by the end of 1939 a feeling of intense annoyance with Britain was manifesting itself both in public opinion and in official circles in the United States, and which many feared might disturb the cordial nature of Anglo-American relations. This arose largely through the insensitivity of British officials in handling Americans; their stiffness in dealing with U.S. mails, the delays in the examination of ships passing through the blockade, and such-like difficulties.

In addition there was a growing suspicion of British propaganda. Memories of the First World War – of the close friendship between Colonel House and Sir William Wiseman, and of the propaganda machine set up by Lord Northcliffe and Sir Campbell Stuart, when the former was British High Commissioner in New York, a position alarmingly independent of the Embassy in Washington, were still green if not fragrant. Americans were warned from all sides not to be 'gulled' into sentimental and emotional support for the Allied cause, and the passage of the Neutrality Act through Congress early in November 1939 was hailed with enthusiasm.

It was to meet this situation that Philip Lothian turned his extraordinary flair for public relations. Watching this at close quarters, I was fascinated by the genius of his almost unerring technique in this field. He was like a great musician playing a complex composition on the organ, sometimes he would use the *vox humana*, sometimes the *vox angelica*, sometimes a soft and appealing *liedlich gedacht*, sometimes a full and challenging diapason and sometimes he would pull out every stop there was and really 'go to town'!

To begin with he knew America from nearly every angle and Americans of nearly every stratum and then he had the priceless gift of being accessible. He was not only on excellent personal terms with President Roosevelt but also with Harry Hopkins, Marvyn Macintyre and others of the White House circle. He always knew exactly the man to go to on any particular subject. On the other hand he expanded the Embassy social circle to a considerable degree. Dining or lunching there one would be as likely to meet the Mayor of Kalamazoo as one of the famous dowagers of Washington, and the Ambassador would display an evident and genuine interest in talking to either. He would see anyone at any hour and though this was time-consuming and took toll of him in his output of energy, it paid off one hundred per cent in dividends.

Philip was especially adept at handling the press. Whereas many of his predecessors had been 'buttoned up' and even hostile to the media, he was expansive and assured, knowing as if by instinct exactly what to say at any given occasion. He never put a foot wrong.

Nor did he omit an occasional tease. There hangs in the stair-well of the British Embassy at Washington a copy of Allan Ramsay's state portrait of George III, and this provided Philip with an endless source of leg-pulling with Americans. Following him down the stairs as he was showing some particularly anti-British Senator, such as William Borah or Burton Wheeler or Tom Walsh, to the door, I have seen him pause suddenly and say in his gentlest voice; 'I hope you recognise the portrait of your last King;' and he would urge especially portentous ladies of the Daughters of the American Revolution to 'pay reverence to the true founder of the American Republic'.

These sallies met with a mixed reception. Some were delighted, some mildly shocked, but the vast majority were utterly perplexed for they had little idea as to who the subject of the portrait was!

I can still hear his warm voice floating up the stairway as he bid good-bye to a friend: 'Good-bye, Ned, you inveterate old intriguer.'

Since 'propaganda' was anathema, Philip Lothian concentrated on the press to make known to the American people, during this period of comparative military inactivity, what exactly the Allies were doing and thinking. He urged the Foreign Office to make full use of the American correspondents in London for this purpose. 'If Britain and France cannot evolve a clear idea for themselves of their purpose in the war and how it is to be won and what is to follow it, no propaganda will do so.'

Nor was he ignorant of the paucity in both quantity and quality of the machinery at his command. 'The S.D. [State Department] is terrified about British propaganda,' he wrote to Ava Wigram (later Viscountess Waverley) at this time. 'If it only knew what our propaganda is really like.' How right he was.

In 1920 the Foreign Office, in liquidating its wartime activities, left intact the British Library of Information in New York. The library was charged with the task of keeping both press and private individuals informed on life and culture in Britain. For nearly twenty years this estimable institution pursued a sort of 'Sleepy Hollow' existence with a decreasing prestige and a diminishing clientèle. 'I don't use the Library,' said Ham Armstrong on one occasion, in his capacity of editor of *Foreign Affairs*, 'because it is not of the slightest use to me – I have never got anything I wanted from it.' That others were of a similar opinion is evidenced by the fact that on 3 September 1939, though the news of the declaration of war by Britain upon Germany arrived at early dawn, not one single press man or member of the general public applied to the Library for any kind of information. Well might Lord Lothian write that the American public had nothing to fear from British propaganda activities!

Before I left London Sir Robert Vansittart had asked me to establish contact with the B.L.I. and let him have a confidential report on it. I told Philip Lothian of this and he concurred. I suggested that, for the sake of the proprieties, my report should be submitted to him and thence to 'Van', and to this too he agreed.

I therefore betook myself to New York soon after my return from the Middle West, and there I found a deplorable condition not exactly of inertia but of a total inability to grasp the idea of what to do and how to do it. The fear of transgressing the Foreign Office injunction to avoid any semblance of propaganda had resulted in a paralysis, the staff of the Library being afraid or unwilling to open its mouth in answer to the most harmless and general enquiry. The place was pervaded by what George Robey used to call 'a deathly 'ush'.

There was, however, one supremely happy consequence of my visit to New York at this time. I met Aubrey Morgan, whose friendship and that of his wife Constance, I am delighted to say, have continued to brighten my life ever since. The fact that we had never met before was due entirely to the well-meaning efforts of Bruce Lockhart, who, with the best of intentions, had assured both of us for years that we really must meet as we should get on so well together. Nothing is more calculated to keep two people apart than the recommendation of a common friend, and we had deliberately avoided meeting one another. When 'Van' told me that I should find Aubrey already installed in the B.L.I., I felt that the horrors of war were already upon me.

Now, however, once we were thrown together, as it were as comrades in distress, we took to one another immediately and the measure of our friendship may be judged from a remark of Aubrey's: 'If I had two cigars left in the world [we were both great cigar-smokers in those days] I'd give you one of them, but if I only had one I'd smoke it myself because to cut it in half would only spoil it for both of us, and I know you'd agree.' And, of course, I would.

Aubrey Morgan is a splendid person. He is one of the best friends I have ever known, warm, loyal, supremely dependable and utterly delightful. He is also, which I find equally appealing, 'a bonnie hater' and enjoys his feuds almost as much as his friendships. Moreover, again and again he proved himself a noble fighting comrade. He was utterly fearless, full of initiative and imagination, ruthless when necessary and having essentially 'the power to mould the manifold of experience into new unities'.

A scion of the family department store of David Morgan of Hayes, Cardiff, Aubrey had forsaken the Old World for the New because, on the advice of London specialists, he took his wife who was seriously ill to Pasadena, California. She was the eldest daughter of Senator Dwight Morrow, a partner in the majestic house of J. P. Morgan, who was a class-mate and close friend of Calvin Coolidge at Amherst College. He served his country with great distinction and success during the latter's presidency, as Ambassador to Mexico, as delegate to the Naval Disarmament Conference of 1930 and as Senator from New Jersey. Aubrey's first wife Elisabeth died sadly and prematurely of an incurable heart disease and some years later he married her younger sister, Constance. Mr Morrow's middle daughter, Anne, became the wife of Charles Lindbergh. I never knew Elisabeth, but Aubrey and Con, Charles and Anne, and Ruth and I became the best of friends; and we have remained friends for over thirty-five years.

This is not to say that Aubrey's and my friendship was one of complete similarity of character. I like to think that both our friendship and our partnership in serving our country on what was as difficult a war-front as any, was an amalgam of complementary talents and based on an irresistible attraction of opposites. He was a Welsh Liberal, I an English Tory. He had been a keen and useful cricketer at Charterhouse and at Cambridge, whereas I was a duffer at games. However we both had many of the same literary tastes. Aubrey's knowledge of the United States was greater than mine and I learned much from him; however I had a wider experience of British officialdom and had perhaps a suaver and more cautious touch in handling it. I acted as both a brake and safety-valve for his zeal for action, his contempt for all pomposity, official or unofficial, and his tendency for driving clean through any difficulty. In many of our forays together against an official bureaucracy I was at one with him in realising that heads might fall in the process, but, whereas he was not deeply interested as to what became of them when they were off,

I was more inclined, perhaps, to give them decent burial. Nevertheless we worked closely, amicably and, I believe, efficiently together as what Bruce Lockhart has described in *Giants Cast Long Shadows* as a 'powerful, formidable and influential combination'.

Both Aubrey and I were appalled at the spirit of lethargy we found at the British Library of Information, and each of us set out to combat it after his own fashion. He recruited his wife Constance, some good friends and his own private secretary and set up on his own initiative (and virtually at his own expense) a survey of the American media, for the use of the Foreign Office and the Ministry of Information in London, so that they should at least be aware of what was being said editorially, by the columnists in the press and by the political commentators on the radio. I believe that this service, unless recently axed as a measure of economy, is still performed from New York – a lasting memory to Aubrey Morgan's early initiative.

As for myself, I carried our troubles to Philip Lothian, explaining that the Germans were getting a head start on us by launching a well financed and competent propaganda campaign. The main theme was that Britain had encouraged the Poles in their intransigent defiance of the Germans by giving them a 'blank cheque' in the form of the treaty of alliance and guarantee, and had thereby rendered any hope of negotiation nugatory and rendered war inevitable. They had also issued a pamphlet entitled *Lord Lothian versus Lord Lothian* setting out in parallel columns contradictory extracts from his speeches both pro- and anti-German. An illustrated booklet traced the term 'concentration-camp' back to the British action during the South African War in interning Boer women and children, relatives of those Burghers whose farms they had burned. Could we not do *something*, I asked, to counteract this enemy propaganda?

Philip, I remember, counselled patience, caution and subtlety. The Germans, he said, had little to lose by indulging in overt propaganda. They had very little sympathy to build on and he doubted in effect whether their line of strategy would prove greatly to their advantage. The British, on the other hand, had much to lose by making a false step. There were very few Americans who really liked the Germans or who were willing to think well of them, but there was a large body of sympathy for Britain. Whereas the Germans were *expected* to use propaganda, we were *suspected* of doing so and were being watched carefully as a result. We could therefore, he thought, allow the Germans a free field for the moment.

But the time would come, said Philip to me, when we could go over more and more to the offensive and we must be prepared and ready to grasp the opportunity when it occurred. For this reason he suggested that Aubrey and I should work out a secret emergency plan for the expansion of the British Library staff and the extension of its activities. At the same time the British consular representation in America should be overhauled and made ready to act as outlets for information about the British war effort. For this reason the Ambassador instructed me to visit all the consular posts throughout the country and to report to him on my findings.

'But first,' he said, 'we will make a manoeuvre of our own. I want you to act as my personal representative at the requiem mass for Cardinal Munderlein in Chicago. You can see why.'

I could indeed and the subtlety of Philip's gambit delighted me. George Cardinal Munderlein, Archbishop of Chicago, who had recently died, had been a bold and trenchant opponent of National Socialism and had not hesitated to describe the Führer as 'an Austrian house-painter – and a poor one at that'. He had denounced the isolationist and anti-Semitic Father Coughlin in no uncertain terms. Since the beginning of the war he had openly expressed his grief and sympathy to many priests and parishes who were of Polish stock within his diocese and had chided the Irish elements who, if not pro-German, were certainly not pro-British. His Eminence had been strongly attacked in the pro-Nazi section of the German-American press and had even been castigated by Goebbels personally on the German radio. Indeed rumours were current that his death was due to poison administered by Nazi agents, but to this I give no credence. He died of a coronary thrombosis.

Lothian's move was therefore admirably conceived and designed to please the maximum number while antagonising the minimum. Both Irish and Poles would be pleased at the compliment paid to a Prince of the Church, as would those German-Americans, of whom the Cardinal had been one, who were anti-Nazi. Even the isolationists could scarcely take umbrage at so unexceptional a tribute to a great American – though they might, we agreed, attribute it to British cunning – but anyway it was worth the gamble.

Thus 6 October 1939 found me again in Chicago, seated in the Cathedral beside the Consul-General, Lewis Bernays, who was representing the British Government. As it turned out we had stolen a march not only on our enemies but on Bernays' colleagues of the consular corps, who, though they attended *en masse* (with the single exception of the German member) were placed in the front of the ordinary rows of chairs. Bernays and I, however, were given seats of honour in the middle of the aisle immediately below the steps of the chancel, where rested the panoplied catafalque, flanked by some half-dozen wax tapers on tall ceremonial candlesticks.

The majestic liturgy of the requiem mass, with the sonorous beauty of its music, the muted mutter of its prayers, and the solemn magnificence of its mourning vestments, lasted for nearly two hours. My reverence for its grandeur was somewhat tempered by the fact that when the time came for the diocesan clergy and members of the religious orders to pass before the bier, many of them whipped out Kodaks and cine-cameras from beneath their habits and brought them into action. I suppose this was for subsequent exhibition in their parish halls, but for me it gave a jarring note.

Apart from the sincerity of Philip Lothian's sending his personal representative to the requiem, which was unquestionably genuine, the political advantage accruing from this move was gained to the full. The whole press next day – even the *Tribune* – bore witness to its courtesy and it was indeed a master stroke. For me personally, however, there was one mildly macabre consequence. At about two o'clock the following morning the telephone beside my bed at the Drake Hotel rang, and to my sleep-fogged senses a guttural voice announced: 'If you know what's good for you, you'll get out of town today and don't come back – or else.'

I was leaving for Washington in any case that day, but I reported the incident to Bernays, who contacted the police, whose principal reaction seemed relief that I was leaving Chicago. I returned there, however, a number of times during the war to address public audiences and have lived to tell the tale, but at the time it brought back unpleasant memories of my experiences in Germany.

Very shortly thereafter I began my consular tour and in three weeks I had travelled from Boston to New Orleans and from New York to San Francisco. What I found was far from adequate. For economic reasons between the wars the consular posts in the United States had been allowed to dwindle to seventeen, of which five were consuls-general, three of these being on the eastern seaboard. This was barely sufficient for a peacetime establishment but totally insufficient for wartime conditions. Moreover the posts were allocated in the most curious manner. For example, apart from Chicago and St Louis, there was no British representation between the Alleghenies and the Pacific Ocean, a distance of some three thousand miles, and none between Detroit and New Orleans. Moreover in the whole of Texas, an area comparable to France and Spain put together, there was but one consul, and he was situated at Galveston, because this had been a main seaport at the time of the American Civil War.

In addition to the disparity of British representation I encountered some very odd types among the representatives themselves. Some of them had never even been to the Embassy in Washington, their lives alternating between their districts and their spells of leave in England. One, having been born and educated in the West Indies, had never been to England in his life and seemed rather proud of the fact. He had sat for his consular examination in Washington. Another had been recently seconded from the Levant Service and had a deep interest in native customs. This led him to travel around the city in which he was located in street-cars, a custom which, harmless in itself, was rendered highly detrimental to British interests by the fact that his bailiwick lay south of the Mason and Dixon line. Consequently, in those pre-integration days, he was not infrequently hauled protestingly out of the 'Coloured' section of the cars, where, he said with vehemence, he had greater opportunities of studying the 'natives' – a term which pleased no one. There was also a consul whose wife was known to go to dinner-parties with a live snake in her bosom ! And another of whom current gossip averred that he had been threatened with a horse-whipping by a local inhabitant.

Philip Lothian used the report which I wrote for him on my return as the first draft of his own great paper on the reform of the consular service and its personnel in the United States, which he subsequently forwarded to the Foreign Office. Though he did not live to see it implemented, he knew that it had been accepted in principle, and shortly after Lord Halifax arrived to succeed him, it was put into force. As a result, the number of posts was increased to thirty-three, more than double the number I had visited, most of them having an Information Officer to deal with enquiries from the press, the radio and the general public.

Alas, economic exigencies have again necessitated a cutting-back in this highly important field.

'The Americans are an ear-hungry people,' Philip Lothian had said to me in London and I was to learn the truth of this statement the hard way. In the period between the opening of hostilities in Europe on 1 September 1939, and the beginning of the Pacific War on 7 December 1941, I spoke in thirty-seven of the then forty-eight states, criss-crossing the continent from coast to coast and from Bismarck, North Dakota, to Mobile, Alabama. At one period I made as many as eight addresses in ten days. All these were in response to specific requests and the audiences were as varied as they were courteous and attentive.

In the first place it must be understood that the English voice is an asset rather than a liability in America. Never have I been asked in that country, as I have in Australia, to 'take the potato out of your mouth, you bloody Pommy'. On the contrary, I have sometimes felt that if I recited the multiplication-table it would be well received and indeed perhaps convey as great an understanding of my meaning. For example, once I overheard a charming if over-enthusiastic lady remark to a friend as they left one of my meetings: 'My dear, wasn't he *too* wonderful? I didn't understand one word he said; and next week it's *Dant*.' I could not help wondering whether the Bard of Florence would suffer any better fate than I had!

Among the infinite variety of my audiences were universities and colleges where one met with faculty discussion groups, seminars of history graduate students and undergraduate classes of two or three hundred. Within this bracket came every stratum of educational institutions from the Service academies at West Point and Annapolis, the Ivy League establishments and the great women's colleges of the East, to high schools and teachers' colleges in Little Rock, Arkansas and Wichita, Kansas. Then there were those organisations which specialised in the study of international relations, such as the Cleveland, Ohio, Council on Foreign Affairs, run by my old friend Brooks Emeny. There were a number of these and their members were informed and intelligent, but it was at one of these meetings that I nearly ran into trouble.

Philip Lothian had been especially anxious to avoid what he called 'gladiatorial combats', that is to say open forums at which representatives of both Germany and Britain (for from the first the French left to us the burden of putting the Allied cause!) should put their respective cases from the same platform and, as a matter of fact, most organisations had the good taste to avoid any such confrontations. One, however, did not, nor did it give notice beforehand of the nature of the meeting. The whole thing was run on what was described as 'sporting lines', which meant that we actually spun a coin as to who should speak first. I lost the toss and had to listen for half an hour while an eminently presentable blond, good-looking young German put forward very plausibly the current German line of Britain's 'blank cheque' to Poland being the real cause of the war.

I had not caught my opponent's name when we were introduced beforehand but had studiously refused to shake hands with him, somewhat to his apparent surprise and greatly to the annoyance of the chairman who was officially our 'referee'. I felt therefore that the dice were rather loaded against me. Nor was I made much happier by the German's performance, for he was both bland and assured as well as plausible, and when he sat down there was more applause than I liked. But my heart leapt up as if I had beheld a rainbow in the sky when, almost unbelievingly, I heard the chairman say, 'Thank you very much, Baron Munchausen, and now may we hear from Mr Wheeler-Bennett's corner?' I thought I had detected a slight ripple of amusement among the audience but I unhesitatingly drove the point home, being careful to use the Anglo-Saxon pronunciation of the name. 'Ladies and Gentlemen,' I said, 'I am sure that during the last half-hour we have all recalled with some amusement the pleasure we enjoyed in our youth from the works of the former speaker's famous and noble ancestor, Baron "Munchorsen", who earned, you will remember, the reputation of being the world's greatest master of prevarication and misrepresentation. It is remarkable to what a degree his talents have been inherited by his descendant. I will make no further comment,' and I paused. That it was a blow well below the belt I am prepared to concede but after all, as General Sherman so sapiently remarked: 'War is hell.' The sequel, however, was really most gratifying. There was a roar of laughter and the Baron was so angry that, purple-faced, all his suavity abandoned, and looking most unattractive, he stamped off the platform and was seen no more. The thought occurred to me that I could 'take the mickey out of the chairman,' who had been so keen on running the meeting on 'sporting lines', by suggesting that I could perhaps claim a victory by default, but I refrained and gave my own speech on the well worn theme of 'Why Britain is at war' to a most friendly and subsequently enthusiastic audience. But in my heart I felt that I might very probably have been 'saved by the gong'.

By far the largest group of the 'ear-hungry' were the 'professional listeners' – the Women's Clubs, the Knights of Columbus, the Rotary Clubs, the Lions and Kiwanis, the Elks and the Shriners. All of these organisations have regular weekly meetings during most of the year each with a different speaker on a different subject; there is also even a tribal ritual called a 'talk-fest' at which some four or five speakers are given twenty minutes in succession on a Saturday afternoon. I once found myself sandwiched on one of these programmes between a dissertation on bee-keeping and a fascinating discourse on how to deal with potato blight. Between two such practical topics 'the British

Case', in the middle of the Phoney War period, seemed, perhaps, a trifle unreal to a mid-Western audience.

There was a procedural pattern about these gatherings. They were usually at luncheon and the menu was depressingly and monotonously invariable – fruit-cocktail, chicken with a green salad topped off by a round of tinned pineapple with a ball of Philadelphia cream-cheese in the hole in the middle, and ice cream for pudding; the beverages were ice-water and very weak coffee. We began unfailingly by singing 'There'll always be an England', after which I would speak and there would be questions, and we closed with 'America', a song immortalised by the popular singer Kate Smith.

I must, however, bear witness to the amazing kindness and hospitality which I received throughout these trying months. The courtesy of my audiences was almost uniformly of the greatest and even those who disagreed with me did so in a civilised manner. After the collapse of France when Britain was 'standing alone', their sympathy and generosity though I appreciated it to the full, was positively embarrassing and I found that it was I who had to sustain their morale, for they had already written us off as defeated, albeit gallantly, and spoke to me in those hushed tones of the 'bowels of compassion' which are customarily used to the lately bereaved.

After a while the constant repetition of my own theme and the circumstances under which I propounded it, coupled with the incessant travelling by air and train became exceedingly exhausting and wearisome. I longed for a change to some other field of action, but there was no letting-up and indeed, in the prevailing state of affairs, there was very little else I could do. In point of fact my burden increased. As the weight of office routine kept him more and more chained to his desk, Philip Lothian found it difficult to keep engagements he had made in advance and would send me in his place, often at short notice. This was indeed a challenge because, in the first place, he was an excellent and persuasive speaker, and secondly an audience who had been expecting to be addressed by the British Ambassador did not always take kindly to his being deputised for by one of his aides.

However, they were extremely tolerant and usually wrote nice letters to Philip afterwards. I had worked out what I hoped was a disarming little opening formula to the effect that I deeply sympathised with their disappointment which was akin to that of a young man who had asked a prima donna out to supper and had suddenly found himself fobbed off with a chorus-girl. This worked pretty well until one morning Philip called me into his study for a talk and at the conclusion said casually: 'Oh, would you go and preach in my place in Pittsburgh cathedral on Sunday week? I'm afraid I can't go. You can choose your own text, of course. Thank you so much.'

I felt myself to be in what one of my post-war colleagues at Oxford, who had an imperfect mastery of the English language, described as 'a pretty soup'. I had never preached a sermon in my life and, to tell the truth, had been a pretty irregular churchgoer for a number of years. Moreover, my opening gambit about the chorus-girl would scarcely be appropriate.

However, as Emerson once sententiously wrote (and there is no one who can outdo old Mr Emerson in sententiousness), 'When duty whispers low: *Thou must*, The youth replies: *I can*.' I put myself through a crash course in the order of Evensong in the Book of Common Prayer, and for purposes of reassurance, went out to Pittsburgh a day or so in advance to reconnoitre the terrain. I made a courtesy call on the Dean and wished I hadn't, for he was a depressing man. 'I've preached here year after year,' he said to me in a weak and resigned voice, 'and have never succeeded in making myself heard. There are the street-cars outside, they rattle; and there are the Presbyterians next door, they will sing; and the congregation, at whatever time of year, seem to be afflicted with coughs. But, if you pitch your voice to the third pillar on the left side of the aisle on the left of the pulpit, the first six rows *may* hear you.'

I thanked him for his encouragement and went to look over the cathedral. It seemed vast, echoing and forbidding, and I returned to the Dusquesne Club, where I had been put up by friends, in a state of gloom. A good and agreeable dinner with my hosts, however, did much to dispel my despondency, though I spent an apprehensive Sunday rehearsing my sermon. On arrival for the evening service I discovered that there were one or two rocks and shoals which hadn't been on my chart. Awaiting me in the vestry was a black silk robe, clearly designated originally for the Ambassador, so bedecked with gold bullion that I could barely stagger under it. Having struggled into it, I was assigned my place in the choir procession, preceded by the chief verger, an elderly grey-haired black man of great dignity, who looked exactly the benign image of Uncle Tom, and who conducted me to a stall in the chancel. The congregation was a large one, the choir sang beautifully and the organist was a master of his art; only the Dean seemed determined to remain inaudible.

In due course 'Uncle Tom' approached, and with a deep bow (I was never sure whether he thought I was the Ambassador or not) convoyed me to the pulpit which was entered by a flight of steps with a door at the top. This he threw open suddenly projecting me before my audience and whispered: 'Yuh stays here till I fetches yuh, suh,' and the door then closed with an ominous click.

Now I had chosen my text from the Book of Ecclesiastes 3:8, 'There is a time ... for war and a time for peace,' and I was determined I would be heard beyond the Dean's estimated target of the first six pews. So I lifted up my voice and declaimed what a clergyman friend of mine to whom I had submitted the text described as 'a very tolerable amalgam of a layman's theology related to an appeal for understanding of why Britain was at war'. It seemed to go all right and at least no emulator of Jeanie Deans threw a hassock at me. With relief I pronounced the ascription and expected to find the door behind me open. Alas, it remained steadfastly closed and I noticed with horror that there was no handle on my side. I had a sudden nightmare vision of being thus marooned on high and in full view of the congregation for an interminable period. With a somewhat sickly smile I turned to them again and joined haltingly in the last hymn. At the same time I stretched out a leg behind me and knocked on the door as hard as I could with my heel. As it seemed from the bowels of the earth, a reproachful and rather breathless voice replied, 'It's all right, suh, I'se acoming; I'se acoming,' and to my great relief I was released.

The proceedings ended on a note of irreverent comedy. As I entered the vestry to rid myself of my borrowed and undeserved finery, I was delighted to find two angelic-faced choir boys rolling on the floor, locked in a most infelicitous embrace. They at any rate were in no doubt as to whether the time was for war or peace.

I have preached on a number of occasions since but I shall never forget the vicissitudes of my first sermon.

But one had one's consolations. Audiences were, as I have said, for the most part kind, sympathetic and complimentary. But the tribute which I most treasured at this time came from a member of a midwestern university group. It occurred later in the war when the details of the Battle of Britain and the subsequent Blitz were grist to our mill. I had spoken with some feeling of the spirit of Britain in this her greatest hour and it had gone down well. As we adjourned a man came up to me and I saw from his riven face that he was the victim of mixed emotions. He sputtered a little and then said with some passion: 'You're a scoundrel, sir, a damned dangerous insidious scoundrel. I've been an iron-bound isolationist all my life – and you've made me feel like a heel.'

During this peripatetic period I lived a sort of triangular existence. My base in New York remained the Chatham but later Aubrey, Con and I were to move into a very pleasant little house on the south side of East 70th Street, between Lexington and Third Avenues. I rented a room in the house of a friend in Charlottesville so that I could see Ruth when opportunity presented, and the University of Virginia still allowed me to hold an irregular and intermittent seminar in the Law School. In Washington I stayed with Keith Officer in Georgetown, and later, when in 1940 he was transferred to Tokyo, with Dwight and Pauline Davis, who most kindly gave me a room and a latch-key.

I had met Keith Officer first in the bar of the Melbourne Club in 1923, and it was one of my most fortunate experiences. We took an instant liking to one another and remained staunch friends until his death in 1969. Our lives were destined to cross and re-cross in many quarters of the world, including London, the United States, The Hague, Paris and in Oxfordshire and Hampshire.

Keith was one of the earliest and most outstanding of the Australian diplomatic service. Had he, like Dick Casey (now the Rt Hon. Lord Casey, K.G.) whom he succeeded as Australian Liaison in London, elected to go into politics he might also have ended by being appointed Governor-General of Australia, as did Dick. But he preferred to remain in diplomacy and achieved the highest success. He was Australia's first diplomatic representative in Washington, being attached to the British Embassy with the special denomination of 'Australian First Secretary'. He was *chargé d'affaires* in Tokyo at the time of Pearl Harbor and interned until duly exchanged at Laurenço Marques. For the remainder of the war he was *chargé d'affaires* in Moscow and Kuybichev, and Minister in Chungking; and after the war Minister in The Hague and Ambassador in Paris. A varied career and one which disinclined him to return ultimately in retirement to Australia, where he owned a sheep-farm in Tasmania. Though he always remained a loyal Australian, he had been away too long, had absorbed European customs and social life too deeply to go back to sheep-raising. Some of the more narrow-minded and parochial of his countrymen criticised him for his obvious enjoyment of the *le grand monde* of diplomatic life and it must be confessed that in the house which we shared in Georgetown, he always collected the richest cream of Washington society and that the best duchesses were to be found in his embassy at Paris, where Ruth and I often stayed with him. This was a harmless form of snobbery, for, though his detractors would untruthfully aver that Keith knew the *Almanach de Gotha* by heart, he chose his friends from a certain stratum not because they were socially impeccable but because they amused him and were amusing people in themselves. I have never known him to give a dull party; he was an excellent host and evoked gaiety in others. Living with him or being entertained by him was a joy as well as an education. Never was there a more shrewd or intelligent observer, nor one who could extract important information by the seemingly most innocent of questions. He was one of the most knowledgeable diplomats I have ever known and his diaries, now lodged in the National Library at Canberra, provide the historian of this period with a rich and glittering vein of vital facts and vastly entertaining gossip.

At the outbreak of the European war the Embassy staff numbered eighteen, including Keith, whose rank was that of Australian Secretary at the British Embassy, and such unorthodox and peripheral persons as myself; at the close of the Pacific War six years later the number had risen, owing to the proliferation of such work as Economic Warfare and also to the necessary additions to the secretarial and clerical staff to close on a thousand. Of the original complement the man who seemed to me to be the most outstanding personality, and who, indeed, was destined to go furthest in his career, was Derick Hoyer Millar (now Lord Inchyra), who is to be numbered among the best and most efficient Permanent Under-Secretaries the Foreign Office has known since the Second World War. Wise and firm, he had all the virtues of the Establishment and he was always fair and of great charm. More than once his orthodoxy was shocked and tried by the more heretical methods employed by Aubrey and myself (to whom he once referred, in a moment of irritation, as 'a pair of tatterdemalion gypsies'), but he was a splendid colleague and I have always greatly valued his friendship.

Gradually our little band of over-taxed, over-tired staff at the Embassy was augmented from the Foreign Office and the Ministry of Information. Among the first to arrive was John Foster, then a flourishing and brilliant barrister, and a Fellow of All Souls, to become a Queen's Counsel, a K.B.E., a member of the House of Commons and a junior minister in Mr Churchill's third and last administration. Now he took over the duties of legal adviser to the Embassy, a position which owing to our vulnerable position in a neutral, if friendly, country was of considerable importance and necessity. He discharged his duties with characteristic brilliance, though he also became suspected of heterodoxy among the Establishment.

In the momentous summer of 1940 an incident occurred which was to prove eventful in the life of the Washington Embassy. Isaiah Berlin arrived in America for the first time. He was *en route* for Moscow to take up an appointment at the British Embassy there and had experienced a gruelling Atlantic crossing, in the course of which his ship had been under submarine attack. On his first evening in Washington John Foster brought him to dine with Keith Officer and me. For me, at any rate, it was a great occasion, for it was the beginning of an unending friendship.

I had never met, nor, I regret to say, even heard of Isaiah before but, as we sat on the garden-patio with our drinks, I fell at once under the spell of his brilliant intellect. He had been in America scarcely forty-eight hours but his comments on the situation would seem to betoken a lifetime of acquaintance with that country. His conversation – and he never seemed to stop talking, though he never bored us, even if we did sometimes have difficulty in understanding him – was of an effervescent brilliance and humour. He sparkled and scintillated, yet not one of us who listened to him felt that we were being overwhelmed or left out. One of Isaiah's most priceless attributes is that he evokes genius in others with whom he talks, giving them the impression that they are really more coruscating and witty than they would otherwise believe themselves to be.

I wondered whether the impression which I had formed of Isaiah's brilliance would be dimmed by the cold light of morning, but it was not so. I was convinced that, come what might, his talents ought to be used in Washington rather than in Moscow, though having been born in Riga, he spoke Russian fluently. I spoke of my conviction to Keith and to Stephen Childs, the newly appointed Press Counsellor, and, with their concurrence, I approached Philip Lothian. He agreed in principle and as a test job, Isaiah was asked by Childs to write a report on the attitude of the Associated Press to what was then going on in England. The result was a masterly, penetrating and droll survey and armed with this we again went to the Ambassador and repeated our plea.

It was now that fate seemed to play into our hands. A telegram from the Foreign Office arrived cancelling Isaiah's appointment to Moscow and to his enquiry as to what he was to do, the Office returned the Olympian response that, as after all he was not an established Civil Servant, they were indifferent as to his movements. He was, as it were, abandoned.

To us in Washington this seemed to be an answer to prayer. Manifestly, we said to one another (Keith, Aubrey, Stephen Childs,

Tony Rumbold, John Foster and I), Isaiah's considerable talents must be used to the full in America, beginning 'as of now'. He would be an invaluable addition and asset to a jaded and overworked garrison, either at headquarters in Washington or in the out-post bastions of New York with Aubrey and me.

We had, however, reckoned without Isaiah's principles. He would have none of our plans for him. He had, he said, been appointed to Moscow and, since this appointment had been cancelled, he must return to Oxford. The idea of working in America interested, and even fascinated, him, but he believed that if he did as we asked he would appear to be *embusqué*, attempting to evade danger at home, and, at best, to have been seduced from the austerities of wartime Britain to the fleshpots of the United States. We spoke to Lothian, we even mobilised the support of Felix Frankfurter. We put to them the arguments that Isaiah would be lost to Government service if he returned to academic life at Oxford and added (though, as far as I know, this was never mentioned to Isaiah himself) that, in the event of a successful invasion of Britain by the Germans, which at that moment seemed all too imminent and probable, he would almost certainly be consigned to the horrors of a concentration-camp.

But Isaiah remained adamant in the face of all our inducements. It was his avowed intent to return to England and then, if officially appointed to America, to come out again. He therefore accompanied Philip Lothian back to London in October, and resumed his duties at Oxford as a Fellow of All Souls. We did not, however, abandon our efforts. Though the dangers of invasion had diminished with the victory of the Battle of Britain, the need for someone in America of Isaiah's gifts remained and increased. Isaiah was appointed, in February 1941, first to New York and later to Washington, where he began that series of masterly reports on the American scene which made his name a byword in Whitehall. After the war he reached the greatest eminence in academic and intellectual circles (not always quite the same thing) and nothing gave me more pleasure than when the Queen appointed him a member of the Order of Merit.

Social life in Washington was naturally restricted for us by the overwhelming burden of work, but there was a limited amount of it. The ambassadors of our original allies, Comte de Saint-Quentin, for France, and Jan Ciechenowsky, whom everyone called 'Chicken', for Poland, were much in demand, so, of course, was Philip Lothian, but he rarely dined out in social splendour, preferring to have a few cronies in in the evening for a quiet meal.

The rest of us were constantly placed in the difficult position of unexpectedly meeting the diplomatic representative of the Third Reich because some Washington hostesses could not quite understand that, while the United States was still a neutral country, we happened to be at war. Since the recall of Hugh Wilson from Berlin in protest against the pogroms of November 1938 and the consequent departure of his German opposite number from Washington, the two embassies had been in the hands of *chargés d'affaires*, of whom the German was one Hans Thomsen, who had been an acquaintance of mine in Berlin. Happily I was never called upon to cut him in public but, had the occasion arisen, I should certainly have done so.

An embarrassing situation did, however, occur early in the war, when the Duke of Saxe-Coburg-Gotha, who, along with other (but not all) of the former ruling dynasties in Germany, had embraced the National Socialist principles with almost indecent haste and fervour, arrived in Washington on a 'good-will mission' in his capacity as head of the German Red Cross. One Washington hostess (not a 'cave-dweller'!) issued invitations on a large scale with 'to meet His Royal Highness, etc.' written on them. She was first bewildered and then pained at the number of refusals which resulted, especially those from the British. She had thought, she was alleged to have explained, that it was quite all right to ask them to meet the Duke as she understood that he was a sort of cousin of King George VI!

It was now that I grew to know well many Americans who became permanent friends. Alice and Dean Acheson, for example, when he was Assistant-Secretary of State, and Mary and Jimmy Dunn, who became the greatest of the veteran statesmen among the career diplomats of the Foreign Service, and Sumner Welles, whose frigid and almost glacial exterior concealed a witty and sparkling humour once he thawed out. All these were agreeable and understanding companions with whom one could relax on a thoroughly informal and intimate basis of friendship – a great luxury in wartime, especially in a foreign country.

Once again, at, I am sure, the instance of young Franklin, I was invited to the White House. On this occasion it was to Sunday supper and the ritual of the chafing-dish was maintained. It was a mixed company which included General Marshall, Sumner Welles, Felix Frankfurter and other luminaries. On Mrs Roosevelt's right sat a charming elderly bishop of the Episcopal Church who was an old friend of the family. I was on her left and on *my* left, rather surprisingly, I found Errol Flynn. He was very pleasant and, as my hostess addressed most of her conversation to the Bishop, he and I talked amicably together. He was greatly interested in the course of the war and asked me various questions of a general nature, which I answered in equally general terms, for, great actor though he was, he was no strategic genius. I felt myself becoming more and more banal, but was absolutely horrified to hear Mrs Roosevelt tap her glass for general silence and announce: 'Mr Wheeler-Bennett is saying something that I think we should all like to hear.'

My mind congealed and I felt a cold sweat on my forehead. To repeat to an audience which included the President and Commander-in-Chief of the United States, the Chief of the General Staff, the Under-Secretary of State and a Justice of the Supreme Court, general remarks on the conduct of the war which had been couched in terms calculated to meet the intelligence of a Hollywood idol, was something of which I had never dreamed even in my wildest and most horrific nightmares. However, there was no help for it and I did repeat what I had said though in terms which I hoped were more appropriate to my enlarged audience. At the end the President caught my eye and if it may be said respectfully of the Chief Executive of the United States that he winked, President Franklin Roosevelt did so.

Nor did this end the curious Alice-in-Wonderland atmosphere of the evening. As we were leaving I followed the Bishop to the great glass doors of the White House. He turned to me with the most charming smile. 'Tell me, my dear boy, who was that young man sitting opposite me on Eleanor's left?' Again a prey to the throes of unreality, I took a deep breath and replied, ungrammatically enough, 'As a matter of fact, Bishop, it was me.' 'I thought you'd know,' he replied with great courtesy, and passed out into the night.

On 16 April 1940, a week after the German invasion of Denmark and Norway had begun, I was at Brown University, in Providence, Rhode Island. I spoke three times that day to groups of faculty and students and, in accordance with the tone of the guidance telegrams we had received from the Ministry of Information, I struck an optimistic note, to the effect that the British were masters of the seas and that the Anglo-French forces were not only holding their own but had gone over to the offensive. A few days later, I was proved tragically and abysmally wrong.

On 11 May 1940, I was at Princeton University for a similar purpose and I read in my morning papers the first reports of the German blitz into Northern France and the Low Countries. Some instinct – and how fervently I blessed it later – warned me against over-enthusiasm and counselled greater caution. I talked, with innocent sincerity, of the superb fighting qualities of the French army but I did warn my hearers that there might be some early reverses as the Allied forces absorbed the German attack in preparation for a counter-offensive. I reminded them of the miracle of the Marne in 1914 and spoke guardedly of the strategic potential of the Maginot Line. On the whole I did better than at Brown.

The next few days and weeks were a veritable *cauchemar du diable*. Isolated in New York, dependent for our news on the alarmist and emotional reporting of the American media, the almost maddeningly calm, detached broadcasts of the B.B.C. and official telegrams from London, which, when intelligible at all, were vastly out of date, Aubrey Morgan and I were a prey to anxiety and frustration. Indeed, I confess to occasional moments of something akin to despair, as the news showed us only too clearly that all hopes of a counter-attack had been abandoned and that our forces in Belgium and France were fighting for their very survival. Aubrey reminds me that on that terrible day when we heard of the fall of Arras, Amiens and Abbeville, I said to him: 'I think we may have lost this bloody war – let's go and have lunch.'

We consoled ourselves, however, with the knowledge that now at last the moment had come to produce our 'secret plan' for streamlining the British Library organisation in general, enlarging its staff, and, in particular, providing for speedy and efficient replies to enquiries from newspapers. Now, if ever, was the time for making what effort we could both to arrest the rising tide of depression which we encountered on every hand and to counteract the exuberance of German propaganda, which was daily becoming more gloatingly blatant and arrogant.

The Director read the plan with due deliberation, then he paled with emotion and his reaction was that of positive horror. 'But this,' he exclaimed in shocked dismay, 'is Teutonic efficiency; this is what we are fighting the war *against*!'

I have rarely been so angry in all my life. I contemplated throwing up the whole thing there and then and going back to England, where I longed to be at this sad moment of her fortunes. At least, I thought, I can find something to do there that will be worth doing. It was Aubrey who was the clearer thinker of the two of us on that occasion. 'You must go straight to Lothian,' he said 'and tell him the situation. He will understand and he'll do something.'

Aubrey was right, of course. I realised at once that, as a result of being overwrought and over-extended, I had temporarily lost my sense of perspective. There was a job to be done there and we had to do it. I took the next plane to Washington, and lost no time in begging the Ambassador to take action to ensure a more virile organisation in New York. Philip grasped the situation at once in his quick, vibrant way. He realised that while there still remained a valuable function for the B.L.I. in serving the needs of academic and cultural institutions and of the general public, it was too set in its ways to adjust to the new task of coping with the quick-fire demands of the press and radio. He promised that all relations with the media should be separated from the Library and vested in a new and parallel organisation to be known as the British Press Service. Availing himself of the ancient device of statemanship in placing responsibility in the hands of the rebels, he put the operational direction of this office in the hands of Aubrey and myself, with Alan Dudley, a young established Civil Servant (who was subsequently knighted and achieved ambassadorial rank), to give the whole thing an appearance of respectability in the eyes of the Establishment.

Even with this encouragement there were still intolerable delays to be encountered. Both the Foreign Office and the Ministry of Information reacted unfavourably, each for its own reasons, and, inevitably obstacles were raised by the Treasury. At one moment it looked as if the whole project was to be still-born, but it was now that Philip Lothian performed one of those acts which made him such an inspiring chief to work for. On his own initiative and authority, and disregarding the objections of London, he gave instructions to rent new office premises and engage staff, cutting the Gordian knot of finance by drawing upon official funds at his own immediate disposal. Faced thus with a *fait accompli*, Whitehall capitulated unconditionally. But it was October 1940 before we were able to go into action.

Our ranks were subsequently strengthened by some distinguished reinforcements. The wholly delightful and vastly entertaining René MacColl, who later became the star correspondent of the *Daily Express*, added his expertise to our armoury, and that redoubtable and almost legendary figure Bill (later Sir Berkeley) Ormerod became famous as our Public Relations Officer. Bill Ormerod had an uncanny ability to take an almost clinically sterile 'situation telegram', assimilate its contents and regurgitate it to commentators and correspondents with such authority and vividness of style that it was difficult to believe that he did not have 'a hot line' to the Chiefs of Staff. Later still, Isaiah Berlin joined us before his translation to Washington. And there were others.

We were also always greatly encouraged by the periodic and

refreshing visits of Ronnie Tree, who served as P.P.S. to successive Ministers of Information. Not only did he give us strong support in regard to the B.P.S., but he also kept us in touch with the inner thinking of Whitehall, which did not always emerge with crystal clarity from the official telegrams. He has given his own intriguing account of conditions in America in his book *When the Moon Was High* (1975).

Thus began the first concerted effort towards providing a 'popular' organisation for the conduct of British public relations in America; an institution which aimed to serve the curious many rather than the enquiring few, and which was based upon the principle of creating an ever-growing demand for its services. It was Philip Lothian's action which had taken the initial step towards the substitution of that compact and smoothly functioning machine which served the interests of Britain in America not discreditably for the remainder of the war in the place of an amorphous group of warring entities.

It was now that my admiration for Philip Lothian's courage and wisdom reached its zenith. From the first moment of the war his profound knowledge of the American scene and his insatiable appetite for the problems of public relations enabled him to direct and inspire a campaign which attained remarkable proportions and had far-reaching effects. His thesis was extremely simple. He concentrated – and bade us concentrate – on convincing America that the survival of Great Britain was vital to the security of the United States and he avoided any attempt to rally America to the side of Britain by anti-German propaganda. His object – and ours – was to create an American appetite for knowledge of Britain; her capacity to wage war, the determination of her people to see it through, her desire that a better world should emerge from the struggle.

The fruits of his wisdom in thus mingling restraint with stimulation became abundantly clear during that fateful summer of 1940. As early as 24 May he could report to the Foreign Office: 'The past week has brought sudden realisation to Washington and dawning understanding to the country of what elimination of Great Britain would mean to the security of the United States,' and in that same month was formed 'The Committee to Defend America by helping the Allies', headed by the 'Sage of Emporia', William Allen White. This title, though cumbersome, was in perfect consonance with

Philip's consistently marked distinction in asking America to 'aid Britain' rather than to 'make war alongside Britain'.

The disasters sustained by Allied arms in May and June gave Philip the opportunity of driving home and emphasising the basic principle of all his Anglo-American thinking, namely that the security of the United States was an illusion without mastery of the seas; that she could not attain that mastery by isolation; that unless she held command of the surrounding oceans, they were not a defensive bulwark but a highway for a naval foe; that she must have access to bases overseas, though not her own, which, if they fell into the hands of a hostile power would imperil her approaches. Their fate was consequently hers and it was to both her and our advantage that they should be denied to the enemy.

This was the teaching of that great American naval historian and strategist, Admiral Alfred Mahan, which Lothian had imbibed from his earliest contacts with America. It was shared, moreover, by President Roosevelt, who, during that historic visit of the British Sovereigns to Hyde Park, New York, just a year before, had discussed in confidence with King George VI the possibility of American naval patrols using British bases in the Western hemisphere in time of war. Whether this fact, which the King had reported to his ministers on his return to London, had been communicated to Lothian, I do not know but I am pretty sure that he was confident of preaching to the converted in so far as the President was concerned. But he was also aware that the President could not outpace Congress in his policies. Succour must therefore be given to those American voices which were now being raised in support of Britain and the great American public must be constantly apprised of the danger which threatened their illusory complacency.

The story of the destroyer-bases agreement has been admirably told by Philip Goodhart in his *Fifty Ships Which Saved the World*. Both this book and Sir James Butler's biography of Philip Lothian give full credit to the part which he played behind the scenes in the White House, with Cordell Hull and Sumner Welles at the State Department and with those newly recruited Republicans, Frank Knox and Henry Stimson, whom President Roosevelt had recently added to his cabinet at the Navy and War departments respectively. But I had the privilege of seeing him in action publicly and can bear witness to the fact that his constant harping upon this issue prepared and conditioned the minds of Americans for the impact of the momentous events which were being matured in secret.

I recall particularly an address Philip gave to the Yale alumni in which he laid the facts boldly and brutally before his listeners. Under Hitler's control, he told them, the seas would never be open to all as under British or American control. If the Nazis gained possession of the British fleet the security which Britain and America had enjoyed for the last hundred and twenty years would disappear. America must have bases far out in the Atlantic as she had in the Pacific and South America. The real Maginot Line for the democracies was for Britain to continue fighting with her fleet based in the British Isles.

This was the line that we took from Lothian and which was also followed by William Allen White's group and by the 'Fight for Freedom' Committee, a more belligerently interventionist body comprising such gallant spirits as George Backer, Peter Cusick, Herbert Agar and James Warburg. The result was that the President and the public were ahead of Congress in their sympathies, but though he enjoyed an increasing degree of public support, Mr Roosevelt still felt it necessary to preserve the greatest secrecy in his negotiations with the British for the exchange of fifty First World War destroyers for the lease of naval bases in the Caribbean and in Newfoundland.

When the final agreement was signed, the ceremony took place under somewhat bizarre circumstances. Since the final decision to act had been taken by the President without Congressional approval, the whole affair took on a clandestine nature. It was considered inadvisable to meet at the State Department for fear of alerting press speculation, so, at seven o'clock on the evening of 2 September 1940 Philip Lothian accompanied by Derick Hoyer Millar, who had been closely involved throughout, drove to the Carlton Hotel, where Cordell Hull lived, and were conducted up the back stairs to the Secretary of State's apartment, for the exchange of signatures on this historic document. This ceremony having been completed the Ambassador and his Head of Chancery returned with some sense of satisfaction to the Embassy to find there a delayed telegram from the Prime Minister directing that certain verbal changes be made in the text of the Agreement. With what I conceive to be a certain relish, for he considered that the negotiations had already been dragged out too long, Philip sent an answering signal: 'Sorry: too late.'

Philip Lothian's calm and courageous example was an inspiration to all of us in this summer of 1940 and, following his example, we went about our business. I still spoke a good deal in various parts of the country, but I felt a strong renewal of the fighting spirit and, though the news from Europe became increasingly disastrous, I felt a new tranquillity of mind. Without abandoning totally the possibility and the hope of victory, I felt a grim consolation in the evident determination of the British Government and people to go down fighting if defeat should be our fate, and this afforded me, at any rate, a strengthened assurance in facing my audiences. Only, in my heart of hearts, I longed to be back in England at this time, to share the exaltation of the miracle of Dunkirk and the preparations for resisting invasion. In spirit I shared the lament of the Jacobite exile and 'pined by Arno for my lovelier Tees'.

Of this fluid period of tension and ever-changing circumstance two incidents stand out with blazing clarity. 10 June was set for the graduation ceremonies at the University of Virginia and my pupil Franklin Roosevelt Jr was to receive his law degree. The President of the United States had consented to make the Commencement Address and great preparations were made for the occasion.

That morning Ruth and I sat in my car and listened to the frenzied oration in which Mussolini declared war on Britain and France. We heard it first in Italian and then in English, and neither of us said anything at the finish. We went home and had lunch very quietly together.

The ceremonies were set for the afternoon and were to be held out of doors, and later that evening I was to fly west from Washington to speak next day at the University of Oklahoma. The President duly arrived and the academic procession was about to take off from the Rotunda down the Lawn when one of those Virginia summer thunderstorms burst upon us. An adjournment was ordered to the gymnasium and thither the President was transferred in his car and was borne up the platform steps by secret service men. Meantime the procession had become a shambles. It was a rush for cover, every man for himself, and in the ensuing confusion I found myself sitting immediately behind the President, so close to him that, but for the guards, I could have touched him and could easily see over his shoulder as he placed his speech on the podium. I watched him turn the pages and at a certain point became aware of a blank in the page of the text, and as he came to it, he drew from his pocket a piece of paper from which he read those thrilling and inspiring words (I learned later that he had originally included these words in his text, then discarded them, and had finally decided during the journey to Charlottesville to reinstate them).

On this 10th day of June, 1940, the hand that held the dagger has struck it into the back of its neighbour.

Philip, Lord Lothian

Aubrey Morgan

On this 10th day of June, 1940, in this University, founded by the first great American teacher of democracy, we send forth our prayers and our hopes to those beyond the seas who are maintaining with magnificent valour their battle for freedom . . .

We will extend to the opponents of force the material resources of this nation; and at the same time we will harness and speed up the use of those resources in order that we ourselves in the Americas may have equipment and training equal to the task of any emergency and every defence.

I recall the shock of excitement which passed through me like a shot of adrenalin as I heard these words. This was it; this was what we had been praying for – not only sympathy but pledges of support. If Britain could only hold on until these vast resources could be made available to her we could yet survive and even win the war. It was the first gleam of hope.

When the President had finished his speech there was an absolute silence and then a crashing roar of applause. The audience – like the nation at large – was first stunned by his frankness and then warmly in support of his challenge. It was a moment of history; a climacteric.

As President Roosevelt turned from the podium, we all stood back, but he recognised me and greeted me genially. I thanked him warmly for what he had said and he smiled that quizzical smile of his. 'What are you doing now?' he asked. 'Well, sir,' I answered, 'I'm driving to Washington to try and catch a plane out to Norman, Oklahoma. I'm due to speak at the University there tomorrow morning.' He smiled again. 'Propaganda, I suppose?' 'We call it information, Mr President,' I answered and he laughed with that leonine backthrow of the head. 'Well you'd better tag along with me,' he said, 'I've just got to see young Franklin and then we'll be leaving in twenty minutes,' and he spoke to one of his aides.

Having come down to Charlottesville by train, Mr Roosevelt was returning by car and my instructions were to join the rear of the presidential motorcade, with two of the motor-cyclist state troopers in front and two behind. In this august company my driver Joe, who was bursting with pride, and I zoomed over the 120 miles to Washington with the greatest ease. As we approached the entrance to the old national airport I got the signal to 'peel off' and with a wave from my escorts, I parted from them. Never have I caught an airplane with greater comfort and less anxiety.

Less than a week later I was back in Charlottesville with permission from Philip Lothian to attend the annual session of the Institute of Public Affairs. Many of my friends were to be among the speakers, among them Bruce Hopper, Ted Roosevelt and Dick Casey, who had recently presented his credentials as the first Australian Minister to the United States. I rented a house for the ten days of the Institute and filled it with these old companions and with my former students. The weather was wonderful. Blazing days followed one after the other and on each magnificent moonlit, magnolia-scented night, we would sit out on the back patio with our drinks, after the evening session of the Institute, and discuss incessantly the ever worsening situation in Europe. Ruth was always with us and she reminds me that at one point someone said: 'I suppose the next time we meet we shall all be in uniform,' and that I made the *sotto voce* comment: 'What's left of us.' This was certainly justified for among that young group that sat about us not a few were destined to die in action.

The star turn of the Institute's session was to have been an address by the British Ambassador on the night of 17 June, but once it became apparent that the Battle of France was lost, he had warned me to be ready to take his place. When I reported back to him on my return from Oklahoma on the thirteenth, he confirmed this warning with a definite instruction. The Germans entered Paris on the fourteenth, and it was evident that it was only a matter of days before the French would be seeking an armistice. He could not leave Washington.

During the few days that remained before I had to speak I prepared and discarded draft after draft of what I was to say. The news grew steadily worse and the question uppermost in the mind of the world was, 'What would Britain do?' I felt I had to have guidance at this critical moment and on the evening of the seventeenth I telephoned to Philip. I must, I said, have some message of hope for the audience I was about to face. I can hear now the cool calm of his voice as he answered me: 'You can say that Britain will fight on under any circumstances. The Prime Minister has just said so. Good-bye.'

With my confidence restored I went on to the platform, tore up my text and spoke extempore, the record being taken down by a court stenographer in attendance for the purpose.

> Tonight my country stands alone, *alone* – before the embattled might of totalitarian Europe, Nazi Germany rooted in hatred and cruelty and perversion, and Fascist Italy standing forth at last in her true colours, wearing a suit of tarnished blackmail and with the bar-sinister upon her shield.

Tonight, for the first time in many years, *your* country sees an unfriendly Power established on the far shores of the Atlantic.

France, immortal and glorious France, has fallen at our side. We pay tribute to her, we salute her, confident that she will rise again. But we declare to the World our intention – and this is the policy of His Majesty's Governments throughout the Empire – that we shall continue the fight to the last drop of our blood and to ultimate victory. Let it be remembered that the Briton never fights better than when standing with his back to the wall, a sword in his hand, and a prayer in his heart . . .

To the British, the answer to the question: 'Why are you fighting?' is clear and evident. We are fighting to defeat and destroy that aggressive and brutal mentality in our enemies which seeks continually to dominate other peoples by force, which wantonly violates the neutrality of inoffensive States, and which justifies the repudiation of its own pledged word whenever it finds it convenient. We are fighting for our lives. We are fighting in defence of our own Empire. We are fighting to bring about restitution for the wrongs done to the long and growing list of the victims of Nazi aggression – to Austria, to Czechoslovakia, to Poland, to Denmark, to Norway, to Belgium, to Holland, and to Luxembourg – and, especially, to France.

But above all else we are fighting in defence, and for the preservation, of that basic factor of our faith – our individual freedom; freedom of conscience and utterance, freedom from arbitrary arrest and punishment; freedom from concentration-camps and firing-squads, and from all the other sneaking, cruel machinery of the secret police system.

We are fighting as the Scots fought for Robert the Bruce – 'Not for glory, not for wealth, but for that freedom which no good man surrenders but with his life.'

This is the cause for which we fight, and in its defence we are prepared to shoulder heavier burdens, to suffer greater sacrifices, to make the offering of 'blood, tears, toil and sweat' which our chosen leaders have demanded of us. In defence of this cause we must either conquer or perish – for to us, at least, it is self-evident that the world cannot exist half-Nazi and half-free.

We need the sense of our cause for many reasons. We need it to give us the resolution and drive and self-sacrifice necessary for victory. We need it to meet, with continued hope and courage, the reverses which are inevitable in war. We need it so that, when the end of the war confronts us with problems as great as the war itself, we can attack them with the confidence which comes from a clear purpose. We need it to keep our minds sweet, when offences against international law and against human decency may turn them bitter, and when personal loss and the grinding hardships and inhumanity of war threaten to deprive us of sane judgement.

Above all we need the sense of our cause to sustain us in

contemplating the future – and the future holds for us but two alternatives, victory or defeat . . .

If our cause fails it will mean that the flame of freedom will have been snuffed out in two continents, and that from London to Vladivostok the human mind will have become enslaved . . .

If this is achieved, the United States will find itself confronted in the West by a Europa Germanica, in the South by a flanking movement – both above and below the Panama Canal Zone, for Mexico is also a fertile field of Nazi operations – and in the Orient, by an enriched and invigorated Japan. Unless America is prepared, both physically and morally, to meet this challenge to her national interests, she will be forced to make a capitulation in comparison with which the Munich Agreement will appear as a diplomatic victory for Great Britain and France.

But there are deeper issues even than these. If we perish in this struggle, the United States will become the last refuge of democracy and liberty, and the American people will become the ultimate trustees of individual freedom.

You *cannot* fail to accept this responsibility; and in accepting it, you *must* not fail to be ready to meet the challenge which it implies. We shall bequeath to you, as sole guardians, that common tradition of 'a deathless attachment to freedom' which our two countries have shared for generations. If we go down, can we do so with the assurance that here, in this land, this tradition will continue to be cherished and championed, and that you will have learned from us the lesson and the penalty of being unprepared?

When the sweetened tones of Nazi leaders declare that Germany is satisfied with what she has gained and has no further ambitions – remember that this promise was made in turn to Austria, to Czechoslovakia, to Poland, to Denmark, to Belgium and to Holland.

This is the warning which will be written in flames above the ruins of Europe, 'Be strong and well-prepared and place no trust in Nazi promises.'

I have tried to portray for you the two possible futures which confront my country, and, if the latter is a gloomy one, I would not have you think that my faith in Britain is faltering. There is a certain spirit in Britain which is indomitable, a spirit which will transcend alike the deepest sorrows and the greatest victories. A shining thing within our very souls which no enemy can ever command, or attain or conquer . . .

Writing in the midst of another great war, John Milton saw a vision of a people 'not degenerated nor drooping to a fatal decay, but casting off the old and wrinkled skin of corruption, to outlive these pangs and wax young again, entering into the ways of truth and prosperous virtue, destined to become great and honourable in these latter ages. Methinks I see in my mind a noble and puissant nation rousing herself, like a strong man after sleep and shaking her invincible locks.' Those who have seen English men and women of all classes ready to resign comfort, occupation, income and life in the defence of their ideals have seen such a people as Milton conceived ...

In some ways it was one of the most tragic moments of my life, in some ways one of the proudest. The speech had an effect far beyond my expectations. On the following day the Director of the Institute, Hardy Dillard, in a telephone conversation with Philip Lothian described it as 'one of the most moving addresses I have ever heard', and that 'its restrained eloquence and deep feeling had aroused so much interest and sympathy' that it had been necessary to run off three lots of mimeographed copies in response to the demand, and 'requests for copies are still pouring in'. Hardy further suggested that it might be 'highly beneficial' to have the speech reproduced 'in a more permanent and dignified form' and made available for the wider distribution of which he felt it to be worthy.

With a certain native canniness Philip Lothian asked to read a copy first, but when he had done so he gave the order for it to be printed and given 'maximum distribution'. Of all the tributes which I received on this occasion the one which gave me greatest pleasure and gratification was Philip's simple: 'Well done, Jack.'

The speech had some interesting personal repercussions. It sent a young man named Frank MacCarthy into the officers' reserve and thus launched him on a career in which he served General Marshall as A.D.C. throughout the war, became an Assistant Secretary of State in the State Department and finally a top executive of Twentieth Century-Fox, for whom he directed the film of *Patton*, among others. Some years later in the war, when I was in London, I encountered General Marshall at dinner. 'I understand,' he said with a crinkled smile lighting up his leathery face, 'that I'm indebted to you for my young aide, Frank MacCarthy. I'm very grateful.'

Perhaps the most comical result was a provincial Virginia newspaper which printed the speech *in extenso* under the banner headline, 'Wheeler-Bennett says Britain will fight on.' This, I felt, was indeed fame.

CHAPTER FIVE

A Whiff of the Blitz

Later that summer I urgently besought Philip Lothian for permission to return to England, at least temporarily. If there were to be an invasion, I said, I wanted to be there but, even if there were not, I felt it necessary, if I was to continue to talk to American audiences, that I should have some first-hand experience of life in Britain under siege. He was understanding – as he always was – and said that he himself proposed to go home in October for a short period. He granted me a month's 'working leave' and asked for my promise to return unless there was an actual invasion, in which case I would be free to seek guidance in London as to where best I could serve. However, he added, 'You are not to hang about waiting for an invasion. I need you here.'

I sailed from New York on 7 August 1940 in the old White Star liner *Baltic*, a vessel of a very early vintage since she bore outside the Purser's Office a bronze plaque to the effect that she had carried General Pershing and his headquarters staff across the Atlantic in 1917! The hand of progress seemed to have passed her by in the intervening years but we reached Liverpool safely and uneventfully after a passage of only seven days. Alas, however, she fell a victim to a U-boat attack later in the war. She was a gallant old tub.

My arrival at Liverpool coincided with an air-raid, my first but by no means my last during my visit. In fact it is true to say that a raid occurred nearly every day or night (and sometimes both) during my time in England. One got oddly accustomed to the intermittent throb of the Luftwaffe machines and tremendously exhilarated by the roar of the anti-aircraft barrage. The crump-crump of the bombs I found disturbing but not terrifying.

As I journeyed southwards to London I was struck by the number of 'Anderson shelters' which had been installed in the back gardens of the houses along the railway, and also by the fact that the Englishman, with his innate love of gardening and genius for improvisation, had discovered that this simple structure of corrugated iron half-covered with earth afforded an ideal means of growing vegetable marrows. These plants, with promise of an excellent crop, decorated the majority of the shelters. Shortly after my arrival in London I found myself sitting next to their progenitor, the great Sir John Anderson himself, at luncheon. I little thought that some twenty years later I should become his biographer; my whole attention was concentrated on finding some topic of interest which would elicit a conversational response. It was hard going. John Anderson had little small-talk and disapproved of anything that smacked of levity. I tried cast after cast with little or no success – the state of public opinion in America; one's experiences in crossing the Atlantic in wartime, etc., all failed to evoke any but the most monosyllabic though courteous replies. Finally, in desperation, I told him about the vegetable marrows. His interest quickened perceptibly but he was still barren of utterance until, some minutes later, he remarked: 'I had not intended the shelters for the cultivation of vegetables.'

My first discovery on arriving in London was that I was homeless. The lease of my apartment in Albany had expired shortly before the war and I had rented a house in Bolton Street, just off Piccadilly. An early bomb had hit it, rendering it uninhabitable, and though my faithful secretary, Margaret Dunk, had arranged for the removal and storage of such of my furniture and belongings as had escaped irreparable damage, I was still without a home. I could have stayed with my mother in Queen Anne's Mansions but I preferred independence and so I went to the Ritz and explained my predicament. Their response was generous and magnificent. They agreed to allow me to leave a couple of suitcases indefinitely and covenanted to guarantee me a bed at a flat rate whenever I was in London. This arrangement lasted throughout the war and I have occupied every kind of accommodation there from a courier's room in the attics to a suite overlooking Green Park; I have even slept on a palliasse on the floor of the grill on more than one occasion during air-raids. It was a kindness I have never forgotten.

My next activity was to subject myself to a medical examination first at the hands of a military medico and then of my own doctor. Their verdict was unfortunately the same. My heart, though not in a state of danger, was not up to army requirements and I was brutally informed that I should be more of a liability to the service than an asset. Dejectedly I abandoned all hopes of a military career, even in an emergency.

My days were filled to the veriest minute. Chiefly my centres of action were the Foreign Office, with 'Van', Alec Cadogan, Orme ('Moley') Sargent and Charles Peake, head of the News Department, with whom I was to be so closely associated sometime later, and at the Ministry of Information, with Duff Cooper, Harold Nicolson, Ronnie Tree and Walter Monckton. I was trying to learn as much as I could in the short space of time allotted to me and also to impart what information I could. I picked up some of my old European contacts again. Bruce Lockhart was British representative with the Czechoslovak Government-in-exile at this time, and with him I used to foregather with Beneš and Jan Masaryk. There were long talks too with Eduard Raczynski, now Polish Foreign Minister and with his Netherlands opposite number, Elko van Kleffens, whom I had first known in Geneva in the thirties. There was also an unforgettable talk alone with Mr Winston Churchill at No. 10 Downing Street. He catechised me about public opinion in America and chuckled when I told him of my adventure in Pittsburgh cathedral.

Lord Beaverbrook sent for me at his Ministry of Aircraft Production on Millbank ostensibly also to cross-question me about America. In effect, however, he treated me to a brilliant dissertation on this subject which indicated that he knew as much or more about it than I did. He asked me to dine at Stornoway House and, more out of curiosity than anything else, I accepted. We were a small, select and curiously assorted group: our host, Leslie Hore-Belisha, Bruce Lockhart and myself. The talk was excellent, provocative and, as it seemed to me, sometimes indiscreet, but I sat and listened with my ears cocked while the three others outdid one another in purveying the 'inner life' of government. In the middle of dinner there was an air-raid warning and we adjourned below stairs to a most comfortably appointed shelter. Champagne flowed, the talk continued unabated, its spice becoming sharper. Later, much later, we were informed of the all-clear and went upstairs. With his own hands 'the Beaver' threw open the great doors of Stornoway House, and there, against the glow of the rising sun, a fire was blazing nearby. Hore-Belisha and Bruce went out before me and as I was about to follow them, Lord Beaverbrook put his hand on my shoulder and, somewhat to my alarm, said in that raucous Canadian accent of his: 'We've been under fire together. You're one of my boys now.' In point of fact I did not see him again until we met at one of the dinners of the 'Other Club' some ten years later.

On another occasion I was dining with Neill Malcolm when the sirens went. My general preserved complete equanimity, refusing to recognise this interruption in our conversation. Shortly thereafter a stick of bombs hit the house at the back of his with a shattering roar and set it on fire. 'That was close,' said Neill. 'Have some more brandy,' and we talked on.

I walked back through the blackout with fires on either hand and the patter of shrapnel very audible. To the east was a brilliant glow in the sky. It seemed curious to be in Piccadilly in evening clothes and carrying a gas-mask while death and destruction rained down about me but somehow no more incongruous than the whole atmosphere which I found in London at this time. It was one of restrained euphoria. The glory of the Dunkirk miracle was still an influence charged almost with the supernatural. Few other nations have the startling British faculty for decking their defeats with laurels and giving them the appearance of legendary victories. There was, moreover, a feeling of overwhelming relief at having got rid of the French and of being, in the words of a Foreign Office door-keeper, 'in the final and playing it on our own ground'. 'Praise God now for an English War', Dorothy Sayers was writing. The distinction of 'standing alone' was still something to be inspiringly proud of and had not yet developed that sense of fatigue and loneliness which made us so ready and willing to welcome the Russians as allies a year later. There was also heroism. Not the demonstrative flag-wagging kind, but the simple quiet heroism in the face of danger and discomfort and homelessness; a grim, quiet defiance of fate and a determination to fight and to win. Though the 'upper brackets' hummed with rumours of invasion, the man-in-the-street and the man-in-the-fields discounted the imminence of this menace and went about his everyday work, giving service to his country in his leisure time. The townsfolk were engaged in A.R.P. work or as special constables, in the country they enrolled in the Home Guard and drilled with pikes and broomsticks.

The preliminary stage of the Battle of Britain had ended and the attack had switched to fighter-fields in the south and south-east. It was not until early September that the assault began on London by day and by night, though she had sustained spasmodic attacks before then.

In the course of one of these I was driven down into an Underground Station by a shepherding A.R.P. warden and saw for myself the conditions there. They were very bad indeed, for this was before the excellent organisation with its bunks and sanitary arrangements, had got under way. I emerged more shocked by what I had seen than I was alarmed by the raid itself.

I was anxious to see as much as I could of the battle and, through the kindness of Duff Cooper and of Anthony Eden, who was then

SPECIAL RELATIONSHIPS

Secretary for War, arrangements were made for me to spend twenty-four hours at Dover. I was driven down to the coast and duly reported to the Commanding Officer at the Castle. He couldn't have been more helpful and issued me with a steel helmet. He also suggested that I should drive down to the end of Admiralty Pier. 'You can practically see them taking off from France there,' he said. 'Only try to get back here before they start strafing.' To the end of the pier I duly went and waited upon events. Almost at once the warning sounded and my driver, an old hand, turned the car. Then he shouted at me: 'Get down, sir, and put on your 'at. Those are Stukas.' It was at this moment that I found I had forgotten to bring my helmet with me. I cowered at the bottom of the car which my driver sent hurtling 'like a bat out of hell' along the mole and up the hill to the Castle. Behind us we heard the strident whine of a diving Stuka, then the anti-aircraft defences went into action and I felt better. As I entered the ante-room the C.O. greeted me genially. 'Ah,' he said, 'just in time for lunch. Did you find it interesting?' Pusillanimously I did not own up to my delinquency in the matter of the steel-helmet.

I found it engrossingly interesting to be permitted to watch the course of an engagement in the Operations Room that afternoon. Gathered around a large-scale map table covered with talc, I watched W.A.A.F. operators wearing head-phones mark off the various losses on either side over the battle area, which was somewhere between Tunbridge Wells and the coast. It had been a sizeable assault by the Luftwaffe and it was repulsed decisively but at some cost to the R.A.F. With my glasses I could see a number of rescues of pilots of 'ditched' planes by dashing little rescue boats, but alas, there were others who did not return.

Before leaving Dover I came under direct shell-fire. The Germans had mounted a long-range gun just outside Calais and well capable of firing across the twenty odd miles of the Channel. At intervals they sent over a number of rounds, which landed at random in the town causing both death and damage. It so happened that one of these bombardments took place just before my departure and for half-an-hour or so I sat in a public shelter. I realised how much worse shelling was than bombing. It was, I found, a greater strain to the nerves and its accuracy made it the more frightening. Yet I was amazed at the resigned patience and courage of my companions. This had become an accepted part of their lives. They played cards; they quieted their children; they discussed their family affairs with an intimacy and a wealth of detail that startled me, but they showed no fear, even though the casualties from shell-fire had been heavy. When it was over they gathered up their possessions, living and inanimate, and disappeared, some with a joking reference to 'next time'.

The question which was put to me from the highest to the lowest was 'when did I think we could expect aid and succour from the Americans?' I could, of course, give no definite answer, save that they had already embarked upon the preliminary stage and were 'tooling up' like mad, and for this we were paying 'on the barrel head', in accordance with the 'Cash-and-Carry' policy which had replaced the Neutrality Act in America.

In return the one query which I put to all my friends likely to be knowledgeable about the answer was: 'When do you expect the invasion?' and the answer became more and more definite as time went on. 'If they haven't tried it by the end of September, we shall be all right till the spring.' Meantime, preparations were apparent on every hand. Machine-gun posts were set up in block-houses at unexpected places. Sign-posts were blotted out in the happy belief that this would mislead Wehrmacht map-readers. Playing-fields, golf-courses, commons and other open spaces were protected against glider landings by scattering large concrete hoops across them, and warnings were issued concerning enemy agents parachuted into the country. A series of splendid Fougasse drawings cautioned all to beware of 'loose talk', and the whole affair was christened 'Operation Cromwell', the general alarm for which was to be the ringing of the church-bells throughout England; bells which had been silenced since the outbreak of war.

On the week-end of 7 September that kindest and most generous of men, Ronnie Tree, had invited me to Ditchley, in Oxfordshire. This truly lovely example of Palladian architecture he had placed with characteristic public spirit and hospitality at the disposal of the Prime Minister as an alternative to Chequers. Both Mr Churchill and Anthony Eden spent many week-ends there throughout the war, as did I when I was in England, for Ronnie and his wife Nancy had given me a standing invitation.

On this occasion, however, neither the P.M. nor Anthony was there, and our company included Duff and Diana Cooper, and Bob Brand (later Lord Brand) who had married a sister of Nancy Astor's, and at whose daughter Virginia's coming-out ball at the Farmington Country Club, Charlottesville, I had danced some years before. After dinner on Saturday the seventh we sat in the White Saloon and I remember thinking that the whole thing was almost a theatrical setting. Something of elegance and graciousness still remained about life at Ditchley and the beautiful furnishings and appointments had not been entirely dismantled. We were all in evening dress. At one end of the room were Michael, Ronnie's eldest son, resplendent in regimental 'dress blues', and a group of his contemporaries playing poker; at the other, a bridge table at which were Duff and Diana, Ronnie and Nancy; and in the middle a 'conversation group' which included Bob Brand, myself and a few others.

War seemed a very long way away and had it not been for the blackout and the uniforms of the young men, one might have imagined oneself in the course of a very pleasant week-end in time of peace. At about eleven o'clock this calm was shattered. Ronnie's immaculate butler entered and, as if announcing a new arrival, declaimed: 'Sir, the invasion has commenced.' At once all was action, we listened and sure enough the bells of the little nearby church were ringing the alarm, and in the great hall we heard noises suggestive of the mustering of the local Home Guard. Duff Cooper made for the telephone and demanded a 'priority call' as a former Secretary of State for War and First Lord of the Admiralty and the present Minister of Information. He failed to procure it on any of these grounds, and returned fuming.

And then we waited. The bells continued to sound their tocsin, for it was afterwards found that the verger-cum-bell-ringer had locked himself into the tower, and Ronnie's distinctive hospitality was extended to the Home Guard. At two o'clock, nothing further having occurred, Bob Brand and I entered into a pact to go to bed. I slept well and, on going down next morning, found the Home Guard still manfully at their posts and enjoying an excellent breakfast. The bells were stilled, it being rumoured that the enthusiastic and dedicated campanologist had collapsed from exhaustion.

Duff and Diana gave me a lift back to London in Duff's official car and we found every check-point between Oxford and London manned by exhilarated Home Guards who checked our papers with meticulous care. The journey took over two hours and when we arrived at the Ministry of Information, which was housed in London University, we found that the whole thing had been a false alarm. The alert had been sent out by the Deputy Chief of Staff at G.H.Q. Home Forces, on the basis of a report that a force of more than 300 German bombers, escorted by twice as many fighters, were droning through an almost cloudless sky towards the docks and other Thames-side targets. To the Chiefs of Staff, who had been warned by

Intelligence that the invasion operation might be launched at any moment, nothing seemed likelier than that Hitler would make a heavy air-raid on London as an immediate prelude to his main attack. When they actually saw this Luftwaffe armada approaching, they waited no longer and assumed quite rightly that the situation demanded a higher state of alert; hence the alarm for 'Operation Cromwell'.

As it happened, Hitler's plans at that moment did not include a cross-channel operation but, throughout the morning, the rumour was current in both the pubs and the clubs that the Wehrmacht had indeed launched an attempted invasion but that their forces had been cut to pieces by the Navy and the R.A.F., a bruit which continued to persist throughout the war.

Mindful of my promise to Philip Lothian to return to America unless there was an invasion and also of his minatory injunction not to 'hang about waiting for it', I concluded that I had pretty well achieved my purpose in coming to England and arranged for my passage back. I left London on a day of particularly lively aerial activity. As we pulled out of Euston Station the great glass roof crashed down on the moving train; when we arrived at Liverpool it was to the blast of bombs, through which – and the black-out – I groped my way to the Adelphi hotel; next morning I sailed in the old *Duchess of Atholl* and, as we made our way down the Mersey, water-spouts of explosions rose from the river around us. Miraculously we were unhit, but my passage back was not as uneventful as my passage over. We were in the same convoy as the *City of Benares*, which was carrying a cargo of children and parents and nannies to the safety of American welcomes. West of the Irish coast our destroyer escort turned back in a very heavy sea and some time thereafter signals of distress were received from the *City of Benares* that she had been torpedoed and was sinking. For the captain of the *Duchess* this presented a hideous dilemma. All his instincts were to go to the succour of his stricken consort, but his orders were explicit. We were carrying a thousand naval ratings, destined to take over the American destroyers for which we had traded bases, and in view of this the captain was strictly charged not to change course under any circumstances. It was essential to the security of Britain that those destroyers should be manned and made operative at the earliest moment. Sadly, we were told, the signals from the *City of Benares* grew fainter.

It took us ten days to make Halifax and another three days by train to reach Washington, but the picture I had seen on entering that great harbour was one that remains with me yet. Not only was it filled with allied mercantile shipping, from the Canadian Pacific Line, Cunarders and White Star vessels to the *Nieuw Amsterdam* and other maritime assets of the allied governments-in-exile, but there riding at anchor in serried ranks was the blessed sight of those ancient American destroyers for which we were so grateful. It was wonderfully reassuring to know that we had their crews, or at least part of them, on board with us, thereby making certain that these tough workmanlike craft would soon be at sea.

CHAPTER SIX

'Good Night, Philip'

I breakfasted with Philip Lothian on the morning of my arrival in
Washington (23 September), and he greeted me warmly. He was avid
for news of Britain and gave me encouraging tidings of the improve-
ment in Anglo-American relations. But I was shocked by the change
in his appearance in the few weeks since I had seen him. He looked
greatly fatigued and to my dismay dropped off to sleep for a brief
spell in the middle of one of his sentences. That he had been working
desperately hard ever since June I was well aware, but this seemed
unnatural and I was the more anxious when I found that this falling
asleep was a recent development and that it had occurred on public
occasions, between courses at luncheon- or dinner-parties and even
when he was dictating. It was disturbing not only for itself but
because it was causing comment in Washington. The odd thing was
that, though he would complain of feeling 'desperately tired', his
resilience was such that, after a short rest, he would boast of being
'fit as a two-year-old'. To me, however, he looked a sick man.

A few weeks later, on 12 October, Philip flew back to London to be
greeted as a hero and a master of diplomacy at the highest level. The
War Cabinet honoured him personally and the Prime Minister
recommended his name to the King for appointment as a Knight of
the Thistle, Scotland's proudest order.

The word that Lothian brought back to London was basically what
he had told me that first morning at breakfast. The United States had
now passed from neutrality to non-belligerency and the margin
between that and co-belligerency seemed to be visibly diminishing.
There was no longer any doubt about America's desire to help
Britain – though none could as yet envisage a declaration of war –
the chief problem was finance. How could payment be made by
Britain for the sinews of war now placed at her disposal by the
'Arsenal of Democracy'? It had long been understood that a time
would come when Britain would no longer be able to find the gold or
the dollars for this purpose. Mr Churchill has described the position
very clearly in *Their Finest Hour*:

Up to November 1940 we had paid for everything we had received.

111

We had already sold 325 million dollars worth of American shares requisitioned for sterling from private owners in Britain. We had paid out over 4,500 million dollars in cash. We had only 2,000 million left, the greater part in investments, many of which were not readily marketable. It was plain that we could not go on any longer in this way. Even if we divested ourselves of all our gold and foreign assets, we could not pay for half we had ordered, and the extension of the war made it necessary for us to have ten times as much. We must keep something in hand to carry on our daily affairs.

Of this crucial problem Lothian was fully aware and of the necessity for its urgent solution. It was uppermost in his mind when he stepped off the Clipper at LaGuardia airport on his return to New York on 23 November. Aubrey and I had gone out to meet him and the press were clamouring for a statement. Aubrey asked him if he would care to make one, and he agreed, but asked for a minute or two to think. In those few moments he took a major decision. He knew that the Prime Minister proposed to write to the President on the subject of payment; he had indeed been asked to draft the letter; but he knew too that the President would require some demonstration of popular support before he took the great step that was hoped for from him and he knew too that this could only be achieved by shock tactics. As in the case of the Destroyer-Bases deal, Philip Lothian took it upon himself to condition the mind of the American people. To the expectant newspapermen he made one of the shortest and most momentous statements in the history of the war: 'Well, boys, Britain's broke; it's your money we want,' and he passed out to the waiting car.

Aubrey and I could scarcely believe our ears. We knew what this would mean for us when it came to interpreting it to the press. Had he, we asked politely of the Ambassador, meant exactly what he had said? Indeed he had, Philip replied. 'Oh yes,' he added, 'I know I shall get my head washed in London and in Washington, but it's the truth, and they might as well know it.'

He was indeed more than accurate in his prophecy. The President and the Secretary of the Treasury, Henry Morgenthau, were annoyed at what they rightly divined to be a 'calculated indiscretion', and the President feared that the effect on Congress might be unfavourable. The Prime Minister was afraid that Philip's public statement might prejudice the mind of the President when he received Mr Churchill's letter. The Chancellor of the Exchequer, Sir Kingsley Wood, took umbrage because he had not been previously consulted and because his emissary, Sir Frederick Phillips, was about to arrive in Washington to follow up the contents of Mr Churchill's letter.

Philip Lothian's biographer has written that the Ambassador 'is said to have felt some remorse at what he had done', but I find it exceedingly difficult to concur in this view. To the best of my knowledge he displayed no signs of contrition. He had pondered deeply the problem during his flight from Britain and had arrived at the final decision to throw his firecracker where it would cause the loudest reverberations, namely into the ranks of the press. His terse, succinct statement had been no casual 'throw-away line' but a premeditated simplification of the position of affairs. Nor had he, as can be seen from his remarks to Aubrey and myself, failed to foresee the effect which his statement would have in high places nor the obloquy which would descend upon him in consequence. Never was an indiscretion more calculated. It was Philip Lothian at his best, appreciating instinctively the reaction of the American people, knowing very clearly what he did.

And, of course, he was absolutely right. His stark assertion to the press at LaGuardia airport on 25 November set off a chain of events which in less than two months had achieved its results. Public opinion snowballed in favour of greater and more material aid to Britain. Within a week even so tough-minded and moss-backed a pragmatist as Jesse Jones, Secretary of Commerce and Chairman of the Reconstruction Finance Corporation, was declaring that 'Britain was a good risk for a loan'. By the middle of December President Roosevelt openly told the press that, in pursuing his policy of aid to Britain, 'I am trying to eliminate the dollar mark'. He was as good as his word; on 10 January 1941, the Bill incorporating what Mr Churchill has called 'the glorious conception of Lend-Lease', was introduced into the House of Representatives. Appropriately it was entitled 'An Act to further promote the defence of the United States', and its number as a Bill was, significantly enough, '1776'.

The Bill was not accorded an entirely easy passage; however, it successfully weathered the rocks and shoals of controversy. It was passed by the House on 8 February, and by the Senate a month later. It became law with the signature of the President of the United States on 11 March.

Such was the ultimate success, the final 'end product', of Philip Lothian's brilliant diplomacy. Alas, he was not alive to enjoy his laurels.

Though his spell of leave in England had been a personal triumph, it had been no real vacation, and though on his return I found him exhilarated and anxious for talk and work, he did not look rested and he did not seem well. The periods of sudden somnolence became more frequent and more commented upon. Yet he lunched and dined out more frequently than before, instituted the custom of 'working breakfasts' and occasionally snatched the time for a round of golf.

Two items were predominant in Philip's mind. The drafting of Mr Churchill's letter to the President and the composition of an important speech which he was to deliver on 11 December at Baltimore to the American Farm Bureau Federation. He finished his draft and despatched it to the Prime Minister and then turned to the speech. He spent the week-end of 30 November at the Maryland house of his Private Secretary, Leander McCormick-Goodhart, and completed the first version. This he brought back to Washington and revised it. Then on 7 December he asked me to go over it with him. 'I'm not quite happy about the peroration,' he said, 'try your hand at it.'

I took his first and second drafts and made some few amendments, somewhat in the vein of what I had said at Charlottesville. Among other small additions, I inserted the sentence: 'If you back us you will not be backing a loser,' and handed it back to him. 'That's fine,' he said, 'but I'm going to change one word. I'm going to say: "If you back us you will not be backing a *quitter*".' And, of course, it was incomparably better.

The speech as a whole was a superb quintessence of all that he had believed in and striven for and for which he was about to die. It was his valedictory to America and to Britain and to the World. It was read to a hushed and deeply moved audience after his death, by the late Sir Nevile Butler, then the Chargé d'Affaires.

The final paragraph over which we had worked together on that gloomy December afternoon was as follows:

I have done. I have endeavoured to give you some idea of our present position and dangers, the problems of 1941, and our hopes for the future. It is for you to decide whether you share our hopes and what support you will give us in realising them. We are, I believe, doing all we can. Since May there is no challenge we have evaded, no challenge we have refused. If you back us you will not be backing a quitter. The issue now depends largely on what you decide to do. Nobody can share that responsibility with you. It is the great strength of democracy that it brings responsibility down squarely on every citizen and every nation. And before the judgement-seat of God each must answer for his own actions.

When we had finished our task I looked up and saw that he was ill. I begged him to go to bed. 'I can't,' he said, 'I have Norman Davis [the veteran American statesman and Head of the American Red Cross] coming to dine.' 'You know him well enough to give him a tray in your room,' I said. 'Do go to bed.' But he would not – at least not then – and summoning up a smile he said: 'Good night, Jack, and thank you.' I had always preserved strict protocol in dealing with him as my chief, calling him 'sir', but now somehow I felt as if I were off-duty. 'Good night, Philip,' I said. I never saw him again.

That evening I dined with Derick and Bunchy Hoyer Millar, to whom I spoke of my anxiety about the Ambassador's health. Could we not get a doctor to see him, I asked, despite his devotion to Christian Science? They shared my perturbation and Derick and I agreed to speak again on the morrow. It is an interesting fact that in these last days, Philip was surrounded by members of his own persuasion. His second-in-command, Nevile Butler and his wife Rose, his lady-secretary, Mrs Fowler, and his chauffeur valet, Winter, were all Christian Scientists.

Next morning we realised that the course of events had been taken out of our hands. The Ambassador was now very drowsy, weak and ill. He had asked on the previous evening that an old friend of his in Boston, a Christian Scientist practitioner, should be sent for, and he arrived on the morning of Monday, 8 December. Philip died during the night of 11/12 December 1940.

His death was announced to the Foreign Office in a telegram from Nevile Butler:

> It will no doubt be questioned why I did not insist on calling in a medical practitioner. As regards this, it was Lord Lothian's clear wish to have the form of treatment he chose ... to have forced a change on him would in my view have been dangerous. I had contemplated calling in today (12 December) an orthodox practitioner in order to give you his opinion as to the length of time Lord Lothian was likely to be out of action.

His complaint was in fact later diagnosed as uraemia.

Philip Lothian was mourned as deeply in America as in Britain. He had come handicapped by a past reputation but had from the first convinced all of his 'apostasy from heresy'. Throughout the fifteen months of his embassage he never failed to gauge the opinion of America to a nicety. He knew when to cajole and when to shock, when to appeal and when to issue a clarion-call of leadership. His humour was irresistible, his sincerity unquestioned, his statesmanship among the most inspired of our time. His was the hand who laid the foundation of 'the Special Relationship'.

Moreover, he made himself liked and respected by all his staff of all ranks and both sexes. This went beyond the mere loyalty to a chief; it was rooted in affection and personal devotion.

One is prompted to reflect what would have happened had Philip lived. Whilst he had been ambassador he had been almost proconsular in his independence. During the Phoney War period, when the British Government was running mute, it was he who had declared to America and, through its media, to the world, what were Britain's aims and why she was at war. When the war became open and disastrous it was he who dared to prepare American opinion for what fate might demand of it. But we were now on the threshold of that period of personal communication and conference between the President and the Prime Minister, which necessarily relegated the Embassy to the level of a post-office and the Ambassador to the status of messenger-boy. It is difficult to imagine Philip Lothian in that role.

As for myself, Philip's death meant more than I can express. The fifteen months during which I enjoyed the honour and pleasure of serving under him are among the most stimulating of my life. I have never known a chief whose inspiration spurred one on to greater heights than one thought it possible to achieve. His understanding, his wit, his rare praise and rarer blame were expressed as he thought merited. He was never emotional; he was always fair.

CHAPTER SEVEN

The Road to Pearl Harbor

The vacuum caused by Philip Lothian's death was not easily filled. So great had been his position in America, so mighty his stature, that it was generally felt that the most careful consideration must be given to the selection of a successor. Nor must this choice be made precipitately, and to give time for cogitation it was, at first, considered feasible to appoint a temporary Ambassador, an envoy *ad interim*, who should act as a 'stand-in' until the right man could be found.

Rumour was rife in both Washington and in New York. The name of Sir William Wiseman, that veteran and mysterious figure of Anglo-American relations in the First World War, was first bruited as an 'understudy' but this suggestion never really got off the ground. The next to be the subject of hearsay was Sir Gerald Campbell, a man wise and experienced in American affairs through having been Consul-General in San Francisco, Philadelphia and New York, in each of which he had engendered great popularity and genuine affection. At the moment he was British High Commissioner in Ottawa. He also failed to find favour in London and the idea of a temporary ambassador was abandoned.

But worse was to follow. From the Foreign Office came the whisper that the Prime Minister, whether out of misplaced loyalty or wishing to get an embarrassing personality out of the country, was about to propose Mr Lloyd George for the *agrément* of the United States Government for the post of ambassador. The idea was, of course, preposterous. Magnificent though Mr Lloyd George's leadership in the First World War had been, he was a very different man in 1940. In the first place he was seventy years old and though, like Lothian – and probably under his influence – Lloyd George had been to visit Hitler in the thirties and had returned not unimpressed, unlike Lothian, he had never followed the road to Damascus. Though he had played a significant role in bringing about the defeat and resignation of Mr Chamberlain ('Let the Prime Minister set an example by sacrificing the seals of office') he had refused to join Mr Churchill's government and at heart he remained a defeatist and increasingly so. Within six months of the events of which I write

117

now, Mr Churchill was to denounce Lloyd George in the House of Commons for making 'the sort of speech with which, I imagine, the illustrious and venerable Marshal Pétain might well have enlivened the closing days of M. Reynaud's Cabinet'.

Never have I witnessed such consternation among an embassy staff as was caused by the rumour of this possible appointment. An overturned hive of bees could not have been more distraught or more virulent, and this amazed alarm was also shared by those of the Dominion Governments who had diplomatic representation in Washington. The alarm developed into a combination of panic and near-mutiny when Nevile Butler received a definite instruction to enquire formally what would be President Roosevelt's reaction to a request for his *agrément* for Mr Lloyd George.

I saw much of Dick Casey, the Australian Minister, at this time and can bear witness to his indefatigable efforts to avoid this disaster, of which he has given an all too modest account in his *Personal Experience, 1939–1946*. Dick had shared my deep admiration and affection for Lothian. Scarcely a day passed without their conferring, and Dick was the last of Philip's friends to see him alive. His reactions thereafter verged upon the ferocious. The British Chargé d'Affaires could scarcely disregard his orders but he did delay in carrying them out and, in the meantime, Dick set to work to mobilise opinion against them. Having first ascertained from the White House that Mr Roosevelt would recoil from such a proposal with 'consternation' but that he did not wish to be placed in the position of giving an explicit refusal, Dick then set the machinery of his own foreign service into operation and thus alerted not only the Australian government but also those of the other Dominions. Within twenty-four hours Mr Churchill had received messages from Mr Mackenzie King (Canada), Mr Menzies (Australia), Field-Marshal Smuts (South Africa) and Mr Frazer (New Zealand) deprecating at length his idea of appointing Mr Lloyd George to Washington, and Nevile Butler's instructions were rescinded.

In the end, of course, we got Lord Halifax, and here again the selection did not appear to be inspired. To send to the United States at this juncture a great patrician, noted as a Master of Foxhounds, who in his political career had been closely identified with the expediency of Appeasement – even though, as Roy Jenkins has written, 'he lent dignity to a squalid policy' – did not at first glance seem to bristle with wisdom, more especially since he was to succeed the democratic, easygoing, informal and ever-accessible Lord Lothian. But Edward Halifax adapted himself very successfully to the

American scene and established for himself a position of authority and popularity for he was essentially a great and courteous gentleman, with a certain shy charm.

He dealt with the delicate and complicated aspects of Anglo-American relations in a highly competent manner, and was adept at co-operating with the other outstanding personalities, who included Field-Marshal Dill, Arthur Salter and Bob Brand not to speak of his Commonwealth colleagues. Throughout, he was greatly helped by Lady Halifax, who was splendid in every way and universally popular.

Halifax came at a moment when, as I have indicated, the status of ambassador was on the wane. Within a few months of his arrival in Chesapeake Bay in the battleship *King George* V on 24 January 1941 to be welcomed by the President in person, there had occurred that first meeting between the two 'former naval persons' in Placentia Bay in August, which ushered a new and far more personal element into the conduct of Anglo-American relations. From thenceforward the President and the Prime Minister pursued the course of their policies for the prosecution of the war on terms of close intimacy; an intimacy which sometimes resulted in Cabinet colleagues, Chiefs of Staff and ambassadors being informed rather than consulted. Philip Lothian could not, I believe, have tolerated such a situation; Lord Halifax accommodated himself to it with facility.

With him as his Personal Assistant Lord Halifax brought Charles Peake, an old friend of mine from the Foreign Office. The two had close affinities based partly on the fact that both were devout Anglo-Catholics and partly because Charles had served Halifax loyally as Head of the News Department during the troublous days of Appeasement, when Halifax was Foreign Secretary. He was a delightful and amiable companion, with the most delicious sense of humour. He was also a brilliant diplomatist when he had to deal with one particular individual, however difficult and complex. This gift he displayed with marked success when accredited to General de Gaulle and to Marshal Tito, with both of whom he got on famously. But he was essentially a European, and America was an enigma to him. Though he was the most amicable and kindliest of men, with a real art in friendship, he was not really designed to deal with any but the most sophisticated Americans.

Moreover Charles's sense of public relations was not attuned to the American wave-length. Lord Halifax's original gaffe, from which it took him some considerable time to recover, namely his acceptance of an invitation from an ancient and fashionable Philadelphia hunt club to chase the fox, was due largely to Charles's lack of opposition. Both Aubrey and I had warned him of the inevitable results of such a caper on that great body of Americans whose support for Britain was based on their admiration for her much advertised austerity and her gallantry in 'standing alone'. Into neither of these pictures did fox-hunting fit easily, and I almost went down on my knees to the Ambassador in a personal appeal not to do it. He would have none of our arguments, saying that 'Charles thought it was all right', and alas, his image suffered accordingly.

For me the changes at Washington meant that I was able to devote much more of my time to the Press Service in New York, where I headed the Research Department, to which I contributed my own extensive library, and staffed it with a variety of experts, paid and voluntary, among them a young man, a Commonwealth Scholar, called Frank Thistlethwaite, who in later years, discharged the unenviable office of Vice-Chancellor of East Anglia University with courage and acumen. We also had our own monitoring service, whose presiding genius was Jack (later Sir John) Rennie, who subsequently rose to be a Deputy Under-Secretary in the Foreign Office where he served with distinction. In those days, however, we were all amateurs and proud of it.

Part of our work was to prepare studies in depth for those media who wanted something more than comments on 'hot news', and to supply information to those Americans who wished to speak in our cause. This we encouraged warmly for not only did it relieve us ourselves but was less suspect. I still, however, did a good deal of speaking myself.

One of my most valuable 'peripheral attachments' was Dr Alfred Wiener, a droll little Berlin Jew, who from a very early date, well before the National Socialist Revolution, had begun an exhaustive collection of Nazi literature. As it became more and more apparent that Hitler would come to power I persuaded Wiener to take himself and his library out of Germany, and he established it in Amsterdam, from where I again uprooted him in 1939 just before the outbreak of the war. He then moved to London where he proved an invaluable asset to our propaganda services and eventually established the famous Wiener Library, which still flourishes, though he himself, alas, died in 1964.

My first contact with Wiener is a delightful memory. He had served with a gallant record throughout the First World War, unexpectedly enough in Persia with that strange figure Wilhelm Wassmuss, the German equivalent of Lawrence of Arabia, of whom

Christopher Sykes has written so fascinating a biography. I discovered this fact from a chance remark of Wiener's: 'In der First World Var,' he announced, 'I haf commanded two hondred and fifty – camels.' This so delighted me that I probed him for further details and thus began our friendship. He always referred to me, somewhat to the surprise of some of my colleagues, as 'Herr General-Oberst'.

Wiener's visits to New York were always welcome, and were fairly frequent, for he was able to collect there a quantity of Nazi propaganda then current in Latin America, which was a useful asset to our people at home. The visits were not always, however, without incident or complications. Wiener had all the puckish humour of the Berlin *Strassenkind*. Once he was sitting in my waiting-room with a distinguished but highly sensitive Zionist lawyer, who was also waiting to see me. Wiener carefully folded the newspaper he was reading (as it was later reported to me) and crossed the room to address himself to a complete stranger with the ominous warning: 'Do not post your letters in der mail boxes. Der spies feesh them out mit feesh hooks,' and left without further comment. My Zionist friend entered my office trembling with anxiety and bewilderment. 'Will you kindly inform me,' he asked in a shaking voice, 'how I am to communicate with my friends and with my office in London if I cannot safely make use of the mail facilities of this country?' I pacified and reassured him explaining that this was just Dr Wiener's little way, and when the Herr Doktor next came in I reproved him for undue hubris; he replied, 'Ach, *aber Herr General-Oberst*, he looked so gloomy, I only wanted to cheer him up a little.'

In mid-summer of 1941, very shortly after the German invasion of the Soviet Union, a decision was taken in London and in Washington which was to have a far-reaching effect on the careers of Aubrey Morgan and myself. It was recognised at last that the British public relations set-up in New York was too amorphous and it must be confessed that, though each was doing its best according to its own lights, the relations between the Library of Information and the Press Service continued to be unfriendly. A good case could be made for bringing all these activities under one hat, thus making for closer co-operation and up-grading the general image of British services to Americans.

The vital question was, who should wear the hat? One of the many inducements which Mr Churchill held out to Lord Halifax in urging him to accept the Washington embassy was the suggestion that, if he thought well of taking on Sir Gerald Campbell as Minister, he would be relieved of the pressure of chancery business and would be able to return periodically to resume his position as a member of the War Cabinet, which he retained. This suggestion could not wholly recommend itself to Edward Halifax nor to the Establishment. A non-career ambassador, with the prestige and eminence of a former Foreign Secretary, was one thing, but the appointment of a member of the consular corps, even though acting at the moment in a quasi-diplomatic capacity as British High Commissioner in Ottawa, as a sort of 'deputy ambassador' was quite another, and the matter was tactfully and tacitly abandoned.

When, however, the question of a head of the proposed new organisation in New York arose, the name of Sir Gerald Campbell again came up and this time with success. In due course he was appointed Director-General of the British Information Services.

On paper he had much to recommend him for this office. There had never been so popular a Consul-General in New York (or for that matter in Philadelphia or San Francisco) and his friendly relations and general amiability had begotten him a legion of god-children. He had a dry pawky wit and was always in great demand as a popular speaker to a Rotarian type of audience, to whom his humour and oratory were exactly suited. Indeed he could get away with saying practically anything. When I was once 'ghosting' a speech for him one of my colleagues bet me that I could not insert the phrase 'nothing is so ferocious as a cornered sheep' into the draft and not have it deleted. In a moment of irresponsibility I did so and when we listened later on the radio to Sir Gerald's performance at the banquet we heard these immortal words duly received with thunders of applause.

But Gerald Campbell's qualities really stopped at personal popularity. He disliked the details of administration and had little sense of the overall picture of public relations. What he really enjoyed was getting around the country, making his shrewd, dry, humorous speeches, at which he was very good indeed. It was apparent, however, from the beginning that both he and the new organisation needed direction and support. Some inspired soul in the Ministry of Information had thought of sending out as his deputy director general, Robin Cruikshank, a brilliant journalist, who later became editor of the ill-fated News Chronicle. Robin was to me almost the perfect type of newspaper man – imaginative, with an unerring instinct for what was good and bad in a story, a marvellous Dickensian humour, coupled with a side-splitting sense of the ridiculous and a flashing wit. Above all, he had an immense capacity for knowing just how to handle individuals and situations in just the right imperturbable manner. He was a delight to work with and that the B.I.S. ever got off the ground as an organisation was largely due to his efforts and inspiration.

I had known Gerald Campbell for a number of years in his three consulates-general and had seen him again during the war, when Philip Lothian had sent me on a mission to our mutual friend John Buchan (then Lord Tweedsmuir), the Governor-General of Canada. John and Philip had been colleagues in Lord Milner's Kindergarten and later in the councils of the *Round Table*. They were close friends and John's sudden death in February 1940 had been a great blow to Philip.

I had always liked Campbell, indeed one couldn't help liking him. I never knew a man with more friends and fewer enemies, and it was my idea that Aubrey and I could give him the help he manifestly both needed and desired; moreover both of us liked being near the centre of power. With very little need of encouragement he appointed us both his Special Assistants and we settled in with Robin Cruikshank, to make the new organisation really hum.

The important thing, however, we all agreed, was to get Gerald Campbell accepted in London as a figure of stature and eminence. It was therefore arranged that, accompanied by me, he should fly back to England for a few weeks' visit. We left New York by Pan-American Clipper on 2 July, and on the following day made the scheduled refuelling stop at Horta, in the Azores. It was always easy to get into the anchorage of Horta but often extremely difficult to get out again. Any storm in the Atlantic resulted in rank after rank of giant rollers coming in and making it impossible for flying-boats to take off. It was not unusual for persons, however Very Important they might be, to be held up there for a week or more. On this occasion, however, our delay was limited only to an extra twenty-four hours, which we spent chiefly in walking along the shore and watching the rollers come in.

It was now that I learned a fascinating aspect of Gerald Campbell's earlier career. He was perhaps the last person one would have imagined to be associated with that notorious eccentric Frederick Rolfe, self-styled Baron Corvo, yet readers of Arthur Symons's *Quest for Corvo* will remember that in his description of Rolfe's death he speaks of 'the horrified [British] Consul', who, in going through the deceased's effects found enough material to cause a hundred scandals and disclosed plainly enough what sort of a life Rolfe had led. I had read this book when it appeared before the war, and when my

Director-General happened to mention that he had once been *en poste* in Venice, I suddenly remembered that the name of the 'horrified Consul' was none other than Gerald Campbell. I asked if he were indeed the same man. He admitted it and told me his side of the story.

When he was summoned to examine the effects of an unknown Englishman on the morning of 26 October 1913, before they were sealed by the Italian authorities, he had indeed been horrified at what he had found. Letters, drawings, notebooks, photographs, books and paraphernalia of all descriptions of pornography and perversion had met his appalled gaze. There was not a moment to lose. In the interests of the prestige of the British raj such obscene evidence must not be allowed to fall into alien hands and the Consul accordingly scooped up what seemed to him to be the worst of it and stuffed it into a suitcase. With the boots of the Italian *carabinieri* clattering on the stairs, he hurled it out of the window and into the canal. At least that was his intention, but in fact the case fell straight into the police-launch moored at the entrance to the decayed *palazzo* in which Rolfe had rented his last lodging. The Consul was equal to the emergency. Leaving the field to the police, he ran downstairs and reclaimed the suitcase from the bewildered policeman left in charge of the launch. Then he destroyed it. The maddening thing was that he could not remember how he had accomplished this. The whole thing was, however, an agreeable diversion from the tedium of our enforced delay at Horta.

We spent the following night at the British Embassy at Lisbon as the guests of Sir Ronald Campbell (Big Ronnie) who had been ambassador in Paris at the outbreak of the war. He gave us a graphic and almost sickening account of those last days of the Reynaud Government in June 1940, with vivid descriptions of the exhausted and diminishing resistance of Reynaud himself in face of the defeatism of Pétain and Weygand, the indecision of Lebrun and, above all, the evil cunning of Laval. I remember his final epitome of the situation: 'The Third Republic began its life in the good claret country of Bordeaux, it concluded its existence at Vichy, a district of a table-water aperient.'

Incidentally Ronnie Campbell was the author of my favourite telegram of the war, which I was shown one day in the Foreign Office. It was at a moment during which we badly needed supplies from the Portuguese Government and the Ambassador telegraphed tersely: 'I am very busy about tungsten and must therefore not be bothered about sardines.' Nor can I forget my equally favourite minute on a file which once reached my table at the Embassy in Washington. The content of the file was of no little importance but the sole comment of the head of the chancery (who was *not* then Derick Hoyer Millar) was: 'I think the "r" of this typewriter needs cleaning.'

Very early in the morning of 5 July Gerald Campbell and I drove out to the Lisbon airfield which in itself was an extraordinary sight. Because Spain and Portugal afforded the only 'free transit' communication centres for the southern part of an Axis-occupied Europe, it was a meeting-place and point of exchange for all the continent. Every airline was represented, Lufthansa, K.L.M., Air France, Swissair, Imperial Airways, and Pan-American, whilst German, British, American, Dutch, Italian, Vichy French and Swiss pilots jostled one another at close quarters. It was an odd sight and a remarkable one.

We took off in a K.L.M. machine with the windows covered by black-out material. We had not been told our route but had been informed that we should be making a non-stop flight. As is my wont when flying I fell asleep almost at once but was soon awakened by the sensation of the plane coming down. I managed to catch an illicit peek around the blackout shutter and what I saw filled me with horror. We were indeed descending and were at that moment flying over an expanse of sand-dunes, among which grew small, stunted, wind-bent pine trees. Moreover, as we came lower, I saw some soldiery clad in field-grey uniforms. I confess I was very frightened indeed. I was convinced that through engine trouble we were making a forced landing in the German occupied zone of France, and that on arrival we should be arrested. Mindful of my record with the Nazis and the danger it had already brought me, I was not happy about the immediate prospect. I do remember praying that I should be shot and not tortured.

The plane came to a standstill and the hatch opened. I summoned up such courage as I could and hoped that I didn't look as frightened as I felt. Then I nearly fainted with relief. We had, in fact, landed perfectly safely at Oporto to take on extra fuel for our flight to England. What they had omitted to tell us in Lisbon was that our flight would be non-stop *from Oporto*. As for the field-grey uniforms, I was later told that shortly before the war the Portuguese government had purchased a consignment of surplus uniform-material from the Wehrmacht quartermaster department.

I do not think I have ever worked harder than in the weeks which followed. The object of the exercise was to sell Gerald Campbell to the powers that be, but he proved to be a none too easily marketable commodity. He had lived in America so long and with only short spells of leave in England, for he enjoyed spending his vacations in the United States and ultimately retired there, that he had lost touch with the nerve-centres of Whitehall and Westminster. He was in fact a repatriate returning home after a long absence abroad. Then his manner was somewhat against him. Though perfectly attuned to the American wavelength he found difficulty in accommodating himself to the British way of thought, which is perhaps slower and more formal than across the Atlantic.

However, I did my best. Throughout the air journey over I had tried to inculcate in him the idea that he was in the position of a general officer taking over the command of a new and difficult front and must act accordingly. I arranged for him to meet half the Cabinet, including the Prime Minister, Anthony Eden, Duff Cooper and Hugh Dalton, and he spent a good deal of time in various departments of the Foreign Office, the Ministry of Information and the Treasury. Ronnie Tree invited him to Ditchley on a 'Winston week-end' and through the good offices of 'Van' with Alec Hardinge, the King's Private Secretary, he was invited to lunch alone with the Sovereign. Later he was taken to see the worst of the bombed-out areas and to inspect aircraft production and munition factories. All possible honour was shown him, but it was clear to me that he wasn't happy. He wasn't at his ease or his best – and it was such a good best when he let it show through. Perhaps he was shy, perhaps he was homesick for his round of popular appearances on American platforms. I sent a despairing telegram to Aubrey in cipher: 'My lion won't roar,' and it came as no surprise to me when he told me that he was returning alone ahead of schedule, leaving to me the task of what he described as 'tying up the loose ends'.

Having taken this decision he became perceptibly more cheerful and I decided to give a farewell dinner at the Savoy at which he could make a speech. It was a 'bang-up' party in his honour. The Chiefs of Staff came and 'Pug' Ismay; Anthony Eden was good enough to spare the time and Bruce Lockhart, who was now the Director-General of Political Intelligence (P.I.D.), and Charles Hambro, the Director-General of Special Operations Executive (S.O.E.). The Ministry of Information was well represented by Duff Cooper and Harold Nicolson, Ronnie Tree and Walter Monckton. In all it was a goodly company.

Unfortunately, however, I had selected the worst date possible – 15 July 1941 – on which day Mr Churchill chose to make major changes in his government one of which was to replace Duff Cooper by Brendan Bracken as Minister of Information and to appoint Ernest Thurtle in place of Harold Nicolson. My predicament was, as may be imagined, severe. Duff and Harold had both accepted my invitation and I obviously couldn't 'unask' them. On the other hand, from Gerald Campbell's point of view it was essential to have the Minister of Information present, together with his Parliamentary Under-Secretary, as they were to be his 'bosses' in London. So in the end I decided to have all four of them, 'the quick and the dead', and Brendan, who was an old friend, saw the point and came, bringing Ernest Thurtle with him.

Gerald Campbell, of course, knew nothing of all that had gone on behind the scenes and seemed mildly pleased at such a good turn-out to speed him on his way. He made an unexceptionable little speech and on the whole the affair served its purpose even though Duff was in the depths of gloom and Harold Nicolson in tears. For the first time since his arrival Gerald Campbell thawed out into his warm and genial self and as he moved around the table after dinner, I could see that he was making his breakthrough at last. I wondered whether I ought not to have given my dinner earlier, but this would have been difficult. I also wondered whether Gerald's *bonhomie* was not to some extent stimulated by the fact that he was leaving for America in a few days' time.

Left to myself I did what I had to do and then sought to see the condition of things in England. The worst of the Blitz had ceased with the German invasion of Russia in June when the might of the Luftwaffe had been transferred to the Eastern Front. There was comparatively little bombing while I was there, especially when compared with the previous year, but the scars remained. Wherever one went, in whatever quarter of London, there were stark shells of burnt-out or bomb-shattered houses, or mere holes in the ground where great masses of scarlet 'fire-weed' were already blooming. Refugees still went regularly to the Underground stations, for want of anywhere else to go, and individuals staked out recognised claims to certain specific bunks or benches. The conditions here had improved vastly in a year, especially in sanitation, but it was pitiful yet magnificent to sense the high courage and patient suffering which still pervaded London in general and the country as a whole. I went into the Midland cities of Manchester, Sheffield and Birmingham and found much the same circumstances: great courage but great weariness, amounting to exhaustion, and a profound relief that the Russians had taken the weight of the Luftwaffe off their necks. Britain had become awfully tired of 'standing alone'.

Food I found to be adequate but odd. Lord Woolton had done an amazingly successful job with rationing, and it was said that more children were getting more milk than at any previous time in the nation's history. Strange new items appeared in the shops which, once one had got used them, proved quite palatable; whale steaks, for instance, looked the part even if they had a somewhat fishy taste, and were infinitely preferable to snoek, a South African fish. Spam we were grateful for as an evidence of Lend-Lease if for nothing else, and there was a mysterious culinary achievement called Woolton Pie into the ingredients of which it was felt to be inadvisable to probe too deeply. Liquor was short, except for whisky and beer. We had to wait until the liberation of North Africa a year and a half later before the perils of Algerian wine fell upon us.

On the whole morale was high; the country saw no end to the war and was resigned to this. I returned to America as before with reluctance. My longing to be in England at this juncture had led me to take some tentative steps in that direction.

Up to the very eve of the Japanese attack on Pearl Harbor on 7/8 December 1941, it is probably true to say that 80 per cent of the people of America were strongly opposed to a declaration of war by the United States on the Axis Powers. A great majority, however, favoured a policy toward Britain of 'all aid short of war'. Yet the debates in both the House and the Senate during the passage of the Lend-Lease Bill had disclosed a strong isolationist minority who withstood the meaning and matter of the Bill on the grounds that sooner or later it would inevitably cause American involvement in the war, a war for which, in their opinion, the country was not prepared and which, it was tacitly implied, was no business of theirs.

The most influential of the organisations that held these beliefs was the America First Committee which had its headquarters in Chicago, numbering amongst its supporters many leading and most respected citizens. Many of them were friends of mine, whom I had met in the years before the war and with whom I had disputed the policy of Appeasement pursued by the British Government throughout the thirties, for all these isolationists were profound admirers of Neville Chamberlain. Their fundamental distrust and virtual detestation of President Roosevelt was openly stated from his first election and matured progressively as he drew nearer to 'all aid short of war'.

Among these friends of mine were General Robert E. Wood, head

Ruth

Robert Bruce Lockhart

of Sears, Roebuck, and Janet Ayre Fairbank, respectively national chairman and national vice-chairman of America First. Janet Fairbank was a delightful person who had campaigned for women's suffrage at an early age. She had been a militant member of Theodore Roosevelt's Progressive Party whose intervention in the presidential election of 1912 had brought William Howard Taft and the Republicans down to defeat and Woodrow Wilson and the Democrats to victory and office. Later Janet had turned to fiction and in a fascinating novel, called *Rich Man – Poor Man*, gave a lucid and exciting account of the founding of the Progressive Party and its consequences. I had often stayed with her and her family, both in Chicago and at their country place on Lake Geneva (Illinois). Her reasons for backing 'America First' were clear and understandable enough. As a mother she did not wish to risk the lives of her two much-loved sons in a 'foreign war'. (I may say that they both served later with gallantry and distinction, one being decorated.)

My relations with General Wood were more formal but we were on good terms and the basis of his support for 'America First' was a combination of a conviction that America got a raw deal from the Allies after the First World War – 'Your Lloyd George and that Clemenceau made rings round that chiseller Wilson,' he once said to me – a hostility toward those European countries who had 'welshed' on their war-debts; a conviction that Hitler would win the war anyway; and a profound dislike of Franklin Roosevelt, amounting to a clear suspicion that the President had every intention of committing the United States to war by hook or by crook – most likely the latter. Despite this galaxy of prejudices, he was a very pleasant man and, according to his lights, one of integrity.

It was owing to my happy relations with these two that Aubrey Morgan and I received an unexpected and somewhat surprising invitation to come out to Chicago and address the Executive Committee of 'America First', a fact, I think, very much to their credit. This was during the interim between Philip Lothian's death and the establishment of the British Information Services. We were, therefore, our own masters and we decided to accept without feeling that we had to inform the Chancery in Washington.

What followed was a profoundly illuminating experience. We stayed with Janet and Kellogg Fairbank, in whose dining-room the meeting took place, and they could not have been more kind and hospitable. Nor could our co-hosts have been more courteous. This curious confrontation between the archetypes of American Isolation and two representatives of belligerent Britain was conducted with the utmost urbanity. We made no attempt to argue with them, of course, but confined ourselves to an exposition of the disastrous results which had all but overwhelmed our own country through our neglect of our armaments and defences and our pursuit of our own particular brand of isolation, which had been Appeasement. We had, said Aubrey and I to these hidebound non-interventionists, continued playing so long in the garden of our false security, disregarding the darkening skies above us, that we had succeeded in closing our ears to all rumblings of approaching danger. We never mentioned the United States, but we left them to draw their own conclusions.

Neither Aubrey Morgan nor I had entertained any illusions as to our success in preaching to the unconvertible but I think both of us were agreeably surprised at the applause which greeted us when we had finished. The enemy, as it were, gave us the full honours of war. They asked one or two questions which indicated that at least some of our shafts had gone home, and then asked us if there was anything we would like to put to them. I judged the atmosphere to be sufficiently amicable to ask at what point they would consider it necessary to resist the Germans with force. There was silence for a moment and then one of them answered, quite seriously: 'When they cross the Rio Grande.'

We parted with an exchange of courtesies, neither side having made the smallest dent in the mentality of the other, but it was a very civilised affair.

This had not been the first contact which Aubrey and I had had with isolationism. Thanks to the kindness of Constance and himself I spent many week-ends at the Morrow house, Next Day Hill, at Englewood, New Jersey, where Mrs Morrow, a captivating person, had taken me into the family. It was not unusual for her middle daughter Anne to be there too, with her husband Charles Lindbergh, with whom Aubrey's friendship had been forged in those searing days of the Hauptman Trial, the fearful sequel to the tragedy of the kidnapping of the Lindbergh baby. In a short time Charles had accepted me as a friend and we remained on these terms for the remainder of his life. Not that we agreed. Aubrey, Charles and I spent many evenings arguing, debating and fundamentally dissenting in the most amicable fashion. Charles has given some account of our discussion in his *War Diaries*; the nature of his entries confirms my statement that though we rarely ever concurred and 'ever more came out by that same door wherein we went', we never lost our tempers nor jeopardised our friendship.

The essential difficulty about Charles Lindbergh's attitude toward world affairs was that all his life he had had to depend on absolute accuracy and complete expertise; nothing could be left to chance, there must always be a margin for safety. He was really a perfectionist and believed in the most meticulous preparation down to the last detail, whether it was as a preliminary to his famous transatlantic flight, or his subsequent exploratory expeditions. Everything in his view of life had to be calculated and tidy; he could neither tolerate nor understand an amateur approach to anything.

The corollary of this type of thinking inevitably led him toward a respect for the Germans, not because he had a political affinity for their political principles but because they thought as he did in terms of expertise. They too were perfectionists, they too had a tidy approach to a technical subject. When he travelled there before the war the Luftwaffe gave him full run of their installations, a fact which incidentally was of the very greatest assistance to the American military attaché, Colonel Truman Smith, in making his reports to Washington.

Charles left Germany during the Czech crisis of 1938, with a deep respect for the German Air Force, which he expressed to the French authorities with whom he was brought together by Bill Bullitt, the American ambassador in Paris. Though his statement that the Luftwaffe was far superior to the French Air Force was technically correct (and was proved so little more than a year later), it was not calculated to stimulate the stamina of an already demoralised French government, and Charles Lindbergh's contribution to the tragedy of Munich was unintentionally calamitous.

It was the same in 1940 after the collapse of France. Charles could not believe that Britain could withstand the might of the Luftwaffe operating with the added advantage of the use of the French airfields. Nothing that Aubrey nor I could say in our many discussions could compel his comprehension of Britain's genius for improvisation and her gift for inspired amateurism. He was not anti-British; he had lived in Britain and had appreciated the way in which his desired anonymity had been respected. He had simply written Britain off as a bad bet. He disapproved President Roosevelt's policies of 'all aid short of war' on the grounds that there was no point in throwing good money after bad. On the other hand, if the Roosevelt programme were pursued to its logical conclusion it must inevitably involve America in war with Germany, a war for which she was unprepared. He was not a pacifist, though pacifism was within his heritage, for his father, as a Congressman, had voted against America's declaration of war on Germany in 1917. His reasoning was more practical than this. It seemed far wiser to him to build up the nation's defences and armaments so as to be able to resist any threat of aggression from a Nazi 'New Order' in Europe. In addition, there was always at the back of his mind the idea that it was Japan which presented the greater threat to American security and, like many men of a military cast of mind, he dreaded the idea of a two-front war. America, he believed should forsake Europe and prepare to face her primary enemy. His considerable and unpublicised wartime services were to be carried out in the Pacific theatre.

There were, of course, other more personal reasons of longer standing for his feud with President Roosevelt, but what I have set out above represents the impression I received over a long period of intimate and uninhibited argument. Charles was articulate and lucid in expressing himself. Though never a demagogue, he was later to become a public speaker who could hold the attention of his audience in a taut grip. But he had entered the lists against intervention and anything which might lead to it, as a lone voice crying in the wilderness. In many ways it was the 'America First' movement which joined him, not he them, a fact that emerges from Wayne Cole's *Charles Lindbergh and the Battle against American Intervention in World War II*; he remained an independent thinker to the end.

Throughout his life he was no man's man, he was captain of his own soul, and although I have greatly valued his friendship, and that of Anne, over the years, I have more often than not been in disagreement with him, until in the later years of his life we found a comradeship as Cold Warriors.

One thing, however, I still find it difficult to comprehend, Charles's anti-Semitic streak which disclosed itself in his notorious speech at Des Moines in September 1941, bringing upon him much obloquy and denunciation. He believed, I think sincerely, that Jews were predominant in interventionist activities. He criticised them in that capacity and not as a racialist. But he handled this sensitive issue clumsily and even brutally; it was an aberration of tact and judgement, a flaw in an otherwise sound structure.

At this time Charles was essentially a pragmatist and a realist. His was a materialistic outlook because these were the things he understood; the imponderables of the spirit meant little to him, though later they came to mean a very great deal. He, Anne, Ruth and I continued to see one another spasmodically in the years that followed, in England, in Connecticut, in New York and in Switzerland. His maturity of thought deepened perceptibly and he became dedicated to science, to exploration and to conservancy. In our talks together I always found his mind to be full of surprises which stimulated one's own thinking. He became gentler and his sense of humour, originally somewhat juvenile, grew more subtle. Towards the end of his life he came to be positively Victorian, which was endearing.

He died on the island of Maui, in the State of Hawaii, on 26 August 1974, where he had gone when confronted with his last and fatal illness. He faced death with the calm courage of a gallant gentleman, having characteristically planned every detail beforehand and leaving his affairs in perfect order. Of him it might be said, as Duff Cooper wrote of Talleyrand: 'having taken all possible precautions, he departed with his credentials in order, his passport signed.'

Throughout the autumn of 1941 the margin between American cobelligerency and outright war dwindled perceptibly and public opinion in the United States rallied more and more in support of the President. A remarkable feature of this was that, since the Nazi invasion of Russia, the Communist Party of America had become as wildly interventionist as it had been previously uncompromisingly isolationist. This change of front proved an embarrassment for the Fight for Freedom Committee, who though liberal and militant were far from Marxist. It was welcomed with relief by the 'America First' movement, whose conservative membership had always looked askance at their Communist allies.

There now were many who not only felt with Alice Duer Miller that:

> . . . in a world where England is finished and dead,
> I do not wish to live.

but who also realised that in such a world the United States would have to fight a grim battle alone for their independence and freedom. This was emphasised when it became apparent that Hitler was prepared to risk an American declaration of war rather than permit the delivery of Lend-Lease cargoes to Britain. On 27 May, the *Robin Moor*, a merchant vessel, was sunk by a U-boat.

There were also a few who clung to the illusion of a negotiated peace, but generally speaking, as President Roosevelt wrote to King George VI on 15 October, 'Public opinion is distinctly better than six months ago. In fact it is more strongly with us than is the Congress.'

Within two weeks of this letter, the Germans sank the destroyer *Reuben James,* with the loss of one hundred and fifteen American lives, causing a change in the attitude of Congress, who, on 15 November, responded to the appeal of the President for the amendment of the Neutrality Act by changing it to permit armed United States merchantmen to pass through the war zones. The interventionists were jubilant; the isolationists almost frantic. The bitterness between them became acute.

It was at this time that someone in the American media suggested to the Ministry of Information in London that the Allies should send out heroes to tour the United States and demonstrate the gallantry of what was already beginning to be called the United Nations. The Ministry was taken with the idea and imperative instructions arrived from Brendan Bracken that all possible publicity was to be given to the project.

The Heroes were to include airmen, soldiers and representatives of the Navy and the Commandos, and they were to come in relays, making a triumphal progress through Canada and the United States. At least that was the idea. As far as I can remember there was only one contingent and this included, among others, a charming and modest young South African squadron leader, who had led the famous 'hedge-hopping' raid on Augsburg, and his tail-gunner. At the last moment there had been added to the party a terrifyingly proportioned formidable Soviet female partisan, who was alleged – and I can well believe it, having seen her – to have killed more Germans than any other woman in the Red Army.

The party arrived at Montreal where they were given a hilarious welcome and then flew to Newark, New Jersey. The Embassy had dispatched the three service attachés as a welcoming committee and on their arrival, they met with a tremendous ovation; cries of 'Here come the Heroes', the clicking of cameras and the flashing of photographers' flares. Whereupon the military attaché cried in a loud voice saying: 'We are *not* Heroes; we are from the British Embassy,' a statement which was greeted with howls of laughter.

The rest of that day was a fantasy for Aubrey and me. Bill Ormerod was the inspirational genius and we enjoyed ourselves in the wings. The Heroes eventually did arrive, the South Africans shy and embarrassed, the Soviet Heroine dour and repellent and some of the others in pretty bad shape, including one of them who, in the course of a thick night in a Montreal night club, had got the worst of an argument with a French Canadian, who had backed his reasoning with a broken bottle. The result was that our hero arrived with nine stitches and a head-bandage which the crowd, of course, thought was the result of an enemy bullet. It did no harm.

But this was the least of the happenings of this unbelievable day. A traditional parade up Broadway had been arranged and the motorcade ploughed its way through bright sunshine and clouds of ticker-tape. After a good luncheon arranged by Aubrey and myself, their afternoon was spent as the guests of Darryl Zanuck of Twentieth Century-Fox, who had persuaded Duke Ellington to put on a 'do' for them at Radio City. To add to the gaiety 'the Duke' pulled the unfortunate military attaché on to the platform to make a speech. In his consternation and embarrassment the gallant officer succeeded in setting fire to his tie with his cigarette, which, amid loud cheers, was extinguished with a soda-water syphon, drenching him to the skin. It had not been quite his day, but it was the best turn of the show.

By this time the Heroes were showing signs of wear (all except the Soviet amazon who still appeared ready for anything). Nervous exhaustion and utter bewilderment made it necessary to have some time off, so Aubrey and I took the South Africans home to East 70th Street and gave them a quiet dinner, before their greatest ordeal yet.

Seventeen thousand people had packed the old Madison Square Garden to do honour to the Heroes, and they gave them an almost hysterical reception. The master of ceremonies, who was himself highly elated, introduced them and as each stood up he was greeted with thunderous applause. (The Soviet warrior looked definitely disapproving. She was clearly longing for her rifle.) When he came to the end of the line of chairs he found that there was one more hero than he had bargained for. 'And who are you?' he asked the very youthful occupant who was in Canadian uniform. 'Oh,' said the youth clearly and distinctly, with a disarming and engaging grin, 'I don't belong here at all, but that's my big brother next me and we met in Montreal, and I just came along for the ride.' He was made very welcome.

The organ pealed; a chorus led the great audience in passionate renderings of 'God Save the King', 'The Star Spangled Banner' (with some pretty grave uncertainties on the top notes), 'There'll always be an England', and 'America'. They sang themselves hoarse and then there was a pause. To my astonished ears I heard the Master-of-Ceremonies reciting the Lord's Prayer with immense pathos. It was listened to in silence and then cheered to the echo.

Such was the end of a day, memories of which still haunt me as a triumph of utter confusion. What benefit it had for the Allied cause, I do not know.

I have always been fascinated by Hollywood. That is, in its days of greatness, when one could mobilise 'a cast of thousands'; when Cecil B. De Mille could have Claudette Colbert enjoying a bubble-bath in the desert in the role of Delilah, in gorgeous technicolor; when the memory of D. W. Griffith was still green and the Gish girls were still heart-throbs and tear-jerkers. It is different now. Much of the glory is departed. Many of the spectacular films are now made abroad with the active co-operation of the Spanish or Turkish armies, and the great studios have become the helots of television, just as the monolithic concrete temple of Belshazzar, which was built for the classic silent masterpiece *Intolerance*, used to stand in Culver City as a monument to past glories, as 'Amurath an Amurath succeeds'.

I had visited the place a number of times before the war and had learned much of its inner working from two friends who had been at Malvern with me. Brian Aherne is almost an exact contemporary of mine, and I remember well his stage debut in London as the 'clean-limbed young Englishman' in *White Cargo*, playing opposite Tallulah Bankhead's voluptuously alluring Tondelayo. It was an almost embarrassingly 'straight' part to play, but he did it splendidly and it launched him on his road to greater achievements. I stayed several times with him and his first wife, Joan Fontaine.

My other friend, who was slightly older than I, had been my fag-master at Malvern, where we knew him as Dikran Kouyoumdjian. It was possible for fag-masters to make life hell for their fags, but he had always been considerate and kindly disposed, and when he left I thanked him for it. His reply was typical 'Do you think,' he said, 'that someone whose family has been chased round the shores of Lake Van by the Turks for generations is going to take it out on you?' Later, when he had become famous as Michael Arlen, with *The Green Hat* to his credit, we had remained friends and now I found him in a sort of exile in Hollywood at the Beverly Wilshire Hotel, paid not to write by one great movie combine in order to prevent his being bought to write by another.

Between them Brian and Dikran showed me the ropes and made it possible for me to spend many happy hours as a privileged spectator on the sets of numerous great films of that day. I watched Brian playing the misguided but romantic 'Maximilian of Mexico' opposite Paul Muni's enigmatic, boot-faced Juarez and John Garfield's dashing Diaz. I contributed one line to the script of the Emperor's final speech in his cell at Queretaro before his execution. It was at the beginning of Brian's exposition of monarchy, to which I suggested adding: 'A king having everything desires nothing,' and it was accepted.

Dikran, on the other hand, showed me culinary Hollywood and especially the Kingdom of Mike Romanoff, a splendid charlatan who claimed to be the Grand Duke Michael of Russia and had played the role for so long that he had, I think, really come to believe it. He owned the best restaurant in Hollywood where he reigned despotically and thought nothing of refusing entry to those of the 'high and mighty' of whom he disapproved. 'You can see for yourself, every table is occupied,' I have heard him say to some couple who had forfeited his favour, indicating to them a practically empty room. But Mike was always a good friend of mine and often asked me to share his own table if I were alone.

I remember, too, Dikran when we were lunching there together one day, interrupting his own seemingly never-ending soliloquy to draw my attention to a passing figure, 'Look, there goes history,' he said. It was Theda Bara.

Early in the war Philip Lothian had sent me to Hollywood to round up the British actors, who kept on writing to the embassy rather vaguely offering their services, and to tell them that at present the best thing they could do was 'to keep on keeping on' and do what they could to stimulate interest in British war charities. Through Brian Aherne I met old Aubrey Smith, the veteran elder of the British film colony, and captain of the local cricket club. He was superb as a caricature of himself, and agreed to call a meeting at his house, over which he presided with the dignity of a pre-1914 county grandee. It was a strange experience to see in the flesh those deities of the screen whom one had so often enjoyed on film. Ronald Colman was there ('I don't think I can play open-neck parts any more,' he once said to me after having seen the first 'rushes' of *The Prisoner of Zenda*), Brian Aherne, Errol Flynn (whose father was, I believe, chief air-raid warden in Belfast), and Charles Laughton ('Never forget, dear boy, that we are mummers, merely mummers'). Cedric Hardwicke was there too, and some half-dozen more. They were charming people and genuinely anxious to help, and they were slightly disappointed when they found I couldn't give them all daring jobs in Intelligence. But between them they raised a lot of money for Bundles for Britain and other charities, and stimulated their American colleagues to do likewise.

Later on I met that fabulous figure Alexander Korda in New York.

Alex was a genius with a touch of magic in his conceptions and direction. He came from Budapest, where he had had a hard upbringing which had made him keenly appreciative of the 'loaves and fishes' in later life. 'When I was a little boy, I was so poor and so ashamed of it, and now I am rich, I *hate* the poor,' he once said to me. He had begun his career in Vienna and had made one of the earliest of the many films centring around the tragedy of Mayerling. As a technical consultant he had engaged an ancient and practically penniless ex-official of the Imperial Household (I think he had been in the Lord Chamberlain's office), to give him accurate details of protocol in scenes laid in the Hofburg and at Schönbrunn. One evening Alex took him out to dinner and in an expansive moment, occasioned by several glasses of champagne, the aged courtier confided to him in awed and reverential tones: 'You know, His Imperial and Royal Majesty the Emperor *deigned* to have the syphilis.'

It was to Alex Korda that I owed very much during my later wartime visits to Hollywood. He and his beautiful wife Merle Oberon lived in what Lord Curzon once, according to Harold Nicolson, called 'unexampled magnificence' in the Beverley Hills suburb of Bel-Air, where only the great abide. It was indeed a beautiful house and superb in all its appointments; it was approached, moreover, by an avenue of chromium perches on which sat (and screeched) gaily coloured macaws. Alex was a sybarite and a connoisseur of food, drink and tobacco. He liked pink champagne, and his cigars were the finest Havanas specially made for him in various sizes and with his initials on the band. 'Never forget, my dear John,' he once said to me, 'that no cigar is worth smoking that has not been rolled on the naked thigh of a beautiful woman.' I took his word for it. I also recall dining with him in a well-known New York restaurant at the time of rationing. Alex read the menu – a tremendous affair inscribed in purple ink – and then handed it back disdainfully. 'Why don't you get into touch with a *good* black market?' was his only comment.

Hungarian by birth though he was, there did not beat a more passionately British heart than Alex Korda's. His British naturalisation was an honour he cherished greatly. Winston Churchill was his hero and there existed a close friendship between the two men, which Winston crowned with a knighthood. This act, though it caused some raised eyebrows, he defended fiercely and loyally, for no one had done more for the British cause, whether by financial contributions or by such excellent films for export as *Fire over England* and *Henry VIII*. Robert Vansittart was another friend who always praised him. (A little known fact is that 'Van' also wrote the words of Sabu's song in *The Thief of Baghdad*.) This confidence in him was justified in every respect. He extolled Britain and Britain's cause on every possible occasion, in fair weather and foul. I have been privileged to listen to a debate on the British way of life conducted in the fiercest of broken English between Alex and David Selznick to my silent delight and satisfaction.

It was under his auspices that I met the really sophisticated element of Hollywood, such as Alfred Hitchcock, together with Ernst Lubitsch and Bruno Frank, both of whom had been luminaries in their own right in Germany before the Nazi revolution and had brought a certain ingredient of European culture in the Hollywood orbit. I soon realised that it was the producers and directors and writers in the film world who were the most rewarding people with whom to talk. I have heard better conversation at their tables than in many university common-rooms.

Two episodes stand out in my memory with great clarity in connection with Alex Korda. My duties took me again to Hollywood later in the war, when I dined with Alex at his house. He had promised me a treat and he kept his word. The German Ministry of Propaganda had made a film of the life of Paul Kruger called, if I remember rightly, *Oom Paul*, with Emil Jannings in the title role, largely for export to South America. A copy had been seized by British Intelligence and had been loaned to Alex for his own purposes. It was really an excellent film judged by technical standards, with some very impressive scenes in Buckingham Palace, in which Queen Victoria was played by one of Germany's best and most ancient actresses. One scene I particularly remember was between the Queen and Joseph Chamberlain (somewhat of a carica-ture with monocle and orchid too exaggerated). The Colonial Secre-tary was urging the annexation of the Transvaal, and the Queen was defending the rights of small nations. Chamberlain was at last forced to play his trump card: 'But, Ma'am, they have found gold in the Transvaal.' The Queen's demeanour changed completely; an avar-icious grin crept over her face. '*Geld, Chamberlain, viel Geld?*' she whispered and then she rang a hand-bell. 'My medicine, Brown,' she demanded of a huge kilted Highlander, who thereupon produced a perfectly colossal bottle of whisky!

Two other scenes I remember, one depicting the Prince of Wales in the stage-box of the *Folies Bergère* clapping his white gloved hands, held forward in the Edwardian manner, and saying over his shoulder: 'I can't understand your objection to whores. I find them charming.' The other was a hark-back to the old line of propaganda about the concentration-camps in the South African War. There were shots of pale and emaciated women and children, obviously on the shortest of rations, watching almost slaveringly, while the camp-commandant, who bore a marked resemblance to Winston Churchill, fed succulent rashers of bacon to his bull-dog.

Apart from the assessment of the film, which, I regret to say, had good entertainment value, there was a certain interest surrounding Alex's other guests, who included Charlie Chaplin, Lubitsch and David Selznick; truly a select and critical audience.

When I returned to the United States after my first visit to England in 1940 Philip Lothian had sent me again to Hollywood to discuss with certain well-disposed movie moguls, of whom Walter Wanger was one, the making of such non-documentary films as *Mrs Miniver* and *Eagle Squadron* (the story of that group of American volunteers, who, modelling themselves on the Escadrille Lafayette in the First World War, had fought as a unit with the R.A.F. during the Battle of Britain giving a very good account of themselves). The theory was that since these were commercial productions and not documentaries, they could have a love interest which would increase their appeal. A number of these films were subsequently made and, it was hoped, had some effect on the imagination of the great American public, especially in the Middle West where contact with the war was tenuous.

It was Alex Korda's idea that while I was there I should talk to some of the 'top brass' in the moving-picture world, whom he would ask to dinner, about the spirit of Britain. This, of course, was just right, and on the appointed evening I drove in my humble Yellow Cab to the Château Korda. The courtyard was filled, rank on rank, with long, slinky black Cadillacs, resplendent with white-walled tyres, and a bevy of chauffeurs stood about them. 'Gee,' said my taxi-driver. 'This is certainly some party. I wonder what the attraction is.' 'I am,' I said, as I paid him off and left him with his mouth wide open.

Alex had certainly surpassed himself and had gathered in the top brackets of Hollywood tycoonery. Even the fabulous Sam Goldwyn had consented to come, a rare event I was told, and with him were the leading lights of Paramount, Twentieth Century-Fox, Columbia, United Artists and other great concerns. There were no actors present, only those magnificos who disposed their fates.

After dinner I made my little speech and laid it on as thick as I could. I spoke, with perfect truth, of the determination, the courage, the patience and the steadfast resolve of the British people. I described the air raids I had seen myself and the fires of London burning. I gave some idea of the conditions in air-raid shelters. I had a feeling that I was having some effect. Tough business men though these grandees were, there lay beneath their toughness a certain emotional sensitivity. When I had finished, one of them blowing his nose in an agitated way, got to his feet and, seizing a box of Alex's best and largest cigars, pressed it into my hands, saying in broken tones, 'My dear friend, I had no idea you had been through such privations. Then it's true what Ed Murrow had been telling us.' They dug down into their pockets and the evening was a profitable one for British War Charities. To give Alex Korda his full credit, he insisted on my keeping the cigars.

Later still, after Gerald Campbell and I had made our visit to England, I achieved one of the minor ambitions of my life. I directed – or, to be accurate, *jointly* directed – a picture. A film was about to be made on the Rise of the Nazi Party. It was to be directed by John Farrow, who had married the lovely Maureen O'Sullivan, and was the father of the now famous Mia. The script had been sent to the British Embassy for comment and had been referred to me. It was fantastically inaccurate and I covered pages of foolscap with criticisms, corrections and suggestions, all of which were duly sent off to John Farrow. His immediate reaction was to cable the Embassy asking 'could he borrow the guy who wrote that stuff?' and I, answering to this description, was asked by Chancery if I would like to go, it being understood that my name must not be publicised and that I must accept no emolument; I could, however, indent for expenses.

I had never met John Farrow but had heard of him that he was tough and Irish and a devout Roman Catholic and that he only liked the British because he was anti-German, largely on account of what they had done to the Catholic Church in confiscating property etc. Despite this reputation, however, I found him a shrewd and delightful companion. Though we frequently differed in opinions, I cannot recall that there was ever a cross word between us and both he and Maureen were exceptionally kind to me.

John was a really great director; he knew the art from start to finish, when to cajole and when to bully, when to sympathise and when to be brutal. To me he was very generous and insisted that I should be his co-director in all but name. It was deeply interesting to me to see the making of a film from the outset. On the morning that the gates of the studio were opened and a mob of extras crowded in all seeking parts – all with screen ambitions and some even with a little training – we sacrificed, in casting, art to accuracy. We chose, I remember, a young blond butcher of grotesque proportions for the part of Goering, and a thin-faced little hairdresser for that of Goebbels. Our Hitler was a genuine German and a seasoned actor, though he had been a professional comedian, and used to make us laugh till we cried with songs and 'break-downs' in the broad Berlin dialect during the rest-periods. Röhm looked as revolting as he had in real life, but our greatest *coup* was in finding a famous veteran of the German stage to play the role of Ludendorff. I recall that we had difficulty in getting him to portray the right degree of contempt for Hitler until, during one of our 'breaks', I asked him if he did not feel almost humiliated to be playing with such a cast of amateurs and half-trained colleagues. At once his expression changed from his usual cynical boredom to one of immense scorn. '*Ach*,' he said, '*diese verdammten Klatschbäser*,' and the disdain in his voice was withering, and exactly what we wanted. I urged him to use just this sneering tone when he played the scene again. He did so and it came off perfectly.

I can understand how easy it is for a movie-director to become intolerable. There is something god-like in sitting in a chair watching a scene and then saying expressionlessly: 'We'll have that again, please,' knowing that no power in that small world could say you nay. Or to be swung out on a gigantic crane over a set on which a big scene was being taken – as it might be the Beer Hall *Putsch* – involving as many as a hundred actors on stage at once. Through one's microphone one criticised and directed until the wretched performers were either successful or exhausted; if the latter, you just said, 'We'll try that again at eight o'clock tomorrow morning.'

As the eventual script had been largely an adaptation from the latter part of my *Wooden Titan*, I was in a strong position, and John always backed me to the hilt, throwing in his own expertise and authority whenever it was needed. But it meant hard work and long hours because John was especially anxious to get it 'on the road' as soon as possible.

At length it was finished to our joint satisfaction. There were, however, two points on which John and I differed. I lost on both issues. The studio stood pat on entitling it *The Hitler Gang*. I considered this unduly vulgar but John considered it had the right 'appeal value'. The second point was more serious, being one of fact. I was not then – nor indeed am I now – at all sure of the story that Hitler had an affair with his niece, Geli Rabaul, who committed suicide for love of him (so it is said) in 1931. There was precious little sex aspect to a film of this sort and for this reason John had insisted on putting considerable emphasis on this incident, while I was for cutting it altogether. I could, I said, go into the witness-box and swear on a stack of bibles for the accuracy of the rest of the picture, particularly the closing sequence of the Night of the Long Knives, of which I knew something at first hand. But I really couldn't vouch for the Geli Rabaul story. We argued backwards and forwards and then agreed to refer the point to the head of the business who was coming out from New York to see the penultimate stage of the picture. We sat in silence in the studio's private theatre and viewed our handiwork. It didn't seem to me to be at all bad and I would have given it three stars out of five, had I been a film critic. At the close, the great man asked to have the Geli sequence played over again and I hopefully thought that he might agree with me that it was the one episode which didn't ring true – which it didn't. Alas, commerce triumphed over art. He turned to me and flashed a smile of gold-filled teeth. 'Gotta keep it in, boy,' he said. 'Only bit of cheese-cake in the picture.' And in it was kept. I am glad to record that the film had a good reception on both sides of the Atlantic. Such was my first experience as a film director. I enjoyed it immensely.

I think the best epitome of Hollywood was a parable which Alex Korda once told me in answer to my question as to whether the life there was really as cut-throat an existence as I had always been told.

'Oh no,' he said. 'It's like the story of the scientific expedition which went to explore a Pacific island of which the inhabitants, a primitive but generally friendly folk, were said to retain certain tendencies towards cannibalism. The expedition arrived and were welcomed to breakfast by the local missionary, who had lived there for years. They were armed to the teeth and were somewhat surprised to find that the missionary's house seemed devoid of weaponry. Breakfast over, their host said that he supposed they would like to walk down into the villages and meet the natives. "You can leave all that stuff here," he said, indicating the rifles, pistols and sub-machine guns with which they were laden. "Is it all right to go unarmed?" they asked. "Oh perfectly," he answered, "they're charming people." So having abandoned their impedimenta they began to descend the verandah steps. Just as they reached the bottom the missionary called to them: "Oh, just one small precaution. Be careful not to fall down; that might be too much of a temptation." And that,' said Alex, 'is Hollywood.'

*

On 25 November 1941, I addressed the Corps of Cadets at the Military Academy at West Point – the American equivalent of Sandhurst. They are not an easy audience because the discipline of their instruction does not – or certainly did not in my time – encourage the cadets to 'stick their necks out' either in the method of question and answer or, as it seemed to me at my initiation, in the appearance of normal intelligence. When I was first invited to speak there in 1934, my host, a certain Colonel Herkomer, then head of the history department, warned me that I should probably find myself talking to a sea of impassive faces but that I should not be discouraged, as behind this bootfaced appearance there was considerable discernment. On that occasion I was talking to them about the Night of the Long Knives on 30 June, from which I myself had only just escaped, as I have described in *Knaves, Fools and Heroes*, and I had certainly succeeded in getting them to ask an encouraging number of questions, mostly connected with the attitude of the Reichswehr towards the dastardly tragedy; I was only too glad to enlighten them in greater detail.

Now, however, the circumstances were more difficult. I was talking to embryo officers of the United States in the course of a war in which they might easily become, willy-nilly, involved and I had to get my facts right. I had therefore obtained an excellent briefing as to our military situation from the military attaché's office in Washington and, having garnished it with a certain amount of moral reasoning, I finally appealed to their higher thinking.

The issues of this war [I said in conclusion] are deeper and more fundamental than can be expressed in phrases. You, gentlemen, are probably tired to death of the endless repetition of the words 'freedom', 'liberty', 'New Order', 'the survival of democratic institutions' which fill the press and the air today. But though they have become trite and hackneyed, they have not lost one whit of their significance.

This is no small enterprise upon which we are embarked. It is not just the survival of Britain, or the security of the United States, or the restoration of France which is at stake, it is no less a thing than the future of mankind.

My country and yours are engaged today in opposing, each in our respective spheres, the imposition of a monstrous tyranny upon the world. We are defending, again each in our own manner, the basic faiths of our fathers, and of ourselves. It is our avowed purpose that this Nazi menace to our common heritage of a 'deathless attachment to freedom' shall be destroyed, and that, from our common effort there shall emerge from the wrack of war, a world in which we and our children can live free, fearless and secure. It is for this reason that we must be, and shall be, victorious.

When I had finished and sat down there was the briefest period of silence, then, as if galvanised by some common spontaneity, my expressionless audience suddenly broke through their carapace of military abstraction and gave me a standing ovation, an event which, Colonel Herkomer assured me, had never occurred during his long period of service at the Academy.

I mention this fact not in a spirit of vainglory but because it was a remarkable example of the mastery of mind over matter. Coming up from New York to West Point I had felt very ill, so faint and dizzy at one moment that I had feared that I should not be able to go through with my engagement. The challenge of speaking, however, had acted as a sort of adrenalin, but I have only a vague memory of the question-period which followed. On the following day, I was still well below par and very weak and, on arriving in New York, went straight to see my doctor. He was an excellent physician and a wise diagnostician, and he divined the cause of my trouble very quickly. I had been overworking to the point of nervous exhaustion and had all the preliminary symptoms of serious anaemia. He also discovered that I had an oscillating blood pressure which produced an imbalance of the heart-action, causing me to faint. This has dogged me all my life since, but it was first diagnosed by this admirable doctor in New York. There was at that time no recognised treatment and there is still no cure.

At any rate, he sent me straight off to the New York Hospital with orders to rest completely for a week, and, I must admit, that the prospect of lying down and sleeping for a prolonged period was surpassingly attractive. It also afforded me a further example of the quiet, unpublicised, wonderful generosity of Americans at that time. I was provided with the best possible accommodation and every comfort – a large and beautiful room overlooking the East River – and before I was given my first sedative, so that my mind could be at rest, it was explained to me that, as I was a British official, my bill would be 'on the house'. 'It's the least we can do,' the hospital almoner told me. Nor, I may say, could I persuade my doctor even to present an account.

I was discharged from hospital on Sunday, 7 December and returned to our house on East 70th Street, feeling considerably better. Aubrey, Constance and I were listening to a symphony concert on the radio when suddenly the performance was interrupted to announce the news of the Japanese attack on Pearl Harbor. The programme was then resumed. Later that evening Aubrey and I went down to Times Square to see what was afoot. There was an enormous crowd watching the electric bulletin board which ran round the high pediment of the *New York Times* building. There was no great excitement, certainly no Mafeking; people just stood there silently watching for the latest tidings of a disaster, the magnitude of which was, of course, still unknown to them. To many it had not penetrated that they were now for all practical purposes at war. But like Mr Churchill, just as we had felt that when Russia had become an ally we could not lose the war, Aubrey and I were aware that, with the advent of America as a fully fledged belligerent, we should be victorious.

Curiously enough the new phase in Anglo-American relations, which opened with the attack on Pearl Harbor and the subsequent declaration of war by America on the axis Powers, a phase of active military and political alliance, did not open on a note of complete amicability. Whereas our activities at the B.I.S. had previously been condoned in Washington and we had been regarded with benevolent encouragement, we were now exposed to a new attitude which, at best, was that of a senior to a junior partner and, at worst, one of frank hostility. The first reaction of the State Department and of certain elements in Congress was to close down such organisations as ours altogether and to send us packing as almost undesirable aliens. All information on the war should now, it was thought, be imparted to the American public by American agencies and it was pretty clearly implied that the American public would from now on be interested only in American exploits.

Indeed a bill was passed through Congress making it illegal for any public relations organisations, other than American, to disseminate even the barest of facts. As a result of the lobbying of our friends, notably 'Ham' Armstrong and George Backer, the President was persuaded to veto this bill, but for it was substituted another which designated us all as 'foreign agents'. This compelled us to register with the Department of Justice and to be finger-printed, and to lodge with the Department of State copies of all material mailed to correspondents within the country. This the President could not oppose and it became law but, restricting though it was to some degree, it still permitted us to keep before the American man-in-the-street the vital fact that Britain was also in the war and had been for some time. We emphasised that, delighted and grateful though we were for their comradeship and alliance, the Second World War had begun on 1 September 1939, and not on 7/8 December 1941.

The tremendous changes which Pearl Harbor wrought in every aspect of the war also affected my own career. I felt strongly that with the entry of the United States as an active belligerent our 'muffled mission' was concluded and that I could legitimately claim that I should be more use in England, where my knowledge of Europe could be utilised. I hated to break up my partnership with Aubrey, which I had vastly enjoyed and which, I am proud and happy to think, had not been without its usefulness. I remembered, however, the wise counsel which Neill Malcolm had given me on our Transib journey, namely that, in the event of war, when my American job was done I should turn again to my German interests.

And then there was Ruth. As long as the United States was neutral and before I had been designated as a 'foreign agent', I had managed to see her not too infrequently on my trips to Charlottesville and although we were not yet engaged, we had what the Victorians called 'an understanding'. With the United States at war, however, I knew that she would be joining one of the women's services and might well be appointed God alone knew where, so that this attraction too was removed. My duty lay plainly before me.

I had, as a matter of fact, had tentative talks with Bruce Lockhart while I was in London with Gerald Campbell, about joining him in the Political Intelligence Department of the Foreign Office, but at that moment I could not count myself a free man. However, it was bread upon the waters.

Fate was to take a hand in solving my dilemma. I had written to Bruce asking him if his offer was firm but before I could receive an answer there had been a general upheaval. The Ministry of Information had come to the conclusion that, though they had been justified 'on form', they had made a bad bet in appointing Gerald Campbell as Director-General of the B.I.S. It was therefore decided, in consonance with the Foreign Office and the Embassy, that he should be transferred to Washington with the rank of Minister and given control over all consular activities throughout America. This was a job for which he was eminently well suited both by temperament and career and in which he served with outstanding success, revolutionising the relations between the Embassy and its far-flung outposts and giving the latter a feeling of belonging to the official family in Washington. It was an inspired appointment.

In his place Brendan Bracken appointed Harold Butler, one of the great family of Trinity College, Cambridge, who had a dis-

tinguished record as Director of the International Labour Office in
Geneva and had close contacts with America. He, too, however, was
to have the rank of Minister (there were I think something like half-
a-dozen Ministers of one sort or another in Washington by the end
of the war), and be based on Washington, while also holding the post
of Director-General of the B.I.S. In Washington, he was bolstered by
Robin Cruikshank as Press Counsellor and the direction of the New
York headquarters was placed under Aubrey as Deputy Director-
General. He retained this position until the end of the war and with
great distinction. Under his direction the B.I.S. expanded into an
active and flourishing organisation serving British interests in
America with efficiency and devotion.

This seemed to me an admirable arrangement, especially as it
coincided with a telegram for me from Bruce asking me to come back
to London as soon as possible. I therefore bade godspeed and a
reluctant good-bye to Ruth and left New York, as I then thought,
indefinitely.

CHAPTER EIGHT

Political Warrior

There is, of course, nothing new about propaganda or political
warfare. Its purpose is to undermine and destroy the morale of the
enemy. According to Plutarch an early example of this art was
practised by Themistocles, who, whenever his fleet touched at places
where the Persians might put in for food and water or safe harbour-
age, caused conspicuously inscribed stones to be set up on which he
solemnly enjoined the Ionians to come over to the side of the
Athenians, who were risking all on behalf of their freedom; but if
they could not do this, to damage the Barbarian cause in battle, and
to bring confusion among them. This sample of political warfare,
dating from 480 B.C., is one of the most perfect, and conformed almost
exactly to the basic technique which we used in the Second World
War. It also conveyed more clearly the subtlety of this art than does
the more blunt and brutal view of that master of the science of war,
General Carl von Clausewitz. He stated that 'the best way of waging
political warfare is to capture the enemy's capital', a natural
corollary to his contention that 'War is nothing more than the
continuation of politics by other means' (*Der Krieg ist nichts anderes
als die Fortsetzung der Politik mit anderen Mitteln*).

Propaganda, on the other hand, has a purely pacific meaning. Its
dictionary definition is 'any association, systematic scheme or concerted movement for the propagation of a particular doctrine or
practice', and from this sprang the initial use of the word as a
missionary term. The Anglican Church has its Society for the
Propagation of the Gospel and the mission work of the Church of
Rome is under the general direction of the Congregation for Propaganda, presided over by a Cardinal, who is known in church
vernacular as 'The Red Pope', in distinction to the General of the
Jesuits who is known as 'The Black Pope'.

At an early date, however, the term propaganda took on a second,
and more sinister, connotation, namely the deliberate perversion of
the truth for some national or party political purpose, including the
gentle art of 'the smear'. If the new approach of some historical
scholars to the rehabilitation of Richard III is to be taken seriously, it
would seem that one of the most successful examples of the evil craft

took place over four hundred years ago and that all Englishmen, including William Shakespeare, have been labouring under its delusion ever since.

It was during the First World War that propaganda in this secondary sense came into its own, illustrating the fact that 'Truth is the first casualty of war'. Badly though the Germans undoubtedly behaved in the invaded countries, the story of the Belgian children with their hands cut off and of human bodies being rendered down to cooking fat have still to be verified. But they did great service to the Allied cause both in England and France, where they aroused the requisite degree of hatred to generate the will to victory, and in neutral countries whose aid was needed for one Allied purpose or another. They were especially beamed at the United States where they were not without results. The efforts of the British propagandists are entertainingly described by Sir Campbell Stuart in *Secrets of Crewe House*. He organised the propaganda under the general direction of Lord Northcliffe, and it had a boomerang effect. The unashamedly overt activities of the Allies to get America into the First World War were the ultimate cause of many of the difficulties with which we were faced in the Second, and accounted for the wariness which Philip Lothian bade us exercise during those months of the Phoney War.

When, however, the United States did enter the First World War it excelled itself in propaganda and in political warfare. President Wilson's enunciation of the doctrine of self-determination, whether he intended it as such or not, proved a sharp and deadly addition to the Allied armoury. It contributed in great measure to the break-up of the Austro-Hungarian and Ottoman Empires, although both had been the target of previous British and French subversion.

It was the development of the power of the press and of the growth of radio as an additional medium which brought about the recognition of the importance of this new, noxious and destructive weapon between the wars in the course of the desperate but fruitless attempts made by the League of Nations to formulate a viable definition of aggression. It is not altogether surprising that it was Poland, finding herself sandwiched between two hostile neighbours, who proposed as early as 1927 the inclusion of hostile propaganda in the Resolution on aggression adopted by the Assembly of the League. It failed of acceptance, as did a further jointly sponsored Polish-Swedish suggestion in 1931, during the discussions which preceded the adoption of the draft of the somewhat cumbersomely entitled 'General Convention to Improve the Means of Preventing War'. It was to the effect that the Assembly should 'study the possibilities of guarding against the dangers which might arise at a time of international crisis from irresponsible campaigns in the Press and publication of incorrect and tendentious information'.

Though these proposals failed to awake a general awareness of these new dangers, pragmatic point was given them by Adolf Hitler in the course of his destruction of Czechoslovakia. First in 1938 among the Sudeten Germans and a year later with the Slovaks and Ruthenians, he used 'all means short of war' to disrupt the authority of the Prague Government by a most vicious but effective campaign of propaganda.

One of the greatest points of difference between the First and Second World Wars was that in 1939 there was no lack of knowledge of the appalling record of crime and cruelty by the Nazi State in the six years since Hitler's coming to power. The press and radio of both Britain and America had given full coverage to the mounting annals of German malfeasance which needed no exaggeration. Few could plead ignorance of them, save those incredible Germans who pleaded at the Nuremberg Trials and elsewhere after the war, that they were totally ignorant of the events which, they said, were now disclosed to them for the first time, although they had taken place around them during the proud and contemptuous days of the Third Reich.

My first contact with this crepuscular world had been at the time of the Czech crisis of 1938 when hurried preparations were being made for war. Campbell Stuart was summoned to reorganise the activities of Crewe House, *mutatis mutandis* after an interval of twenty years. He formed a small committee which included Bruce Lockhart, Stephen King-Hall and myself and, in the deepest secrecy, we propounded and matured somewhat amateur plans to use our modernised weapon against the enemy. We had not made much progress when the surrender at Munich put an end to our existence. Mr Chamberlain, convinced that he had achieved 'Peace in our time' and that Anglo-German agreement had removed all cause for anxiety as to the relations between the two countries, instructed Campbell Stuart to suspend all operations. This decision was reversed in the summer of 1939, but by that time both Bruce and I knew we were destined for other war stations.

The complex history of these eccentric activities between 1939 and 1941 has little to do with this narrative save in its subsequent repercussions. Briefly it is this. Campbell Stuart was restored to his command in 1939 and, as he describes in his autobiography, *Oppor-*

tunity Knocks Once, moved his entire organisation to Woburn Abbey where they were held *incommunicado* in supposed secrecy. I say 'supposed' because I was later told how the staff of the new organisation gathered at a local pub before being taken by bus to the Abbey. They eyed one another suspiciously, studiously observing their orders not to discuss their future work in public. Desultory conversation of a banal nature was suddenly interrupted by the entrance of the bus-driver who, in ringing tones well audible in the adjoining tap-room, announced, 'Now will all you secret service gentlemen who are going to Woburn Abbey come along with me, please?'

During the Phoney War period life was easy and uncomplicated, for they did practically nothing at all. Campbell Stuart had the greatest difficulty in getting any decision on policy from Mr Chamberlain and when decisions were finally given, they were continually revoked. At that time it was widely believed that many Germans, especially elements in the Army, were not fanatical in their support of Hitler and might, if encouraged, overthrow the Nazi régime. Few who had known Germany at any time during the Third Reich were of this persuasion, but during the years 1938 and 1939 various envoys of political dissidents in Germany had visited London and had given highly coloured accounts of embryo conspiracies. This was the basis of the first British venture into propaganda – a primitive, clumsy and amateurish attempt to drive a wedge between the German people and their Führer. On 4 September, the day after the British declaration of war, Mr Chamberlain made his now historic broadcast. After recounting the crimes of the Führer and his government, he declared: 'In this war we are not fighting against the German people, for whom we have no bitter feelings, but against a tyrannous and forsworn regime which has betrayed not only its own people but the whole of western civilisation and all that you and we hold dear.'

The Prime Minister's remarkable statement had little or no effect on his German listeners; its most deleterious result was on the British public who entered upon the war bewildered as to what they were really going to fight about, and confused by the thought that, if they had no quarrel with the German people, why had Britain gone to the trouble and discomfort of going to war at all?

With the advent of Mr Churchill to office, however, and the formation of a National Government, the situation improved somewhat. The activities of propaganda were divided into 'overt' and 'covert', the first being, as was natural, placed under the aegis of the

Ministry of Information, and the latter, less logically, under the Ministry of Economic Warfare. At that time the Minister was Hugh Dalton, an enlightened Labour leader, who had decided views about this aspect of his job. The official title of the organisation at Woburn was Special Operations, and Dalton divided it into two branches, S.O.1, charged with organising and equipping the secret armies of the Resistance Movements in German occupied territories, which he placed under the direction of Gladwyn Jebb (later Lord Gladwyn); and S.O.2, under Sir Reginald (Rex) Leeper, concerned with propaganda to the enemy and occupied countries.

It was not unnatural that friction should arise in matters of temperament first between Dalton and Duff Cooper, later between Dalton and Brendan Bracken, between those in charge of 'overt' and 'covert' propaganda, and also between S.O.1 and S.O.2! The situation became so dissonant that a complete reorganisation of these services became inevitable, since the battles on a high level were repeated at a lower level to the detriment of the efficiency and value of their war services.

Such was the position in the July of 1941 when I arrived in London with Gerald Campbell. I saw a good deal of Bruce Lockhart at this time but he was not able to tell me much about what was going on as in the first place he was under oath of secrecy and in the second the position was still fluid. However, when we were lunching together at the Carlton Grill, shortly before my farewell dinner for Sir Gerald on 15 July General Sir Hastings (Pug) Ismay came across from his table to ours. After greeting me, he said to Bruce, 'The P.M. very much hopes you will accept,' and having delivered himself of this cryptic message he left us.

It was then that Bruce told me what was in the wind. S.O.1 and S.O.2 were to be separated entirely; the first becoming S.O.E. (Special Operations Executive) and remaining under the aegis of the Ministry of Economic Warfare, and the second re-christened P.W.E. (Political Warfare Executive) under, madly enough, three Ministries, the Foreign Office and the Ministry of Information, with a watching brief held by the M.E.W. Bruce was to become the Director-General of what was, for some extraordinary reason which I never mastered, sometimes called P.W.E. and sometimes P.I.D. (Political Intelligence Department) and was also to be appointed a Deputy Under-Secretary in the Foreign Office. 'Will you join me?' he asked. 'I should love to have you with me.' I answered that I would like nothing better but that I regarded myself as committed for the time being to the B.I.S.

Once that was satisfactorily launched I should have a freer choice, and on that note we parted.

A year later the whole position had been changed by the course of history. The ensuing reorganisation of the British Information Services gave me the freedom of choice I needed and it was with 'pleasurable anticipation' of seeing the war at closer quarters that I joined what I still prefer to call the Political Intelligence Department of the Foreign Office. My expectations, however, were not destined to be fulfilled *in toto*. Having left New York in July 1942, as I believed indefinitely, I was back again, to my intense surprise and partial chagrin, within six weeks but wearing a different hat, and there I remained based for another eighteen months.

The reason was not difficult to find. In the wholly new situation which followed the American entry into the war, the first essential was to co-ordinate and integrate the Anglo-American war effort at all levels. The British Joint Staff Mission in Washington became closely affiliated with the heads of the American army and navy. The Combined Chiefs of Staff (British and American) came into being. Liaison and integration became new watchwords and what was at first something of an uneasy partnership soon developed into a well organised, closely co-operative war machine.

As a part of this process Bruce Lockhart felt it necessary to appoint a British Political Warfare Mission in the United States to establish a working partnership with the American propaganda activities carried out by the Office of War Information (O.W.I.). The head of the Mission was David Bowes Lyon, the Queen's brother, who had been associated with the Woburn outfit from the beginning, assisted by Walter Adams, who in later life discharged the thankless task of Director of the London School of Economics with courage and devotion.

The headquarters of the Mission were in the British Embassy, adjacent to the office of the Director of the O.W.I., Robert Sherwood, who knew the wisdom of sticking close to his friend and boss, President Roosevelt, in the inter-departmental jungle-fighting which had developed in Washington. The operational base of O.W.I., however, was in New York and so it was obviously necessary for the Mission to have an office there also, and to the head of this I was appointed.

The reason for this appointment was that I alone of the staff of the Mission had any knowledge at all of the United States. None of the others had ever been there previously. Moreover, the leaders of the O.W.I. in New York were all personal friends of mine, especially

James Warburg and George Backer, who had been firm friends of
Britain in the 'Fight for Freedom' movement.

I was exceedingly fortunate in the two colleagues who had been
assigned to me, both of them seasoned veterans of political warfare.
The first of these was Leonard Miall, who had been with the B.B.C.
before the war and in later post-war years became Controller of their
Overseas and Foreign Relations; the second was Russell Page, perhaps
one of the best landscape-gardeners of our day. Leonard had a good
knowledge of Germany and of the German language, while Russell
was familiar with France and was bilingual; both of them possessed
the expertise of three years of political warfare. We all three became
good friends and I learnt a lot from both of them.

This arrangement suited me very well but I suddenly found that,
through no fault of my own, I was caught between two, if not four,
fires in the fierce guerrilla warfare of Whitehall and Washington.
The bitter and jealous rivalry which had been engendered in Hugh
Dalton's time between S.O.1 and S.O.2, was carried over and intensified when both of these departments became independent agencies.
Co-operation between P.W.E. and S.O.E. was restricted to the barest
minimum commensurate with the effective prosecution of their
common aim of winning the war. But they were uneasy allies and
fraternisation was discouraged.

I had never felt this to be a very intelligent or adult mode of
conduct but so long as I could view it as an onlooker I was content to
do so. Now, however, I had become involved in it as an occupational
hazard of my new job, and I was not prepared to tolerate it.

At an early date in the war, even before the reorganisation of
1941, S.O.E. had established an office in New York under the
direction of Bill (later Sir William) Stephenson, of whom
Montgomery Hyde has given such an accurate and pleasing picture
in *The Quiet Canadian*. I knew many of his staff from pre-war days
and, with the tacit cognisance of the Embassy, though not of the
Ministry of Information, I had maintained a fairly close contact with
them.

One of the most valuable assets of this efficient outpost was the
close friendship between Bill Stephenson and that fantastic, glamorous, wonderful figure, 'Wild Bill' Donovan. So close was their comradeship that they were always referred to as Big and Little Bill – Big
Bill being the large powerful figure of Bill Donovan. I know of no
better example of Anglo-American integration, nor one more fruitful
for the Allied cause, than that between these two men, so different in

personality yet so closely affiliated by their common empathy.

A first-class biography of Bill Donovan remains to be written, and a most rewarding assignment it would prove, for no man had a more venturesome or exciting life. Born in Buffalo, New York, of devout Catholic parents, Bill sang in the choir of his local church and then turned his good looks and his vocal talents to the entertainment world as a means of putting himself through college and law school. Eventually he became a partner in a famous law firm. His record in the First World War was amazing, for he commanded the old Sixty-ninth New York Regiment, the 'Fighting Irish' which could also boast of the Fighting Chaplain, Father Duffy, whose statue now stands on Times Square. Bill emerged with every conceivable decoration for valour, including the Congressional Medal of Honour, the highest award any American serviceman can achieve, and which carries with it the privilege that all ranks, including those senior to the recipient, must salute its wearer.

After the war Bill specialised as a divorce lawyer and amassed a fair-sized fortune. He also entered politics and unsuccessfully opposed Herbert Lehmann as the Republican candidate for the Governorship of New York. His private hobby, however, was the art and science of war, on which he became a proficient authority, and throughout the inter-war years he observed *in situ* almost every outbreak of hostilities from Ethiopia to China.

It was this interest which brought us into touch. Someone had given Bill an introduction to me in the late twenties and he looked me up in A14 Albany. What he really wanted was to meet General Hans von Seeckt, whom he considered the greatest exponent of the military art since von Clausewitz. This I was able to arrange without difficulty and the meeting resulted in mutual satisfaction. From this grew a warm and lasting friendship between Bill and myself, for when he became your friend, it was no mere fair-weather affair, it was for life, through thick and thin; contrariwise if he became your enemy, he was implacable. I found him a most diverting and pleasing companion, combining the wisdom of a serpent with the heart of a child and the daring of an arrested adolescent. He did not know fear though he was no snob about it and was considerate of other people's minor deficiencies of courage.

I have only once seen him discomposed. It was in June of 1940 when President Roosevelt was broadening the basis of his administration by appointing outstanding Republicans to his cabinet. Bill and I met at the National Airport at Washington and found that we were to fly in the same plane to New York. As always happened when one travelled with Bill, you got the V.I.P. treatment and we were soon ensconced in the two front seats where we could not be overheard. Shortly after we had become airborne, he said to me: 'John, I know I can trust your discretion and I have complete confidence in your sense of security, I think I can therefore tell you that I saw the President very recently and he asked me whether I would like to be Secretary for War. I said that there was nothing I would like more. Keep it under your hat, of course, till it's officially announced, but I thought you'd like to know.' I was profuse in my congratulations and sincere in my good wishes. I also said that the President had shown great sapience in his choice.

As we approached LaGuardia airport Bill offered me a lift into town in his car and I willingly accepted. Needless to say, we some-how managed to be first off the plane – in time, indeed, to hear a radio newscaster announce the appointment of Mr Henry L. Stimson as Secretary of War. I made haste to find myself a taxi.

I have never to this day known the whole truth of this story. Certainly Bill Donovan would not have invented it. Why should he? But had he misinterpreted through too great a desire to believe, what the President had put in the form of a non-committal question? Or was it an example of that strange streak of almost sadistic humour which, we are told, sometimes characterised Mr Roosevelt's dealings with certain persons? All I can say is: *Je constate.*

Bill Donovan, however, was resilient, indomitable and, indeed, 'unsinkable'. In July of the following year, nearly six months before the tragedy of Pearl Harbor, he secured from the President an appointment as Co-ordinator of Information (C.O.I.). As a measure of war-preparedness, he was given an all-embracing charter which gave him control over all intelligence, propaganda and war research services and also censorship of the press. When he told me about it I remember saying that he had secured himself too great an empire. I quoted from *Puck of Pook's Hill* – for we were both great Kipling addicts – the warning given to the Emperor Maximus that one could never ride three mules (Rome, Britain and Gaul), one might straddle two, but it was best to stick to one.

This turned out to be true. Bill's vast dominion lasted less than a year. On 13 June 1942 – at a moment when he was conferring with his opposite numbers in London – a 'palace revolution' took place in Washington. By Presidential Executive Order the office of C.O.I. was liquidated. Elmer Davis, a former Columbia Broadcasting comment-ator, was appointed head of a new agency, the Office of War Information (O.W.I.) charged with propaganda and censorship, with Bob Sherwood running its Overseas Branch.

Nevertheless, despite these amputations, Bill was left with a very sizeable domain which comprised the British equivalent of an amalgam of M.I.6, S.O.E. and some aspects of P.I.D. This, however, had the same effect as the separation of S.O.E. and P.W.E.; the agony lingered on. The O.S.S. (Office of Strategic Services), which was Bill's remaining charge, were not easy colleagues with O.W.I., and the situation in Whitehall was duplicated in Washington. For good measure Bill Donovan and the O.S.S. were at permanent loggerheads with J. Edgar Hoover and the F.B.I.

From the first, however, Bill had sought my co-operation and I remember his surprise when he introduced me to his Planning Board, because all of them turned out to be old friends of mine: Hugh Wilson, until recently Ambassador in Berlin; James Grafton Rogers, a former Assistant Secretary of State and more recently Master of Timothy Dwight College at Yale, with whom I had spent many a week-end in informal sessions with his undergraduates; Colonel John Magruder whom I had first met when he was military attaché in Peking and later as Commandant of the Virginia Military Institute at Lexington; and Jim Baxter, President of Williams College, Massachusetts, a mutual friend of Bruce Hopper's and mine, whom Bill Donovan had corralled as his Director of Research, to be succeeded later by Bill Langer, whom I had also known at Harvard. Bruce himself was also a recruit to O.S.S. as were many other of my friends, colleagues and pupils. It was like 'old home week' and Bill was kind enough to ask me to sit in with them whenever I could, so I used to fly down from New York once a week, breakfast with him and then attend his meeting.

This highly agreeable but completely irregular state of affairs was fine while I was with B.I.S. but, on becoming Head of the New York office of the P.W.E. Mission, I found I was supposed to have inherited the feuds as well as the loyalties. Because O.S.S. and S.O.E. were closely affiliated, as were P.W.E. and O.W.I., I, as a P.W.E. body, was supposed to have nothing to do with O.S.S., because of the enmity between P.W.E. and S.O.E. on the one hand and of O.S.S. and O.W.I. on the other. It was as easy and as uncomplicated as that!

I pointed out that this would entail severing what I had been told was a useful link in the chain of Anglo-American co-operation against the people who were after all our real enemies: the Germans, the Italians and the Japanese, but I had to fight hard and long before I could get my view accepted. At length, however, David Bowes

Lyon, with his native good judgement and understanding, and Bruce Lockhart himself, realised the common sense of my argument. My relations with Bill Donovan were permitted to continue as long as I remained in America, provided I kept both Bruce and David informed of what went on, something which it would never have occurred to me not to do.

I enjoyed immensely working with this group of highly intelligent men, who combined the practical experience of diplomacy with the wide range of academic learning. I found the work engrossing and agreeable partly because I had a certain flair for it and partly because I have always enjoyed working with Americans. In the course of it I developed a theory, which I found proven later in the war, that while the Americans might be better at acquiring intelligence material, the British were superior in analysing and interpreting it. It was for this reason that a combination of the two was so powerful and efficient a weapon of war.

When I was with the British Press Service the Embassy in Washington asked me to undertake the job of maintaining contact with the many eminent refugees who were arriving in America as their respective countries were overrun and occupied by the German army, or those who had prudently left the Axis countries before or shortly after the establishment of régimes of terror. In carrying out this task, which I continued from the P.W.E. Mission in New York, I had to be exceedingly careful not to fall foul of the State Department on the one hand, and the F.B.I. on the other, both of whom resented greatly any tampering by 'foreign agents' with American nationals. This presented no small difficulty because some of the refugees had acquired United States citizenship and all of them had integrated themselves to some degree or other with the hyphenated element of their several national origins, many of whom were second or third generation American citizens and in some cases longer still. However, I established a survey of the foreign language press – and a volu-minously polygot collection it proved – which gave one at least some idea of what, let us say, the Serbs, Croats, Slovenes, Italians, Germans, Hungarians, Arabs, Poles and Czechs were thinking and were telling their fellow linguals to think.

Our first and most complicated problem was the French. At the outbreak of the war the French Government had established an Information Service and had placed over it an old acquaintance of mine from Tucson Arizona (where he had gone to die of tubercu-losis), whose name rang down the ages from the Crusades – the

Comte Raoul de Roussey de Salle. Raoul answered his country's call with great courage and the ultimate sacrifice of his life, and during the Phoney War no one could have been a more amiable friend nor a more able colleague. He had a dry sophisticated sense of humour which gave me much pleasure, though when discussing affairs with Aubrey Morgan and me he was deeply pessimistic as to the moral fibre of his country to sustain a long war. Then came the collapse of France, which in his heart of hearts I believe that he had always foreseen, and Raoul seemed to go into a state of shock. He would support neither Pétain nor de Gaulle; he would pledge his allegiance to neither the régime of Vichy nor the Free French Committee in London. He was loyal and dedicated to France as an ideal but he was too shattered to do more than this. He died, as much, I think, of a broken heart as of phthisis, shortly thereafter. I attended his funeral at the bare little French Church on Park Avenue.

I mention the case of Raoul because it illustrated the attitude of many French-American citizens or long-term residents at that time. When Aubrey and I went out to California together a little later to get something of the climate of ideas on the Pacific coast, we were disturbed to find this same negative attitude strongly prevalent in San Francisco. Here there was a rich powerful French colony whose interests lay mostly in the commercial world, and who were sufficiently numerous to maintain a French Club and a French repertory theatre. Here we found the same reaction as Raoul's, though sometimes from different motives. Most of these men had contributed generously and often to French war charities but, at six thousand miles from their afflicted country, they were not disposed to jump to conclusions. For one reason or another they maintained an attitude of neutrality to the *actualités* of the situation, while retaining, like Raoul, their mystic faith in the ability of France to survive. When one recalls that, since the execution of Louis XVI in 1793, France has experienced the First Republic and the Terror, the Directory, the Consulate, the First Empire, the First and Second Restorations, the 'Bourgeois Monarchy' of Louis-Philippe, the Second Republic, the Second Empire, the Commune and the Third Republic, the Vichy régime and the Free French Committee of de Gaulle and the Fourth and Fifth Republics, it is understandable that Frenchmen are conditioned and calloused to changes of political régime. They naturally cling to the belief that France, which has endured so many varieties of fortune and government will survive anything.

This was not the attitude of those who had escaped from Bordeaux and other southern French ports at the risk of their lives; journalists such as Geniève Tabouis and 'Pertinax'; politicians like André Philip and Charles de Kérillis; and such artists as Henri Bernstein, whose boast it was that when the Germans entered Paris they found the placards advertising his play *Coriolanus* on the kiosks and *pissoirs*. Above all there was the noble and beautiful Eve Curie (now married to Harry Labouisse, of UNICEF) whose ardour was unabated and whose faith never faltered.

All these plunged into action to mobilise sympathy and support for de Gaulle and his Fighting Free French. They were horrified by the trenchant and hostile attitude adopted by Mr Cordell Hull and the State Department to the occupation of the islands of St Pierre-Miquelon, off the Canadian coast, by the Free French Admiral Emile Muselier during Christmas 1941. It was then that the Secretary of State made his slighting reference to the 'so-called' Free French Committee, which provoked a flood of protests addressed to the 'so-called' Secretary of State.

With these ardent patriots I maintained the closest contacts and rendered them any small assistance in my power. I also, with reluctance, met with the egregious Camille Chautemps, who set up an office in New York and proclaimed himself a 'reasonable French-man', which meant that he was more inclined towards Vichy and Pétain than to de Gaulle. He collected something of a following among those who disliked both the Germans and de Gaulle, and were therefore persuaded that Marshal Pétain had made the best of a bad job. I refused, however, to shake the hand of Henri-Haye, the former mayor of Versailles, who arrived in Washington as the official representative of the Vichy Government and especially of Pierre Laval. He did not have a very warm reception in Washington social life except at the hands of the less sophisticated.

So much for the French. There were also the Italians and amongst them the monumentally boring Count Carlo Sforza, the veteran anti-Fascist leader. When he had exhausted even the professional and well-trained courtesy of the Chancery at Washington, they saddled me with him, and I coped as manfully as I could. Not only was he a withering proser but also inordinately vain and a crashing snob. After a two-hour luncheon at which the conversation had consisted largely of interminable anecdotes about King Victor Emmanuel III ('he always addresses me as "*Carlo mi*", you know, because as a Knight of the Annunziata I am a cousin of the Monarch') he would turn suddenly upon me, with his beard bristling and his monocle flashing, and say in a preceptive tone: 'And, of course, you will

F

report *all* that I have told you to your embassy.' I generally spared them.

I have rarely been more pleased than on one evening in 1944 when I was dining with Harold Nicolson and he told me a story which he has repeated in the second volume of his *Diaries*. Harold in the House of Commons that afternoon had referred to Sforza as 'a faded old peacock' and when later Winston Churchill had congratulated him on his speech, Harold had said he hoped he hadn't gone too far. 'You did not go too far,' the Prime Minister replied. 'That is exactly what he is. When he came to see me on his way through London he wasted ten minutes in explaining to me how far older the Sforza family was than the House of Savoy. I was obliged to interrupt him. I was obliged to say to him, "Count Sforza, these dynastic personalities have little to do with the prosecution of the war." I was rude to him, I was very rude', he added with relish. All my sympathies were with Mr Churchill, but he had only had ten minutes of suffering, and I would have given anything to have been 'very rude' just once to Count Sforza.

There were, however, other lighter, if macabre, moments. The Italian refugees were often at odds with the Italian-Americans, not a few of whom were at one time or another admirers of Mussolini. Max Ascoli, that distinguished political scientist and a power in the Mazzini Society, was from the first a firm and valued ally of the British and there were others less prominent who were threatened and victimised by Fascist organisations. I remember one such, an inoffensive little man of some humble calling who came to see me in obvious distress and yet with that curious nervous giggle which sometimes afflicts those who have suffered severe shock or sorrow. Also he had only a sketchy knowledge of English and virtually no command of the nuance of the language. As he came in he first wiped away a tear and then suddenly began to titter; then he said: 'Oh please, I have something so funny [strange] to tell you. My brother, he has just been murdered in the Lincoln Tunnel; hee-hee-hee.' After some further elaboration of this unexpected and remarkable statement, which convinced me of its truth, incredible though it might seem, he went on to ask what he should do about it and looked crestfallen when I suggested seeking the aid of the police. 'I thought the British would help', he said dolefully. 'My brother, he was murdered by the Fascists. You are at war with the Fascists. The New York Police is not at war with the Fascists; it is no good going to them.' And he left saddened and disappointed.

But it was of course with the Germans that I was most interested and there were many of them, good and bad. After Pearl Harbor many offered their services to O.S.S. or O.W.I. and also to those embryonic training centres who were preparing United States officers with professional backgrounds for the work of military government on that happy and longed-for day when the Allies carried the war beyond the frontiers of the Reich.

I saw many of all degrees of anti-Nazi opinion during these years and among the most bizarre was also perhaps the most unexpected. Putzi Hanfstängl, of the great art-print-makers of Munich, had been among Hitler's earliest and staunchest supporters. It was he who had hidden the Führer in his house after the ludicrous episode of the Beer Hall *putsch* of 1923, and who in later years had brought relaxation and solace to that evil soul by his exquisite piano-playing. As I have described in *Knaves, Fools and Heroes*, I had known Putzi well and was aware of the increasingly strained relations between him and other hierarchs of the Nazi Party, due largely to his inability to restrain his very comical sense of humour. Such jests as his question to Goebbels, which I heard, at the première of the latter's propaganda film called *Hitler Jugend Quex*, whether his next triumph was to be entitled *Hitler Mädchen Quatsch*, had not endeared him to those who had been the butt of his wit and there had been general agreement that he should be got rid of. It is alleged that neither Hitler nor Goering, whom he had never ridiculed, were privy to the plot, but in 1938 it was arranged for him to be forced out of a plane en route for Portugal and dumped seawards. Warned by some friend in the Lufthansa who heard of the projected assassination, Putzi prudently left the plane when it put down at Croydon and threw himself upon the mercy of the British authorities, who granted him asylum.

We saw one another infrequently at this time and Putzi gave exceedingly interesting information about the inner workings of the upper strata of the Nazi 'top brass', together with their intrigues, peccadilloes, sex-lives, etc. It was useful gossip and later it was made use of, but he was able to contribute no military information of any value. With the general arrest and dispersal in 1940 of all Germans who might be considered suspect, Putzi Hanfstängl was deported to Canada where he remained in detention until it occurred to Bill Donovan that he might have information from which O.S.S. could profit. After some triangular negotiation between London, Washington and Ottawa, it was agreed that Putzi should be paroled 'on loan', as it were, to Bill and he was forthwith transferred in great secrecy to the military reservation of Fort Meyer, just outside Washington where he was housed in considerable comfort. Here he wrote endless rambling reports and memoranda which were utterly worthless and Bill ultimately decided that he had made a bad bet. Before however returning Putzi to Canadian custody he asked me if I would like to have a talk with him. I naturally would, of course, and when Putzi was apprised of my projected visit he expressed considerable pleasure.

I found him, large and amorphous as ever, writing busily. As soon as the soldier on guard had left us alone, Putzi made a great show of secrecy, seeing that the doors and windows were tightly closed (it was a hot day, by the way), and even drawing the curtain across the one window that looked on to an open green space. Then in a conspiratorial voice he said: 'I have been waiting to be contacted by the British. These Americans are fools and have no appreciation of Nazi psychology. You know Germany and I know the only way to stop this bloody war. It is a very easy way.' He paused and I waited breathlessly for this magic formula for peace. As he did not further confide in me, I thought justified in needling him. 'Well, what is your plan?' I asked bluntly. Putzi seemed to come back from some long vista of thought down which his mind had wandered. 'I will tell you,' he said. 'But you must not tell the Americans. They would not understand. It is this: If King George VI will give Goering the Order of the Garter, the Reichsmarschall and the Luftwaffe will overthrow Hitler and end the war.' Scarcely able to control my emotions I congratulated him on the simplicity and brilliance of his plan. Then I bade him farewell and drove to the Embassy, there to report to Lord Halifax, who was then Chancellor of the Order, and to ask him whether he would like a new recruit for the Blue Riband. Whether he told the Americans I have no idea but I never did. I kept my word, and fortunately I was saved from embarrassment by the fact that when we next met Bill Donovan had forgotten all about it. Putzi is still, I believe, alive and living at Munich at the age of 88.

On a droller note were the dissensions among the Bavarians. I have described in Knaves, Fools and Heroes how, at the First Quebec Conference in 1943, there was some discussion of the possibility of partitioning Germany by creating a Catholic state out of Austria and Bavaria. It was generally assumed that this should be a monarchy and, whereas Mr Churchill had mildly romantic inclinations towards the Habsburgs, President Roosevelt had a preference for the Wittelsbachs.

Now the House of Wittelsbach, which ruled Bavaria for some

eight hundred years until dethroned in November 1918, was itself divided. There was the King of Bavaria, who was promoted from the rank of Elector-Palatine to that of monarch by Napoleon, and there was the Duke in Bavaria (*Der Herzog im Bayern*) whose title derived from a collateral branch. The claimant of the royal house was the Crown Prince Rupprecht, who had been an able Army Group commander in the First World War and had at no time 'bowed the knee in the House of Rimmon' in response to the blandishments which Hitler had frequently dangled before him. I had known him both before and after the Nazi Revolution, and had lunched on more than one occasion at the 'Little Residence' where he kept state in Munich. He had always been unrelentingly anti-Nazi and, after Hitler had become Chancellor, had steadfastly refused to raise the Swastika banner over his palace, always flying his own 'house-flag'. Indeed so militant had Prince Rupprecht's opposition to the Third Reich become that the Führer had him deported to Florence in the final years of the war and kept there under house-arrest.

Despite this fine record of non-compliance with National Socialism, which would have satisfied most people, there was a section of the Bavarian monarchist movement who conspired, in the event of a restoration of the monarchy, to vest the crown in the ducal branch of the Wittelsbachs to the exclusion of the Royal House. Finding little support for their cause in official Washington, they laid siege to the British Embassy, who smartly sidestepped the issue by referring them to me.

I duly received a deputation of somewhat seedy-looking individuals who looked as if they had stepped out of the murkier shadows of *The Prisoner of Zenda* (the followers of 'Black Michael', perhaps!) who did their best to sell me a bill of goods on the Herzog. I was disinclined to be sympathetic, having a personal preference for Prince Rupprecht, and in any case it all seemed wonderfully unreal, but when they suddenly disclosed the fact that their claimant to the throne was actually in New York, I became more interested. I agreed to see him but insisted that we should talk alone. I didn't want this yodelling chorus to be present at our discussions.

Very reluctantly they agreed and in due course there arrived in my office the most charming little old gentleman, very clean and dapper, who looked as if he belonged in the pages of the pre-1914 *Tatler*. He was smartly dressed in a double-breasted grey-flannel suit, brown and white – what used to be called 'co-respondent' – shoes, and, unbelievably, an M.C.C. tie. He was most typically the European royalty who had graced the British Court before the First World

War and were really more at home in England than in their own capitals.

His Royal Highness spoke beautiful English of a 1910 vintage (rather like the Kaiser but less slangy) and was obviously very unhappy at the prospect which loomed – however improbably – before him. I asked him to tell me frankly whether, in the hypothetical event of a South German Catholic state being created he would be remotely interested in ruling it. 'Not in the least,' he replied. 'My cousin Rupprecht has the prior claim. He is known and loved in Bavaria and would make a good king. I have no desire to press any claims against his.'

I began to like this nice little old gentleman very much. He was simple and sensible and loyal and extremely pleasant, though essentially a *grand seigneur*. I asked him what he would really like to do when the war was over. He looked almost embarrassed, like a schoolboy about to confess to a somewhat childish ambition. Then he smiled engagingly. 'Do you want to know what I would really like to do when it is possible? I would like to come to London again and watch cricket at Lord's. Then I would like to live very quietly on my little New England farm and forget about politics altogether.' I told him I thought that, given time and occasion, both these desires could be gratified and I hoped they would be. I never saw him again, nor his shabby supporters, but I was able to assure the Embassy that no further trouble need be expected from this quarter.

My closest personal connection was, of course, with Heinrich Brüning, whom I saw frequently throughout my wartime service in America. I found him moving progressively towards the Right in his thinking and already displaying those ultra-conservative views which he had not expressed during his Chancellorship, though they appeared in intensified form in his posthumous memoirs, published in 1971. He was as anti-Nazi as ever, but remained a patriotic German nationalist – far removed from the attitude of Dietrich Bonhoeffer, who believed and said openly that Germany must approach the future in a spirit of contrition and penitence.

In February of 1943 I spent seven hours with Brüning during a weekend at Harvard and subsequently wrote a report on our talk for Lord Halifax, which he repeated with commendation to the Foreign Office. (It is now in the Public Record Office: F.O. 371 34413 4127.) I had found Brüning greatly depressed as to the course of the war and resentful of the official British attitude towards Germany, condemning the formula of Unconditional Surrender and the heavy bombing. I thought him wrong when he alleged that a German victory was still possible and I attempted to disillusion him when he sought to emphasise the difference between a National Socialist State and a 'New Germany'. It was essential, I told him, for the elements in Germany who claimed to be anti-Nazi to eliminate Hitler, destroy the Nazi state and re-establish the *Rechtsstaat* and then comply with Unconditional Surrender before they could expect leniency from the Allies. The day had long passed when the overthrow of the Third Reich could be followed by a negotiated peace with a new German régime. This made him very angry, and he told me I had become a chauvinist. To this I contended that what I was was a realist and that what I had told him would follow as the night the day, if Germany persisted in fighting to the end. In this case the terms of surrender and peace would be even more draconian. I concluded my report:

> It is my impression that there is growing within Brüning a desire – and perhaps even an ambition – to play the role of a German Talleyrand at the peace table and to win for a non-Nazi Germany better terms than she would otherwise be granted. I think he regards it as a patriotic duty to save, if he can, for the New Germany as much as possible from the shambles which will follow the collapse of National Socialism.

I have always believed that the ultimate *froideur* which arose between Heinrich Brüning and myself, and which I very greatly regretted, began from this conversation in the spring of 1943. As I left him, I had a presentiment that it was the last time we should meet as close friends. From then on our paths were too diverse.

Before this occurred, however, I was able to bring Bill Donovan and Brüning together. Each had for some time wanted to meet the other but Brüning was suspicious of being 'used' by the General and had 'jibbed' at the previous attempts I had made to arrange a meeting. At length, however, he weakened and it was agreed that we should all three lunch together in Bill's suite at the St Regis Hotel.

The circumstances were not, however, wholly felicitous. I have mentioned that a state of strained relations existed between O.S.S. and the F.B.I., and there was acute personal rivalry between Bill Donovan and J. Edgar Hoover. Both were tough, hard men; patient and deadly enemies. It so happened that, on the evening before our luncheon engagement, on the way to the Union Station in Washington, Bill's car was run into by a drunken driver 'proceeding' (as the police say) on the wrong side of the street. Unfortunately he turned out to be an F.B.I. man (personally, I believe this fact to be irrelevant and gratuitous, though Bill would never accept this view); more unfortunate still was that both Bill's legs were badly crushed. He refused, however, to forgo his engagement and continued on his way to New York, where he summoned his doctors and received belated treatment. When Brüning and I arrived for luncheon next morning, Bill received us in bed with both legs in splints and we ate in his bedroom. He was geniality itself and his Irish charm melted Brüning's Westphalian reserve. Soon they were chatting away, exchanging experiences as old front-line fighters in France and Flanders, and from this they passed to more immediate problems in the conduct of the war and the making of the peace. Bill spoke well and listened well, and I could see that behind his extreme courtesy was his lawyer's skill in eliciting information. Apart from his grey, drawn face and the fact that he took two stiff whiskies and sodas – a rare thing for him, for he was almost a teetotaller – there were no signs that he was in the greatest pain. It was one of the most remarkable performances of physical endurance that I have ever witnessed.

In this same spring of 1943 what both Ruth and I had come to regard as inevitable actually came to pass; she was ordered abroad. She had been commissioned in the American Red Cross shortly after Pearl Harbor and had been through a course of intensive training and service both in Washington and in New York. Now she was fully qualified to take over the direction of those clubs and rest centres which the American Red Cross provided for the armies abroad. We had both known that she would be sent overseas and both of us had hoped against hope that her application to be assigned to the European Theatre, and therefore based in London, would be granted. We really should have known better, for any request of this sort is immediately rewarded by the authorities by a posting in a diametrically opposite direction. And so it proved. Ruth received movement orders for Washington as a preliminary to going West, a direction which could only mean embarkation from San Francisco. After a phenomenal voyage of forty-eight days, which took her by way of Australia, the Indian Ocean and the Suez Canal, she eventually arrived at Alexandria where, and in Cairo, she served throughout the remainder of the war.

All this was unknown to either of us at the time, or at any rate to me, for Ruth is very discreet, and we only knew that she had to report to Washington. On the night before her departure we went with Aubrey and Constance Morgan, and with Mrs Morrow to see

Oklahoma (then in its first weeks of triumph) and the following day (Easter Sunday, 25 April) I saw her off at Pennsylvania Station. In these unromantic and sordid surroundings we 'plighted our troth' with that gold ring with a Hittite seal which I had bought from old Kaiky at Aden sixteen years before and had worn as a signet ring ever since. It was another two years before we were married.

Later that year, in June, I returned to England for a 'refresher course'. I found great changes since my last visit. Bruce Lockhart was now firmly in the saddle and had effected a number of important and far-reaching reforms. In the first place he had obtained from the Foreign Office and the Chiefs of Staff a clear definition of the tasks entrusted to the P.W.E. They were simple: firstly to undermine and to destroy the morale of the Axis powers and secondly to sustain and foster the spirit of resistance in the enemy-occupied countries. For these purposes a voluntary agreement had been reached with the B.B.C. giving policy control over all foreign broadcasts to these territories to P.W.E.

This was in itself an achievement, but Bruce had done more. The ludicrous situation by which authority over political warfare was vested in three separate ministries had been resolved on Bruce's initiative by mutual agreement among Anthony Eden, Brendan Bracken and Lord Selborne (who had succeeded Hugh Dalton at M.E.W.) to act as a trinity, with the Foreign Secretary as *primus inter pares* – or, as it might be called, 'Elder Brother'. This made for smoother working at the highest level, and as both Anthony and Brendan were on terms of intimate friendship with Mr Churchill, his favourable influence in the work of the Department was generally assured.

I have never believed, however, that the Prime Minister really comprehended the mechanics of political warfare. I should not be surprised if, in the deep recesses of his mind, he had a vague conception of a man – or at most two men – standing on the White Cliffs of Dover and shouting into a megaphone towards enemy-occupied Europe. But he was intrigued by its secrecy and 'cloak-and-dagger' aspect and warmly defended its privileged status as an essential part of national security. Indeed, one back-bencher, having been refused further information about our activities on the grounds of secrecy, put a 'supplementary' to the Prime Minister asking for a definition of the difference between a secret and an awkward question. Mr Churchill replied with asperity: 'One is a danger to the country and the other is a nuisance to the Government.'

Having secured his position at the highest level, Bruce had then faced the internal problems of his department. When I had joined him in the previous year and had been initiated into the workings of the organisation I had been appalled at the restriction placed on their efficiency by reason of their geographical dispersal. The political wing of P.W.E. under Rex Leeper, was housed at Woburn; the military wing, directed by Major-General (later Sir Dallas) Brooks, was located in Landsdowne House; the European Services of the B.B.C., of which Ivone Kirkpatrick was controller, were lodged in Bush House, Aldwych; and the office of the Director-General was in the Locarno Room of the Foreign Office. Each of these separate sections exercised local autonomy; jealousies were rife and co-operation impaired.

When Bruce asked for my opinion and advice I told him frankly that one of his first and most pressing actions must be the concentration of all these contumacious entities in one place, preferably London, and that their control must be co-ordinated under his direct authority. He agreed, but told me some of the difficulties. Rex Leeper and what had become known unkindly as Leeper's Sleepers were loth to leave the comforts of a rural life for the austerities of an urban existence. Dallas Brooks, a gallant Marine who had won a D.S.O. in the Zeebrugge Raid of 1918, played cricket for the Navy, and was destined to become Commandant of his Corps and later Governor of Victoria, was a consummate 'Whitehall Warrior', who was an invaluable liaison with the Chiefs of Staff. He knew all the tricks of the trade but was unwilling to share the sources of his knowledge. Ivone Kirkpatrick, a future Permanent Under-Secretary at the Foreign Office, though under Bruce's operational control, was not then an integral figure of P.W.E. In addition there was the inevitable opposition from the Treasury on grounds of finance and the Ministry of Works in regard to accommodation.

Nevertheless, Bruce, having taken a major decision always stuck to it, though he might vacillate on minor judgements. Those who judge him by his own published diaries, wherein he appears as his own worst enemy, have no concept of the courage and deft diplomacy which he displayed in dealing with the deities of Whitehall and the prima donnas of his own department. He concentrated all the various divisions in quarters at Bush House and set up an Executive Committee composed of himself as Chairman, Leeper and Brooks, to which Kirkpatrick was later added, as, later still, I was myself. This body met weekly to receive guidance and counsel from the Ministerial Committee, which was then passed on in the form of directives to the operational staff.

The execution of these reforms took all Bruce's tact and patience, and there were delays and disappointments and frustrations which occupied weeks and months. Not all of them had been put into operation when I arrived in London in the summer of 1943 with a plea to be transferred to the new headquarters, but Bruce though he promised that in six months' time or perhaps less he would have a place for me, told me that until then I must be patient. I assured him that I was perfectly happy in my New York job but that I felt I had spent quite enough of the war out of England and was eager to make a contribution at home. 'Believe me, I need you,' were his last words to me as I made ready to fly back to America.

I took wing from Poole on 4 August, and we made Shannon – then far from the imposing international airport it is today – in perfect weather. All seemed set for a good passage to New York, when I was both alarmed and disconcerted on looking out of the cabin window to see one of the four engines of our flying-boat suddenly fall off and disappear with a mighty splash into the estuary. We made a perfect landing, considering our handicap, and were informed that it would take the better part of a week to get a new engine out from England and fitted. We were advised to go away and enjoy ourselves, reporting each morning to the authorities at Shannon for the latest information on the continuation of our journey.

Most of my fellow-passengers departed for the delights of Dublin or Limerick, but I remembered a little inn at Adare, some fifty miles from Shannon where one could stay in uninterrupted peace. The Dunraven Arms was not then what it is today now that it has been modernised and tastefully redecorated by the American skill of Nancy, Lady Dunraven, but it was just what I wanted and I have never enjoyed anything more than the days I spent there. I was very tired and was not feeling very well, and I slept late. I found a most adequate mount on which I explored that lovely country of County Limerick. I also revelled in reading the local press, which, owing to Eire's neutral status and consequent censorship, carried scarcely any news of the war but was filled with the problems of Ireland and local scandal. I was particularly delighted to discover behind the counter in the tap-room a wooden box which the landlady told me had been left with her by a commercial traveller in settlement of a bad debt. On closer examination I found it to be a case of Moët-Chandon 1928, which I secured at a nominal rate and drank with my local acquaintances until there were only two or three bottles left which I took back to Aubrey and Constance Morgan.

Bruce was better even than his word, for I was told in November that I could report for duty at Bush House as from 1 January 1944, and I gladly made my preparations for departure. But here again I was doomed to frustration. I was due to fly on 21 December, in order to be able to spend Christmas with my family, but on the day before I developed an agonising ear-ache, with a mounting temperature. I have little clear recollection of what immediately followed but, thanks entirely to the kindness of Leonard Miall, who took charge of the situation with masterly efficiency, the next thing I knew I was in the Manhattan Ear, Nose and Throat Hospital, having been operated on for a mastoid infection and feeling very weak and ill. Leonard's prompt action may well have saved my life.

Once again I was recipient of wonderful and generous kindness from Mrs Morrow and Aubrey and Constance Morgan. They would not countenance my spending Christmas in hospital and as soon as I could be moved, I was bundled in blankets and driven – petrol being strictly rationed at that time – out to Englewood, to Next Day Hill. Here I was cosseted and spoiled until I was able to stand the journey out to California under wartime conditions, where I was to recuperate with some other friends of the Morgans, Dick and Eleanor Griffith, who were equally considerate in taking care of me.

Altogether it took nearly five months before I was pronounced fit enough to fly, though I was allowed to work in my office. Then on 8 May 1944, I reported for duty at Bush House.

The first thing I noticed about my new colleagues was the infinite variety of their backgrounds and their talents, amounting in some cases to genius. It was a forcing ground of gifted aptitude, a dynamo of creative power, and most of them were young. Many rose to positions of eminence in later years. Dick Crossman, who had been a Fellow of New College, Oxford, subsequently rose to be Lord President of the Council in Mr Wilson's Cabinet; Duncan Wilson came to us from the British Museum, Ralph Murray from the B.B.C. and Con O'Neill, who had courageously risked his future by resigning from the Foreign Service in protest against the Munich Agreement, hied more immediately from Printing House Square. All three became Ambassadors and all three were knighted, and Duncan was elected Master of Corpus Christi College, Cambridge. Alan Bullock, like Dick Crossman, came from New College and returned to Oxford to be Master of St Catherine's College, and Vice-Chancellor of the University. He was author of *Hitler, a Study in Tyranny*, which, despite its recent spate of competitors, still remains the most outstandingly penetrating analysis of this evil creature. Alan, too, was knighted. Our Director of Planning, Ritchie Calder, was recruited from Fleet Street and was created a Life Peer for services to scientific education. Our Director of Intelligence, Eric Sachs, a barrister, is now a Privy Counsellor and a Lord Justice of Appeal. We also numbered Dilys Powell, who has become one of the most brilliant and discerning film critics of our day, and David (Bunny) Garnett, whose important and singular first novel, *Lady into Fox* (published in 1922) assured him at once a high place among literary writers. It also provided Lord D'Abernon with his memorable quip at General von Seeckt's expense: 'General into Fox', he once remarked. Rarely can a galaxy of intelligence have so remarkably fulfilled their early promise.

My second impression was that most of the staff of the Department were too fine drawn. There was a tremendous keenness about them but they were really working too hard, under a sense of strain and a certain febrile activity. This was partly the fault of Bruce Lockhart. Never sparing himself he never spared others, and he set an example of hard work which was inspiring. Moreover he was self-conscious about his earlier reputation as something of a playboy and was determined that it should not arouse hopes or illusions among his staff that they could get away with anything. In this he was successful. Many were frightened to death of him. Even the dashing General Brooks walked Agag-like in his presence and Rex Leeper was markedly deferential.

The fact was that Bruce was an excellent and inspiring chief endowed with extraordinary insight, but the role of disciplinarian – and it must be confessed that such was needed among this highly-strung aggregation of stars – did not come naturally to his normally kindly, gay and easy-going nature. He had to force himself to become a martinet *malgré lui* and, oddly enough, the synthetic nature of the act made it the more effective. Doorkeepers trembled as he entered the office, unsmiling and walking very fast; messengers flattened themselves against the wall at his approach; his secretaries trembled before him. It was magnificent and it was certainly war, but it was really not the way of getting the best out of a staff.

I felt that, as a newcomer and an old friend, I was in an advantageous position to tackle the Director-General on this all-important issue and Bruce has left his own account of what happened:

The legend is [he has written in *Giants Cast Long Shadows*] that during the war I was a tough, unobservant boss who thought only of the day's work and took no notice of my staff or of my three secretaries. We were supposed by envious officials to have the best bevy of beauties' of all government departments. They worked long hours, and I plead guilty to indifference, partly because I was busy and partly because, as head of a department of mixed sexes, I felt I had to be both prudent and stern.

One day when there had been tears, Jack [W-B] ... came to me and suggested firmly that I might be a little more human in my relations with our secretaries. It would make, he said, a great difference. Full of remorse, I reversed my tactics and the very next evening I went into the secretaries' room which was next door to mine, chatted with them, and then, when conversation flagged, I spotted a very neat little hat and a tiny lady's umbrella on a peg behind the door. I put on the hat, took the umbrella, and did a shuffle dance down the corridor. Jack came in during the perform-ance, looked dumbfounded, and asked if I wanted a doctor.

This account is substantially correct. I was indeed aghast at the fruits of my labours to humanise our Chief and feared that he might go too far, if he had not already done so. Bruce should have added to his record the fact that, having assured myself of his sanity, I repeated to him Talleyrand's historic warning to an over-enthusiastic colleague – 'Pas trop de zèle, mon cher!' He soon got on to an even keel, however, and we were a much 'happier ship' in consequence.

My first appointment in P.I.D. bore the embracing title of European Adviser, which meant that I had a roving liaison commission. Each national section of the department had its own staff of experts, who were steeped in the details of their particular region to an incredible degree, but, apart from Bruce himself, there was no one who had an over-all knowledge of Europe until I arrived, bringing with me what he has been kind enough to call my 'immense knowledge of men and affairs.' I quote him because I should have put it more modestly; but it is indeed true that I did know on terms of intimacy many in Whitehall and in Westminster and that I was on terms of friendship with the premiers and foreign ministers of more than half the governments-in-exile and of the British representatives accredited to them, and had immediate access. I also resumed my old relations with George Backer, now head of the O.W.I. mission in London, and, more circumspectly, with the office of O.S.S., then under the direction of the delightful David Bruce, who must hold the record for ambassa-dorial appointments, having later held them in Paris, Bonn, London, Peking, and N.A.T.O.

I do not mention these facts out of personal conceit; the reason was simply that in the past twenty years, as readers of *Knaves, Fools and Heroes* may recall, I had travelled extensively in Europe and elsewhere and had acquired a wide circle of acquaintances and contacts, many of which had ripened into friendship. As a result I could write – again the words are Bruce's not mine – 'most valuable reports' for him which were helpful in his sessions with the Ministerial Committee and also to the various sections themselves. It was work after my own heart and I delighted in it.

But there were changes ahead. When I arrived Bruce's Personal Assistant, and his official link with the Foreign Office, was Peter Scarlett, a charming and tranquil diplomat, who had been captured by the Germans at Boulogne in 1940 whilst trying to return from leave to his post in the Embassy at Brussels. For fifteen months he was interned at Bad Eilsen, together with his ambassador, Sir Lancelot Oliphant, who in an attempt to escape had also been overrun and taken prisoner in France – and therefore 'off base' as far as diplomatic immunity was concerned. Peter, who was later to be Ambassador in Norway and Minister to the Vatican, was translated to the Allied Headquarters at Caserta and I took his place as P.A. to Bruce. This came at a moment when, as a result of strain and fatigue, he had developed an acute and very painful form of dermatitis, which, apart from making him both miserable and crotchety, necessitated his painting the affected parts, including his hands and portions of his face, with a gentian preparation which made him look like an ancient Briton decorated with woad. As soon as he could get about Brendan Bracken ordered him to Scotland for a month's rest – his first real leave since the war – while I made a weekly night journey to Speyside and back to keep him informed on the work of the department, and the situation and gossip in London. As this was the only condition on which he would stay put, I paid my visits to him gladly, but it was a wearing life.

Shortly thereafter Bruce made two further additions to my duties. I was first nominated as representative of P.I.D. on the British delegation to the European Advisory Commission (E.A.C.), which had been set up by the Conference of Foreign Ministers at Moscow in October 1943. The leader of our delegation was William (later Lord) Strang and his chief colleagues were the American and Soviet Ambassadors in London, John Winant and Ivan Maisky. The seat of the Commission was at Lancaster House and the chairmanship changed each month. Although I came lately to its deliberations, I was very soon aware of the fact that greater progress was made when William Strang presided than under either of the others. He had a great ability to get his own way by quiet and patient pertinacity; always knowing when to concede on points which he deemed unimportant in order to stand firm on what really mattered. His was an excellent example of careful and successful negotiation. John Winant was ably seconded by George Kennan and Phil Mosely, both friends of mine from earlier days. The Ambassador was the most silent man I have ever known. He was also obviously unhappy and later became unbalanced, committing suicide shortly after the end of the war. With Maisky I had had friendly relations during the Czech crisis of 1938 but these had cooled to frigidity with the Nazi-Soviet Pact, to blossom again after Hitler's invasion of the Soviet Union. Now, however, he proved as enigmatic and obdurate as any other Soviet official at a conference-table.

My second new hat, under the general umbrella of P.I.D., was as No. 2 to the British Political Adviser at Supreme Headquarters Allied Expeditionary Force (S.H.A.E.F.), which functioned at what was known as 'Wide Wings', at Bushey Park in Hertfordshire. Both jobs were interesting because, whereas my work at S.H.A.E.F. involved planning for the government of parts of Germany which came under our occupation before the conclusion of hostilities, that at E.A.C. was largely concerned with the Unconditional Surrender and post-war control of the German state, and the future of Germany interested me greatly.

To give me the necessary status for this dual role I was appointed Assistant Director-General, responsible directly to Bruce, which gave me the equivalent rank of Assistant Under-Secretary in the Foreign Office, and my position at S.H.A.E.F. gave me the assimilated rank of Brigadier and Rear-Admiral! These latter postings led to some entertaining sequels. For a military headquarters, S.H.A.E.F. had one of the best senior messes I have ever known. It was called the 'Yankee Doodle Mess,' in which the food was largely provided by the Americans and the service by the Household Brigade, *but*, to my horror and humiliation, I found that its membership was open only to the rank of major-general and above. One-star generals might stand at the door hat in hand, begging bowls rattling, weeping 'like Paris at the gate disconsolate', but they could not enter the sacred portals nor taste of the flesh-pots; they were relegated to the outer darkness of 'brigadiers and junior ranks'. This I felt was deplorable and must be rectified, so I guilefully suggested to my chief, who was none other than my old colleague from Washington days, Charles Peake and who held the rank of major-general, that it was high time he was promoted, a view with which he readily concurred. He worked the oracle and in a very short time acquired the stars and badges of a lieutenant-general. From this it followed as the night the day that I too should be advanced in rank and, sure enough, I was awarded my second star and what was definitely more important, became eligible for membership of 'the Yankee Doodle Mess'! It must have been the shortest time on record for anyone to have held the rank of brigadier, but, as John Foster once remarked of a similar situation, 'You have to start somewhere.'

This question of rank caused me further embarrassment. I had all my life longed to be a soldier and the fact that I had been a civilian casualty in the First World War and had been decisively rejected on grounds of health in the Second had made me the more sensitive and envious on the subject. Now I found myself getting in by the side – if not indeed the back – door and holding moderately senior rank. Moreover, when we were actually at S.H.A.E.F., we were required to be in uniform and this I found I simply could not do, so I continued to wear my usual subfusc office attire. I got away with this for some time but eventually received an order to report to the Chief of Staff, General Walter Bedell Smith, than whom a nicer man never walked, and one of the same high standing in his job as Napoleon's Chief of Staff, Marshal Berthier, Prince of Wagram. He was a tough martinet, however, with the Prussian discipline of West Point still upon him, and a vocabulary which, as somebody said, would rout an armoured column. He wanted to know what the —— I meant by not complying with regulations and wearing uniform. I explained the reason to him, adding that I really was only a civilian and concluding with: 'And, anyway Sir, aren't you pretty tired of being surrounded by phoney major-generals?' (There were a lot of us civilians holding this rank around at the time.) Bedell was, as always, kind and understanding. I think he appreciated my reasoning. But regulations were regulations and so we reached a compromise that I would wear battle-dress without badges of rank and that seemed to satisfy both of us.

Bedell Smith later confessed to me that he never knew when I was being serious or frivolous, but he only held this against me on one occasion. Among all the plans and preparations for D-Day there were to be a series of broadcasts by General Eisenhower, as Supreme Commander, to occupied Europe, to the French people and to the Germans, all of which were under the operational direction of P.W.E. and were called the 'Voice of S.H.A.E.F.' We were periodically bothered by air-raids at 'Wide Wings', and particularly so when Hitler's 'secret weapons', V-1 and V-2, were brought into play. Our warning system was excellent and on receiving the alarm a powerful Middle Western voice would bellow over the loud-speaker: 'Enemy aircraft approaching; enemy aircraft approaching. Take cover; take cover,' and would go on repeating it interminably. We were all supposed then to go down into a series of dugouts and wait until either the attack had passed over us or had been turned back. Meantime the master-sergeant from, as it might be, Dodge City, Kansas, continued his threnody of admonition.

On one of these occasions I found myself in the same air-raid shelter as General Bedell Smith and after we had been there some time, I shouted to him through the sergeant's blaring cautionary tale: 'General, I think this must be the Voice of S.H.A.E.F.' He looked at me for a moment in breath-taking fury. Then he recovered. I saw a smile break over his crinkled, weather-beaten face. He laughed loudly, called me 'an impudent bastard' and stood me a drink at lunchtime.

If I write of the lighter side of life at S.H.A.E.F. it is but to emphasise its more serious aspect. When I had arrived in England preparations for D-Day were already well advanced and I was made aware of some, though by no means all, of the aspects of the undertaking. It was prodigious in the might of its assault potential and magnificently prepared in every detail. General Eisenhower, his Deputy, Air-Marshal Sir Arthur Tedder, his field commanders Generals Omar Bradley and Sir Bernard Montgomery and their respective planners brought their preliminary evolutions to the highest point of efficiency, taking into consideration the inevitable handicap of the 'fog of war'. It was a wonderful achievement and it had been the fruit of the talents, labour and inventive genius of a host of devoted workers, great and small.

There was something quite remarkable about the climate of ideas at S.H.A.E.F., which owed very much to the personality and character of its Supreme Commander. General Dwight Eisenhower, though he may not rank as a master of war with Alexander the Great or Napoleon, and was certainly not a world statesman, was nevertheless absolutely ideal for the highly unusual job he held. S.H.A.E.F. was not only an allied military headquarters but also a kind of joint stock company of allied activities. The success of both was dependent on the new formula of 'integration', which did not come entirely easily to many British and to many Americans. General Eisenhower, however, not only understood its vital importance but was the personification of its principle. He seemed to have deliberately thought himself into a state of mind in which he literally did not know the difference between the two major allies under his command and woe betide the offender, be he American or British, who transgressed the spirit of co-operation. He reconciled two such diverse personalities as Montgomery and Bradley and on occasion asserted his superior rank over the former's somewhat overbearing independence of mind. In his relations with junior ranks or peripheral members of his staff like myself, 'the Ike' displayed a courtesy and good humour, and a knowledge of what the right thing to do was and when to do it, which justifies his place in history.

Nor would he tolerate the slightest breach of security and in this he was no respecter of persons. An old friend and class-mate of his at West Point, with the rank of major-general, was guilty of 'loose talk' at a cocktail-party at Claridge's on one occasion and the incident was reported to Eisenhower. The transgressor had scarcely drawn breath before he had been reduced to the rank of colonel and sent back to the United States. Without Eisenhower's extraordinary and particular type of leadership 'Operation Overlord' might never have achieved that wonderful state of preparedness which later led to its conclusive victory.

My own work lay under the direction of Lieutenant-General Sir Frederick Morgan, who, as C.O.S.S.A.C. (Chief of Staff to the Supreme Commander), had performed the stupendous task of preparing and setting up S.H.A.E.F., while Eisenhower was still completing the defeat of the German and Italian armies in North Africa. When 'Wide Wings' was officially established Freddie Morgan became Deputy Chief of Staff under Bedell Smith, one of his principal tasks being, as I have said, planning what to do with Germany when it came under military government. Apart from his military staff he was assisted by the junior political advisers, Sam Reber of the State Department for America and myself for Britain. We were in close touch with our immediate chiefs, in my case Charles Peake and in Sam's, the Hon. William Phillips (universally known as Uncle Billy), and with our departments. Much, however, was left to our own discretion in following our directives and in keeping General Morgan fully informed. It was a fascinating job and proved a most fortunate one for me because both Freddie Morgan and Sam Reber remained close friends of mine until their deaths.

Such was my work at S.H.A.E.F. up to the eve of D-Day.

From the moment I was informed of the date of the forthcoming 'Operation Overlord', life became a nightmare for me. I was obsessed by the fear that, through some hideous inadvertence, I might betray the secret, and I know that many others felt as I did. Security was necessarily very strict and became stricter as time went on. The assembly areas for the invading armies were cut off from communication with the outside world, save only under exceptional circumstances. For the first occasion in modern times the immunity of the diplomatic bag was suspended and communication between foreign missions with their governments was subject to censorship. All southern England became an armed camp, and as my friend and fellow Malvernian, the late John Moore has so poignantly written:

> And lo, on Hampshire hill and Devon combe
> The beacons spoke to friend and enemy.
> The call to arms was lit on gorse and broom
> That time when all hills ran towards the sea.
>
> I never saw the lanes look lovelier.
> The English earth was prodigal as we,
> Sparing no umbelled flower nor crucifer
> That time when all lanes led towards the sea.

So deeply was I imbued with the need for secrecy that I dropped out of social life altogether. I wanted only to be with people who knew as much and more than I did about what was imminent and with whom I could talk with freedom. I worked late at my office, got a tardy meal at one of my clubs and sought refuge in my hotel bedroom. It was the life of an exile from society.

One relaxation only I permitted myself. When we were three young men in our early twenties, of whom I was the youngest, Michael Arlen and I used to meet at the Café Royal for periodic lunches and he then introduced me to Noël Coward. Gradually as they rose to fame we drifted apart but I had kept up friendly relations with both of them and, as I have recounted, Dikran (Michael) had been a tremendous help to me in Hollywood. With Noël Coward I had picked up connection only since my return to London where I found him in rooms at the Savoy and he welcomed me warmly.

It was here that I occasionally paused during this time of stress and strain as I walked back from Bush House to the Ritz. In Noël's sitting-room, where a few kindred spirits often gathered, I used to sit quietly and listen as he played old familiar favourites from *Bitter Sweet* and his other pre-war triumphs, as well as such songs as 'Don't put your daughter on the stage, Mrs Worthington' and 'Imagine the

Duchess's feelings', which had not yet been published. It was indeed a haven of peace in a naughty world and I was very grateful for it.

All our plans for P.W.E. were now complete, all that we waited for was the Big Day, which was originally set for Monday, 5 June 1944. We were all on the *qui vive*; then came the ill-tidings that the weather had turned against us and that the Supreme Commander had taken the courageous and momentous decision to postpone the invasion for twenty-four hours. Bruce, Dallas Brooks and I dined together on the night of the fifth, at the Savoy where Bruce, who revelled in this sort of thing, had booked a room under the name of 'Mrs Deacon'. At 10.0 p.m. we had a final meeting at Bush House at which Bruce took the Regional Directors into full confidence. He had had a hard day, part of the problems of which I had shared with him. There had been difficulties between the Foreign Office and the Ministry of Information and S.H.A.E.F. as to who should control the announcements by the Supreme Commander which were to be released at 10 o'clock next morning. There had also been difficulties between the Foreign Office, P.W.E. and General de Gaulle, as to *his* broadcast to the French people. Nerves were frayed, tempers had run high, but at last all seemed to be composed.

Somewhere about midnight I returned to the Ritz and went to bed. I was too tense, too imaginative for slumber. After all the fate of the world might hang in the balance in a few hours' time. Finally about four o'clock I did drop off but by seven o'clock I was roused by Bruce telephoning to say that the German radio had already announced that the Allies had landed in France. My first reaction, I remember, was one of supreme relief. All our plans were now in operation. The greatest invasion the world had ever seen had begun – and I was released from my nightmare of the danger of breaking security! By noon we heard from S.H.A.E.F. that the landings had been exceptionally successful and there was a general relaxation all round. 'Victory,' as King George VI once wrote in his diary, 'is a good cure for nerves,' and we had at least won the first round.

But scarcely had we had time to savour the welcome taste of our success in establishing a bridge-head on the beaches, when Hitler launched the first of his 'secret weapons', the V-1.

I must confess that these diabolical machines of death scared me skinny. The Blitz had been terrible but there had been a certain exhilaration about it; and when the V-2s were later loosed upon us, one at least knew that if you heard them you had a chance and if you didn't you were dead. These wretched V-1s, however, 'Doodlebugs' as they came to be named, were quite different. There was something eerie about a pilotless aircraft which had a distinctive noise and then shut off as it began its descent and exploded shatteringly on impact. They had the malevolence of an H. G. Wells mechanical monster or a figment of Karel Capek's imagination. It almost seemed that, though they might not have pilots, they did have an uncanny sense of direction which could change with terrifying effect.

I remember my first encounter with them when I was walking up Haymarket and one came over, fairly high up. I increased my pace and turned into Piccadilly, whereupon the wretched thing turned with me. Fortunately it overshot me and came down in Hyde Park, but there seemed to be something personal about its behaviour.

On another occasion, I recall, I was in a taxi in St James's Square when one of the infernal things came over and as one man the driver and I were out of the cab and taking cover underneath it in comradely company.

The V-1s had also a beneficial side to them, if only a temporary one. They brought out the unashamed self-protective instinct in all of us. One warm and sunny afternoon I was in the throes of a tripartite meeting with the Americans and the Russians at Bush House on the subject of a co-ordinated propaganda policy to Germany. The Soviet representatives, two intransigent 'boot-faced' individuals in drab uniform, though I thought they were really civilians militarily disguised, had been at their most obstructive and we had seemingly been wrangling for hours. We could record no progress whatsoever.

Suddenly the menacing sputter of an approaching V-1 became audible. Then it cut off and as one man we went under the table. I found myself gazing into the scared blue eyes of the blond Ukrainian colonel with whom I had been arguing interminably all day, and I knew that I felt no more courageous than he did. The V-1 exploded in a different part of London, though near enough to rock our building, and when we all emerged, rather sheepishly, from our shelter, it was to find that a remarkable degree of accommodating co-operation had become manifest among us as a result of what Mr Kipling has so aptly called 'Ties of Common Funk'. We actually reached unanimous agreement on several of the points that had appeared impossible to concur upon earlier in the day, and we parted with the mutual amiability of those who have shared a common danger. I am bound to admit, however, that, with the dawning of the morrow, the spirit of amiability had evaporated and the Russians took back all the concessions they had made under the influence of fear.

It is true too that these horrible inventions evoked certain selfish elements in a human make-up. There was a tendency after one of these flying bombs cut out, to wait in agonised silence until one heard the explosion somewhere else and then to breathe a sigh of relief. There was a spirit of 'I'm all right, Jack' which, although most understandable, was not edifying. We discovered that, as a people, we were very tired, and that we had got used to the absence of bombing which had come upon us with the Nazi invasion of Russia in June 1941. There had been, to be sure, certain sporadic raids but nothing like the intensity of the Blitz, and to have the 'air-front' reopened with bombing by night and by day was not good for the national morale. We went short of sleep and the greatest kindness any friend could extend was to invite one down to the country for a good night's repose.

Dick Law (now Lord Coleraine), then Minister of State in the Foreign Office, was generous enough to do this one week-end in asking me down to his place in Sussex, over which the V-1s regularly passed but had never fallen. It was like heaven to get down to the peace of a part of England which although it has seen much fighting is also steeped in a rural tranquillity which seems ageless. I went to bed early with the promise of a good night's sleep, but unfortunately this was not to be. Unknown to us all, General Pile, commanding the defences of London, had moved the outer anti-aircraft barrage to exactly our locality. With the appearance of the first V-1, all hell broke loose. The bag was a good one and one of them fell and exploded in the meadow which was overlooked from my bedroom window! So much for a night of rest, but I was nonetheless very grateful to Dick for the kindness of his thought.

My last and major conclusion with a 'flying-bomb' was too close to be comfortable. I had come into my office at Bush House, having slept badly and feeling considerably below par. At lunchtime I told Bruce that I thought I would have a sandwich at the bar of the Waldorf Hotel across the street and then get some sleep on the camp-bed which I kept in my room in case I had to be on night-duty. Bruce disapproved of this plan and told me I should be the better for a breath of fresh air. He would, he said, stand me lunch at the Carlton Grill. I accepted, I remember, with rather a bad grace.

The Carlton Grill at that time was one of the places to eat in London where one saw much history being made. The hotel, which had had such happy pre-war memories for many of us, had been bombed during the Blitz in a raid in the course of which several members of the Belgian government-in-exile had been killed. But though the superstructure had been wrecked, the grill, which was well below stairs and as safe a shelter as one might get, catered to a varied and distinguished clientele. One had one's own table there and rang up to release it if lunching or dining elsewhere. The King of Norway lunched there daily; 'Pug' Ismay was a regular customer, and in a corner there was always a large fat man, wearing clerical clothes and a white watered-silk stock, who was alleged to be the Primate of the Lithuanian Church. I suppose he was living off the offerings of the faithful or the Lithuanian equivalent of 'Peter's Pence', and it was obviously a substantial amount for he had a voracious appetite.

Bruce and I had a regular table there too, and we had just started our lunch when a page approached and said that Sir Robert Bruce Lockhart was wanted urgently on the telephone. 'You take it,' he said to me and I did so. When I returned it was to tell him that a V-1 had fallen at the bottom of Kingsway, very near to Bush House and that there had been casualties among our staff. We were lucky enough to get a taxi, which we had to abandon at the cordon in Aldwych which the police and A.R.P. people had thrown around the building. With the aid of our passes we were allowed through and then we met the first contingent of 'walking wounded' on their way to Charing Cross Hospital. They had received first aid at our own station but there were a fair sprinkling of bloody head-bandages and arms in slings and many walked with the Zombie-like gait of those in shock.

Our next encounter was at the entrance to Bush House. A bus had been almost exactly at the point of explosion which had neatly cut off its upper deck and had blown the occupants into a plane tree on the pavement. Many had been killed and the upper branches looked like a butcher's shop.

In silence, and feeling rather sick, we entered and climbed the stairs to our offices, the lifts having been immobilised by the explosion. Bruce's had escaped fairly lightly – windows broken, furniture smashed and disordered, but no major damage – but my room must have caught the full force of the blast. My office safe had been blown across the corridor (but had remained locked) and across the camp-bed, on which I should have been lying had it not been for Bruce's insistence, lay a steel girder and its twin had smashed my desk chair to smithereens, so that wherever I had been in the room I should have been almost certainly killed. It was, as the Duke of

Wellington remarked on a more important occasion, 'the nearest run thing you ever saw in your life.'

The liberation of Paris provides one of my most bewildering and muddled episodes of the war. By the middle of August rumours were rife in London that German resistance in France had virtually collapsed and that their evacuation of Paris was imminent. On Wednesday the twenty-third, General Koenig, commanding the F.F.I. (French Forces of the Interior) under Eisenhower's supreme authority, issued a communiqué that Paris had been liberated. This news went out on the French Service of the B.B.C. as a straight news item without 'editorial comment', because Bruce's instinct was that all was not well. I was at S.H.A.E.F. and received a message to ask Charles Peake for corroboration. There was none. The official oracle remained silent and it was rumoured that General Koenig had received a wigging.

I returned to Bush House to find that Bruce had seen Anthony Eden, 'Pug' Ismay and Orme (Moley) Sargent, then Deputy Under-Secretary at the Foreign Office, and that none of them had confirmation of or confidence in Koenig's statement. Moley, not a natural optimist, was apprehensive lest Paris should suffer the fate of Warsaw. Meantime the French members of the B.B.C. were already celebrating in no uncertain manner.

Next morning, Thursday, S.H.A.E.F. was still silent, Anthony Eden had agreed to record a broadcast in French, pending verification, but in the afternoon S.H.A.E.F. in a curt message announced to us that the French were not masters of the situation and that for practical purposes Paris was still in German hands. All our preparations were cancelled and Bruce and Moley went off to dine, leaving me to hold the fort. Scarcely had they left when a message arrived from the B.B.C. that President Roosevelt and Secretary of War Stimson had just broadcast messages on the recapture of Paris by the French. I relayed this to Bruce who ordered that the Eden broadcast should be put out at once. It was, and this united radio performance on the part of the Allied leaders touched off the world-wide rumour that Paris was free.

In far away Beirut, Ruth, then on leave from her base at Alexandria, was dining in the French Club and saw the outbreak of hysteria which greeted the news. So great was the celebration that she was compelled to stay in the club until the small hours of the morning, it being considered unwise for unprotected females to return to their billets. In any case, few French were, I gather, in a fit state to act as escorts.

Friday, 25 August dawned without solace. S.H.A.E.F. was still running mute. The French section, though sobering up, were still in the throes of euphoric enthusiasm – and hang-over. Everyone was insisting that Paris *must* be free, but nobody knew for sure, and General Koenig, having said his piece and blotted his copy-book, was vouchsafing nothing further. So the day passed and once again I was alone in the office. Then at about 9.30 I was rung up by the B.B.C. This, they said, was authentic. Paris was indeed free. General Choltitz, the German Commandant, had surrendered and General de Gaulle was already in the city.

The fantasy was over, but it was followed by a mild anticlimax. I rang through to Bruce at precisely the same moment that he rang through to me, with the result that we had a series of crossed lines and deadlocks. When this was finally resolved we hailed one another with delight, relief and exaltation.

When in mid-September S.H.A.E.F. moved to Paris, I had to become a commuter. I was flown in the smallest and least protected of machines and piloted by what seemed to me to be the youngest and most recently qualified officer in the R.A.F. or the United States Air Force. They were all trigger-happy and seemed to delight in taking risks which filled me with terror. For example they greatly enjoyed flying over the Channel Islands. These were still occupied by German forces who seemed to have inexhaustible supplies of flak, which they loosed off at us with equal enjoyment and enthusiasm. This mutual sport continued until one of my less fortunate American colleagues had his foot shot off, when a halt was called to these dashing adventures.

The main headquarters was in the Palace of Versailles, with the rear echelon in the Hotel Crillon. I shall never forget my return to Paris for the first time since the spring of 1939. I had asked for one day's leave so that I might renew my memories of a city which I had once known and loved well. This had been granted and I was soon sorry I had requested it.

I had left London early that morning, a battered, shattered city, pock-marked and scarred, war-weary and monstrously bored with the monotony of its wartime diet, however nutritious it might be. Yet, notwithstanding all this there was a spirit and a pride which was unshakeable and magnificent, a supreme faith in the ultimate victory in our test of endurance. Paris was anything but this. Plate glass windows gleamed in guilty splendour; the gravel paths in the

Tuileries gardens were raked with meticulous perfection and in the Bois sleek saddle-horses in splendid fettle flaunted their paces. Though they were cold and hungry, the Parisians looked smart and almost elegant beside the 'utility' outfits of most Londoners. The Resistance in Paris had been gallant and effective and in the last days of German occupation had fought fiercely. The fact remained, however, that, whereas General de Gaulle had given back to France, and especially to Paris, her fighting spirit, her panache and the arrogance of her egotism, she had not, then or at any later date, succeeded in rediscovering her soul. She is still searching for it, without success.

I slept that night at the Crillon where I had spent so many visits in the past. The place had been the seat of the Military Tribunal of the German Occupation authorities, and many had been condemned to death in those sumptuous public rooms in which all European society had once exercised its fancy and indulged its pleasure. The staff, all old familiar faces, though emaciated and worn, had worked long and hard to eliminate all traces of the enemy occupants, and now, wearing their liveries for the first time in four years, they stood ready to offer a heart-warming welcome. I was kissed on both cheeks by the *concierge* and saluted and my hand shaken by some half-dozen ancient retainers. It was a very moving moment, especially when the *concierge* whispered conspiratorially: 'Would Monsieur like a hot bath? They are not easy to get, but for Monsieur, one of our oldest clients, it can be arranged.' I realised that, under the prevailing conditions, I had been accorded an accolade of distinction. I accepted gladly and gratefully. They could do no more; they had given me of their best.

The same was true when I visited my favourite restaurant and my favourite book-shop. At the first I was made welcome almost like a lost son (though their only real son had been executed, I learned, in the Resistance and by the Vichy Militia – a particular cause of hatred), and made free of the house and what remained of its *caves*. Some of these had been walled up with their contents and we celebrated their liberation. The same technique had been adopted by my bookseller, a little old Armenian, now frail and worn but still full of good humour. In the past his shop had been famous for its supply of English and American, as well as French, editions, and in the back quarters there had been a little secluded room, beautifully furnished in the Louis XVI period where, if one were so disposed, one might browse through his priceless collection of high-class erotica. I asked him what had become of it during the occupation. 'Oh, I bricked up the archway,' he replied knowingly. 'My treasures are not for the

Boches who could not appreciate them. Now I have unbricked it for the Americans, though they too have no real taste – but they have plenty of money.'

At Versailles I found my old colleagues well established in offices which still bore traces of German equipment. I was made a member of Sir Arthur Tedder's mess in one of the most agreeable of circles. Tedder himself, Freddie Morgan, Charles Peake and Sam Reber, with two junior officers and myself. The two officers, one American and one British, were the mess managers and very efficiently they did it, but it would be scarcely possible to imagine two men of more different temperaments. The American, who came from Oregon, a very serious young man, made one trip into Paris and never ventured there again. He did not cease to sing the praises of Portland where he had a law practice and longed to return there. The other, a delightfully humorous, puckish, somewhat irreverent young R.A.F. officer, was Tedder's P.A. He feared none and found something to laugh at in nearly everything. Today he is a dignified and distinguished, though still delightfully humorous, ornament of the Bench – The Rt Hon. Lord Justice Scarman.

We were housed in the villa of the famous decorator Elsie de Wolff, Lady Mendl, and our surroundings were therefore highly tasteful. I remember, however, a large blood-stain on the stair-carpet which was alleged to be that of a German staff officer who had been assassinated by the Resistance in the last frantic rush of evacuation. On the terrace outside the drawing-room window was the camp-bed of Marshal Ney.

An invitation to dine at S.H.A.E.F. was the greatest favour one could bestow on a French friend, for they were very short of food. I used to dine at our mess, then return to Paris where I slept at the Crillon before flying back to London early the following morning.

Duff Cooper was then our Ambassador in Paris, having returned there with the General from Algiers and London, and on one occasion he most kindly gave me a lift back in his official car. He had been dining with the Supreme Commander, who appeared to have done him very well, for despite the scintillating brilliance of my conversation he fell into a deep sleep. It was a perfect night, bright moonlight, and as we drove through the Forest of Saint-Cloud the trees cast black shadows across the road. Petrol for civilians was virtually unobtainable even on the black market at that time and all sorts of vehicles were pressed into service from tricycles to a rickshaw. Suddenly I noticed driving towards us through the moonlit forest a hansom-cab drawn by a dilapidated old horse, very gone at the knees.

As it came abreast of us Duff suddenly woke up and began to apostrophise it: 'A hansom-cab, by God,' said he, ' "the gondola of London" Dizzy called it. It is said to be the ideal vehicle for love-making. If they tell you this, my dear Jack, don't believe them. The damned driver always opens the trap.' And he relapsed once again into slumber.

'How Jack's physique stood the strain and the bombing I do not know. He looked tired, and every day his face became more and more like the colour of yellow blotting-paper. But he worked harder than ever,' my Director-General was kind enough to write of me at this period. 'I owed him much. P.W.E. was a difficult department and Jack was the one man on whose judgement and loyalty I could rely implicitly.'

To tell the truth the problems, logistic and otherwise, of wearing three hats at once, especially when one of them was in Paris, was a very considerable strain and, like everyone else in England, I was dead tired. By 1945 Whitehall had lost much of its spring and efficiency and, in many cases, it was barely ticking over. In addition to fatigue and nervous strain, there was the disappointment caused by the fact that, when the Allied forces had overrun the launching sites of the V-1s, Hitler immediately weighed in with the V-2s.

We had all hoped that we could look forward to a period of at least moderate surcease, especially when Duncan Sandys announced on 7 September, with what proved to be unwarranted jubilation, that 'the battle of London is over'. It was bad luck for him that the first of the V-2s fell the very next day. These were dispatched from sites in the Netherlands and were, in fact, real bombs, with a much greater danger potential than their predecessors, because there was no defence against them. On the other hand, as I have said, they were less terrifying because there was none of that frightful 'cut-off' and deadly waiting which the V-1s had had. You simply could not know when the V-2 was coming.

To give some idea of what the people of London went through at this time it is worth remembering that, according to official statistics, the results of Hitler's 'secret weapons' were 15,760 killed and wounded and over 200,000 houses damaged and destroyed.

Both Bruce and I were showing signs of wear and tear and the ever-perceptive, understanding and considerate Brendan Bracken decided that something must be done about it. In July of 1944 he commandeered a small house belonging to Lady Yule, called Little Hansteads, mid-way between Watford and St Albans. It was a pleasant place with three bedrooms, two bathrooms, a dining-room, sitting-room and study. A small garden sloped down to the river Vale. It was peaceful enough and the only sign of the tragedy of war was that each evening we would see the bombers returning from their raids on Germany, flying in formation with gaps indicating the losses. We also saw part of the aerial armada on its way to take part in the ill-fated Battle of Arnhem.

Brendan's thoughtfulness was not only prompted for the welfare of our health by giving us an opportunity at least to sleep at night, but also for our safety and security. After the conclusion of the war in Europe, when we moved back to London, we were told that in the desperation of his final realisation of defeat, Hitler had evolved a crazy plan of dropping parachutists, who were dedicated Waffen-S.S. men, on suicide missions the object of which was to assassinate certain specified persons before they themselves were captured or killed. A list of those to be thus eliminated had been furnished by allied intelligence and it was found that both Bruce and I had the honour of figuring on it. Hence our rural retreat, though I have never quite understood why we were supposed to be safer when together in a rather isolated country house, albeit with a certain degree of security protection, than separately in hotels in London. Somehow I can never conceive of being assassinated in the Ritz.

However, as I was to discover after the war, this seemingly unlikely idea may have had some factual basis. When the Nazi documents fell into our hands there was found among them the 'Black List' of those who were to be liquidated in the event of a successful outcome of an invasion of Britain. I was flattered to find my name among them, albeit somewhat inaccurately described as: 'Bennett [sic] of the Royal Institute of International Affairs'.

More unpleasant than this potential though improbable threat to our life and limb was the fact that, while Bruce's nerve-induced skin trouble persisted in plaguing him, I at last succumbed to a severe attack of jaundice, which kept me house-bound for some weeks. I was still able to have papers sent down from the office by dispatch-rider and Bruce brought a further batch of them home with him each evening. What really did me most good was to be alone and quiet, though I was always delighted to greet an ebullient Bruce, who I knew, exhausted though he was, was putting on a special act to cheer me up and raise my spirits from that deep depression which is an inevitable concomitant of jaundice.

I see from my Visitors' Book that we did quite a little entertaining at our 'country seat'. Moley Sargent, and Van and Dick Law and Vernon Bartlett and numerous others spent nights with us to share the peace of our retreat, though we generally tried to keep our week-ends to ourselves. I remember particularly the Christmas of 1944, and its complicated repercussions. The Greeks, it will be remembered, were in the throes of a civil war following their liberation from the Nazis. It was felt necessary to resolve this chaos as quickly as possible lest 'Uncle Joe' should be tempted to back the Communist elements and thereby add Greece to his 'bag' of Balkan States, despite the 'Percentage Agreement' he had reached with Mr Churchill. This left Greece in what used to be called, but is now a dirty word, our 'sphere of influence'. Moley Sargent was then in charge of Southern Europe at the Foreign Office and throughout their journey down from London had regaled Bruce with the gloomiest and most apprehensive views on the Greek situation for which he saw no solution. 'Russia will have all the Balkan Peninsula,' he had said, 'and there is nothing we can do about it.'

This jeremiad continued throughout dinner and at nine o'clock we turned on the B.B.C. news, to hear the important announcement that the Prime Minister and Foreign Secretary were *en route* to Athens to sort out the situation and effect some settlement. Moley was furious. No word had been said to him of their projected move and here was he, the responsible official in the Foreign Office, without a clue as to what was in the minds of his chiefs. He was angry both on grounds of personal pique and also because of what he considered the discourtesy of Anthony Eden in not taking him into his confidence. We did our best to calm him down but he would not be placated and rumbled away for the rest of the evening like a petulant volcano about to erupt.

As a matter of fact, Mr Churchill's decision to go to Athens was taken virtually on the spur of the moment and even Anthony Eden had very little warning of their departure, which, of course, was shrouded in secrecy. It was a complete success and Winston and Anthony succeeded in setting up Archbishop Damaskinos as Regent and effected, at least temporarily, a reconciliation between all parties. For the record, let it be said, that Stalin behaved impeccably during this particular episode. Not a word of criticism of the British solution appeared in *Izvestia* or *Pravda*, whereas the British and American press fulminated like a clutch of angry chickens.

When I had at last recovered from my jaundice, I had every intention of resuming my crowded schedule, but Bruce had other ideas. 'I made him go on leave,' he had written 'but it needed two doctors to make him obey.' As a matter of fact, it took two doctors and the Secretary of State for Foreign Affairs. Anthony Eden summoned me and confronted me with the medical evidence Bruce had passed to him. 'You have got to go,' he said. 'Where do you want to go to?' 'Can I go anywhere I like?' I asked. 'Within reason,' he answered cautiously. 'Then I'd like to go to America and get married,' I said somewhat to his surprise. It was arranged therefore that I should go on both invalid and compassionate leave! I had to promise, however, to return at once if Bruce sent me a cable with a certain wording which would indicate that he needed me urgently.

I had heard on the grapevine that Ruth was due to come home to Virginia in the spring. I had not seen her for two years – not indeed since we had become engaged in the noise and squalor of Pennsylvania Station, New York – and I looked forward tremendously to this chance of our getting married. It was my idea that I would do my recuperating at the Arizona Inn at Tucson and then join her as soon as she had arrived in Charlottesville from Egypt, but things did not turn out quite as I had planned.

Aubrey Morgan too had succumbed to war strain and he and Constance had gone down to Cuernavaca to the enchanting house, called Casa Mañana, which her parents had built as a retreat from Mexico City when Mr Morrow had been American Ambassador there. They insisted that I should join them, saying that Isaiah Berlin would be coming later. I had been there with them earlier in the war and I knew how perfect a place it was, with its beautiful quiet gardens and its wonderful views of Popocatepetl and of the plains between. I accepted with more gratitude than I could express. It was something sublime to which to look forward. But first one had to get there.

The doctors had prohibited my flying, so there remained the *Queen Mary* which was due to sail from Greenock on 20 January, with a contingent of American wounded going 'States-side'. Having been provided with the most senior of priorities I was able to obtain a cabin to myself, a considerable luxury in wartime.

My travelling companion, also a victim of war-weariness, was Tommy Stone, who had been a much-liked colleague in London. He too had worn several hats, being the Canadian representative on P.W.E. and also No. 2 in the Canadian Mission to the allied governments in exile. 'I'm dining with ten Canadian diplomats this evening,' I had once remarked, 'and they're all called Tommy Stone.'

Tommy and I had known one another since 1927 when he had

been Private Secretary to Vincent Massey, the first Canadian Minister to Washington and later the first Canadian to be appointed Governor-General of his country. During the war Tommy's companionship had been a great joy to me. Together with Charles Ritchie who was No. 2 in the office of the High Commissioner (who happened again to be Vincent Massey!), Lester ('Mike') Pearson and Norman Robertson, he formed one of that little group of brilliant Canadian diplomats whom I had known and greatly liked for many years.

At this moment, however, Tommy and I entrained at Euston for Glasgow on 19 January 1945, with something of the feeling of boys let out of school. It was bitterly cold and I hope I may escape the charge of ostentation when I say I then possessed two fur-lined coats, one of which I lent to Tommy. I had also obtained one of the last bottles of the Ritz stock of Napoleon brandy. We were met at an early hour by a bright young Canadian Army officer who told us that the *Queen Mary* would not sail until the late afternoon and he therefore suggested that we spend the morning at our pleasure in Glasgow, then lunch at Greenock and then go on board; meantime a Canadian staff car was at our disposal.

We did just this. We dawdled in book shops and chemists and finally drove to a very pleasant little pub in Greenock, where a table was reserved for us for luncheon in a bay window overlooking the Firth: I was sitting facing the water, with Tommy on my right and the Canadian boy opposite me, with his back to the window. Suddenly, in a break in our conversation, I became aware of the *Queen Mary* making down stream towards the boom. 'Don't look now,' I remember saying, as if in a dream, 'but I think we've missed our ship.' Whereupon the Canadian officer turned the colour of an over-ripe Gorgonzola, plunged his hand into his breast pocket and withdrew an official envelope – unopened. He glanced at it then and became sticky about the lips. 'My God,' he said, 'I'm most terribly sorry, Sir; this arrived just as I was starting to meet you this morning and I forgot to open it. It says that the sailing time has been advanced by two hours.'

We did not stand upon the order of our going; we went. As we drove as if pursued by Furies to the dock where our baggage had been sent, a gleam of hope came to me, and I blessed the system of assimilated rank which obtained at S.H.A.E.F. Was I not a titular major-general and therefore equally a titular rear-admiral? And were not these ranks set forth on my movement order? It was just possible that I should indeed rank as the Senior Naval Officer on board; anyway it was our only chance.

'Can the officer in charge of the boom be reached by telephone?' I asked. It seemed that he could. Then call him up and ask him to hold the *Queen Mary* for half an hour. Explain why and get the admiral's barge alongside and our luggage stowed on board,' I told the agonised young Canadian, who seemed galvanised by the suggestion. Tommy Stone in re-telling the story, which he did frequently, always said that in the course of this interview he stood 'silent but admiring'. But, as I once caused Sir Gerald Campbell to say publicly, 'Nothing is more ferocious than a cornered sheep.' I have rarely felt more fierce, more ovine, or, indeed, more cornered, than at that moment.

The young Canadian carried out his orders to the letter. The *Queen Mary* stopped; the barge appeared and willing hands began to stow our baggage.

It was at this moment that an over-zealous *matelot* dropped Tommy Stone's Louis Vuiton wardrobe-trunk into the harbour.

Mercifully it remained just afloat long enough for boat-hooks and grappling-irons to be brought into play and with infinite effort it was dragged back on the barge, but with detriment to the paint-work which the midshipman in charge considered it would be difficult to explain away even in wartime. (Be it recorded in tribute to the great M. Vuiton that when opened not even a pair of Tommy's socks was damp. The trunks were advertised as water-proof and they were.)

In addition to the cold, it was now blowing great guns and the sea even within the Firth was very rough. There were moments when our quarry was hidden by clouds of spray and flying spume. I felt sicker and angrier at every heave and moment.

Finally we arrived. It was not until one had seen the *Queen Mary* from water-level that one realised to the full her majestic proportions and her awe-inspiring height. She seemed vast in length and gigantic in her loftiness. A tiny aperture about three quarters of the way up her side opened and from it descended a rope-ladder, which fell smartly into our barge. I gazed in horror at the ascent. Then I turned to the Canadian. 'You're the junior officer, therefore you embark first. Up you go. 'But I'm not travelling,' he answered. I am not, I think, a naturally brutal man but the after-effects of jaundice rarely make for a 'sunny temperament;' I had been tried hard that day and I was feeling very sick. 'No,' I said to our miserable and abject young escort, 'but you're going to apologise in person to the S.N.O. for all the trouble you've caused. You're going up and you're coming down again.' 'My God,' he said with great fervour. 'Mine too,' I answered. 'Get going.'

To climb a rope-ladder up the side of the *Queen Mary* in a rough sea, wearing a fur-coat (astrakhan collar and all!), with a bottle of Napoleon brandy in the pocket, and a black *chapeau Eden*, and encumbered by an umbrella and a brief-case has remained with me as a vision of hell which I trust never to encounter again. My impedimenta were lashed to me so that my hands were free. I was boosted on to the ladder with the rise of the barge on a wave. I remembered not to look down and I climbed upward for what seemed an interminable period, swinging from side to side in the wind and praying fanatically when I had time. At last I saw faces above me and heard Tommy shouting encouragement. (He, by the way, had gone up with the agility of a chamois, but had left his brief-case in the barge, whence we had to rescue it later. It was not any of our days!) My hands were seized in a friendly grasp and I went aboard, I am proud to say, in an upright position. A glass of neat brandy was pressed upon me, and Tommy and I were whisked up in the lift to the captain's quarters, where I recovered sufficiently to enquire for our Canadian officer. He, it appeared, had arrived on hands and knees – no welcoming grip for him! – and remained prone for sometime. His apology had been accepted and I thought he had been disciplined sufficiently. In any case he was in no condition to cope with the rope-ladder again, so we arranged for him to be lowered down to the barge with a loop round his shoulders. I daresay he got safely back to Greenock. I have never seen or heard of him since.

We took six days to cross the Atlantic in one of the worst storms I can remember. At one moment we had to heave to, despite the fact that a U-boat 'wolf-pack' was known to be in our vicinity, but had the captain continued to ride out the storm the ship would have been very badly damaged. I had crossed many times in the *Queen Mary* before the war and was to do so many times more later, but this was a passage unique for something more than the weather. She was a hospital ship crammed with young Americans on crutches, in splints and bandages, all thankful to be alive, all glad that they were out of the war and all longing to get back to their 'mums' and 'dads', their 'sweet-hearts and wives', in New England or Dixie, or Chi' or 'Frisco. They were incredibly cheerful and wonderfully compassionate and helpful to one another as we pitched and tossed our way across the ocean. I have seen two men with three legs and two arms between them keeping one another upright in the nature of a drunkard's promenade, but cheerfully and carefully, and the surgeons told me of the amazing courage and patience of those who were 'bed-bound' in the sick-bay. Each evening we foregathered in the great hall, most of us sitting on the deck, for chairs were not plentiful enough to go round and were naturally reserved for those who needed them most. There we would watch movies, old and new, or sometimes sing in chorus songs which had become famous during the First World War and the few that had emerged from the Second. *Lili Marlene* still recalls these occasions to me. Or we would just sit and talk, chiefly about home, and they would shyly show one photographs of their wives and children or their girl-friends. The conversation was usually about the future and one could not help wondering how many of their dreams would be fulfilled.

We landed in New York on 26 January, and I spent a week recovering and realising how very ill I had been and how very tired I was. Then I went to Mexico City with joy in my heart at the prospect of seeing Aubrey and Constance again.

With their usual kindness and foresight they had sent a car to the airport to drive me the some fifty miles to Cuernavaca, and, to make recognition easier, Con had told the Mexican driver to look out for a man with a 'slight stutter'. This he chose to understand as a 'small daughter', and some confusion was caused and time consumed by my failure to produce this expected form of identification! Aubrey has always said that I arrived at the great wooden and iron nail-studded gateway of Casa Mañana 'petulant as a snapping turtle and asking irritably "What's all this about my daughter"'! I hope I was more courteous than this.

I cannot describe the delight of the next few weeks. How glorious it was to do nothing and to do it in the sun, amid beautiful surroundings and in the company of two and later three, of the nicest people in the world. Cuernavaca was still undiscovered by tourists in those days, and life was simple, happy and restful. Wednesday was band-night in the plaza and we would go down to listen to a ragged local orchestra in a somewhat dilapidated bandstand playing strange tunes which, if one listened carefully, were recognisable as Viennese waltzes and polkas introduced during the reign of Maximilian and Carlotta. There were no scores, so obviously they were handed down from memory from father to son, like Homer's tales of past heroes.

We sat in the gardens either gossiping, arguing or just being silent together, for our friendship is of that nature, though when Isaiah arrived, welcomed by all of us, there was not quite that same degree of hushed contemplation. We drove about the surrounding country to charming forgotten places like Quatla, where a warm sulphur stream bubbles out of the very bowels of Popocatapetl, and which has been respected for its curative powers since the days of Montezuma. It was an unforgettable episode in my life; memorable chiefly for the pleasure of friendship and the joy of peace. But like all good things it had to end.

We began our return to our various jobs in the middle of March, the first stage taking us as far as St Louis, Missouri, a four days' rail journey. We crossed the border into the United States at Laredo, Texas, where we encountered the vigilance of the Immigration Service and the F.B.I. Though our papers were in perfect order we had to answer a questionnaire giving the more intimate details of our lives.

'Where were you born?' an official asked Isaiah. 'In Riga,' was the unexpected reply. 'Where is that?' came the suspicious query. Isaiah was feeling puckish that day. 'It is,' he replied with literal accuracy, 'a port of the Eastern Baltic.' 'Who does it belong to?' With the air of one delivering a lecture to a backward class, Isaiah answered, 'My native country of Latvia, when I was born in it in 1909, was indeed a part of the Russian Empire. However, during the First World War it was annexed, along with the other Baltic States, by Germany under the Treaty of Brest-Litovsk, but only, as you doubtless recall, for a short time. At the Peace Conference the independence of these states was recognised and they remained in this happy state until re-annexed by Russia in 1940. However, they were reoccupied by the Germans in 1941.' 'Are you a German then?' the F.B.I. man interrupted. 'Certainly not,' was Isaiah's emphatic answer. 'Allow me to proceed. I understand that these lands are about to be "liberated", I believe that is the word, by Soviet troops. After the war is over who knows? who knows?' 'But,' said the F.B.I. man, sticking to his original question, 'they are part of Russia, aren't they?' 'So you would think and so I personally believe,' replied Isaiah, 'but I assure you that there is a Latvian diplomatic mission in Washington which is still in relationship with your government.' 'Now listen,' said the voice of Justice, now 'faint but pursuing', 'are you a Soviet citizen?' 'Certainly not,' repeated Isaiah, with immense dignity. 'I am a subject of His Britannic Majesty, and if you will look at my passport, which you are holding in your hand, you will see that I am an official of the British Foreign Office'.

This was game, set and match and the exhausted representative of the F.B.I. withdrew, muttering something about, 'Why didn't you say so in the first place.' I note from my diary that our halt in Laredo occupied ten hours. I attribute most of this delay to Isaiah's sense of humour.

At last we reached St Louis and I was able to telephone to Ruth in Charlottesville, where she had but recently arrived by air from Egypt, via the Sudan, West Africa and Brazil. She was as anxious as I was for us to get married and we arranged to do so as soon as I could get to her, which was not for three or four days. Then it was fast work, but as a result of the superb organisation of Ruth and her mother, whom I adored, and the efficient and kindly co-operation of our friends, we were at last married in the Chapel of the University of Virginia on Monday, 26 March 1945.

It was no ordinary wedding, because so many of our friends were on active service including the local rector whom we would have liked to perform the ceremony. But there were enough to make it a gay and, I honestly believe, a rather glamorous affair. My best man was my oldest friend in Virginia, Robert Kent Gooch ('Bobbie' to all), a former Rhodes Scholar at Christ Church and then head of the Department of Political Science at The University; Isaiah represented my family on the bridegroom's side of the aisle. Some of Ruth's many beaux actually went A.W.O.L. in order to be present.

Thanks to Mr Jefferson's wisdom in making his University non-denominational and in forbidding religious instruction to be included in its curriculum, we were eventually married by a Presbyterian Minister reading the Episcopalian service.

We were both about to embark on new adventures.

These adventures did not have a wholly felicitous beginning. Scarcely had Ruth and I begun our honeymoon when I received through the Embassy the specially worded cable from Bruce Lockhart recalling me to duty. As my promise to obey this signal had been the only condition placed upon my going on leave in the first place, I was, of course, in duty bound to do so, and having dispatched my bride of only a few days 'back to mother', I left Baltimore by sea-plane for England. I arrived in Bermuda the same afternoon in the most dazzlingly beautiful weather – and there I remained for the next seven days. Heavy storms over Poole and over New York prevented our going either forward or back; meantime the weather in Bermuda remained perfect and I was alone to enjoy it. An added trouble was that because of security I was not permitted to telegraph to Ruth or let her know of my whereabouts and, as I had promised to cable from England on arrival, I knew she would be anxious. Eventually it was owing to the kindness of my host, the Governor,

Lord Burleigh (later Marquess of Exeter), that a message of reassurance was sent to her.

Lord Burleigh was most kind and sympathetic in every way to an enforced guest who, having been invited for an overnight stop, stayed for a week, and would not hear of my moving to a hotel. He provided every form of diversion available and so I possessed my soul in patience and, like Ferdinand the Bull, 'just sat quietly and smelled the flowers'. However, I never ceased to tease Bruce Lockhart about his compelling me to spend my honeymoon in Bermuda by myself.

When I eventually reached London on 16 April, I discovered what it was that had caused all this pother. Among my duties as Assistant Director-General of P.I.D. one had been to keep in touch with any approaches which might be made by the German Resistance movement, many of whom I knew personally, and also to be ready to comment on any peace-feelers which should emanate from the German Government. I had to provide briefs for Bruce at his meetings with the Committee of Ministers, and he knew that my views did not always coincide with those of the Foreign Office.

It had always been thought that during the Phoney War, we might have reached a negotiated peace with a non-Nazi Germany which had restored the *Rechtsstaat* and also agreed to re-establish the frontiers of the Reich as they had been in 1937. There might have been, perhaps, a certain latitude in respect of the Polish Corridor. Any possibility of this had faded with the opening of the Blitzkrieg in May 1940 and had vanished altogether with the enunciation of the principle of Unconditional Surrender (with which I wholeheartedly agreed), at Casablanca in January 1943. I had always emphasised that we should never make promises to the German Resistance. This had been the fatal mistake in November 1918 when the correspondence between President Wilson and the German Chancellor, Prince Max of Baden, preliminary to the German surrender, had been subsequently interpreted as a 'Pre-Armistice Agreement', by which, the Germans claimed, an understanding had been reached for far more lenient peace terms than were ultimately imposed by the Treaty of Versailles. Almost all German Chancellors from Ebert to Hitler had made play with this thesis, and it seemed to me vital that there should be no similar misunderstanding or misinterpretation this time. The German army must be convinced of their overwhelming defeat in the field and the German people must have brought home to them Dietrich Bonhoeffer's courageous admission: 'We do not wish to escape repentance.'

I therefore insisted that any attempt to overthrow Hitler and the

Nazi régime must be undertaken by the German people themselves alone and unaided, in Bonhoeffer's words, their 'action must be considered as an act of repentance.' There must be no bargaining with the Resistance, and, though every encouragement should be given them to perform this 'act of repentance' it must be 'for the very deed's sake' and unaccompanied by any preliminary promises. As I had said to Brüning in 1943 (and had raised his great resentment thereby), the German Resistance must do their own job in their own way and alone, and then, having gone through the process of Unconditional Surrender, must trust to the judgement of the Allied Powers as to the future of Germany.

All this became academic after the failure of the coup of 20 July 1944, and I remember being summoned on the following day by Lord Cranborne (later Marquess of Salisbury), then Under Secretary of State for Foreign Affairs, and his P.P.S., Paul Emrys Evans, to talk to them about it. I said that in the long run it was a good thing that the coup had failed. It was regrettable that so many 'good Germans', some of whom I had known personally, and who might have played a useful part in a new Germany, had sacrificed their lives in vain, but had they succeeded the complications would have been incalculable. At once there would have arisen rival schools of thought in both Britain and America advocating a 'soft' as against a 'hard' peace with the New Germany, which would have missed no chance of playing one off against the other. And the inevitable clash with the Soviet Union would have produced its own problems. On the whole, I said, I believed that things were better as they were and that the war should end with the Unconditional Surrender of the Third Reich.

Events of history, therefore, had removed one of my duties but there remained the second and it was in this connection that Bruce Lockhart had summoned me home. By January 1945 Himmler had seen the writing on the wall. His dread of defeat envisaged the nightmare of the Reich being handed over to the Russians, and he got in touch with Count Folke Bernadotte, representing the Swedish Red Cross. They held secret meetings in and around Berlin in February and again in early April. Allied intelligence was informed, and it was in anticipation of the second encounter that Bruce had sent his telegram.

When I arrived in London on 16 April, I found that Bruce had retired to his Scottish retreat at Grantown with a recurrence of his nervous dermatitis, and was in great discomfort. He had left instructions for me to keep in touch with the Foreign Office and to come up to report to him if occasion demanded. I have recounted the story, as we knew it, in *The Semblance of Peace* in some detail; but, briefly, Count Bernadotte and Himmler met at Lübeck on 23 April and a tentative proposal was put forward that the Führer should be declared *non compos mentis* and that the German forces in Northern Europe and in Italy and Yugoslavia should surrender unconditionally to the Western Allies but not to the Soviet Union. These terms were communicated by the Count to the Swedish Foreign Office and by them to the British and American Ministers and were in the hands of the British Government by the twenty-fifth. After consultation between President Truman and Mr Churchill it was agreed that no such capitulation could be considered unless made to all three of the principal allies and that Stalin should be informed at once. Thereafter the whole thing petered out, and the next that was heard of Himmler was that he had personally surrendered to the British and had committed suicide by taking poison during medical examination, unrecognised by his captors.

I was given the outline of this exchange to take to Bruce in Scotland, which I did at the end of April. I found him a sick man, depressed and weary. I wished I could stay to cheer him up, but I could only spare twenty-four hours before returning to London to resume my other hat with the E.A.C. I do not propose to repeat here what I have also written in detail in *Semblance of Peace*, of the shambles which attended the actual circumstances of Unconditional Surrender, nor the fate with which our E.A.C. labours met, through no fault of their own but as a result of the acceleration of the pace of history. The work of William Strang and his colleagues, however, proved of great subsequent value as guidance for the activities of the Allied Control Commission for Germany.

We were not to achieve peace, however, without the seemingly inevitable wrangle over communications. Bruce returned to London from Scotland on Saturday, 5 May and the following day was spent in an atmosphere slightly reminiscent of that which preceded the liberation of Paris. Word came privately that the Unconditional Surrender of the German armies had been signed at Rheims by Jodl on behalf of the High Command in the early hours of that morning. No representative of the rump régime of Grand-Admiral Doenitz at Flensburg had been present, as it was not considered that its writ could be said to run throughout the Reich. The official word was that the formal announcement of V.E.-Day would be made at 6 p.m. London time but until then complete secrecy must be preserved. We waited in feverish impatience, but an hour later came a second message to the effect that, in order to placate Stalin, who wanted to delay the announcement of victory until after the Soviet Armies had had their parade in Berlin, the B.B.C. would continue to be gagged until 3 o'clock on the following day (7 May). Great was the feeling of frustration and disappointment, but before nightfall two events had occurred which gave general satisfaction. The first was the daring of an American correspondent at S.H.A.E.F. who broke the order for secrecy and revealed the fact of the surrender. The second was provided by the last of the Nazi Foreign Ministers, Count Lutz von Krosigk, a former Rhodes Scholar who had entered von Papen's cabinet in 1932 as Minister of Finance and had remained so until after Hitler's suicide thirteen years later. Doenitz had then appointed him to his present position and he now broadcast the news of Unconditional Surrender to the German people. In the welter of argument which had ensued between London, Washington and Moscow as to when the official announcement should be made, the possibility of the German government getting a 'news beat' had been overlooked.

Jubilantly the B.B.C. gave the whole story on the six o'clock news as had originally been arranged and at once the British and American public and all liberated Europe began to celebrate, though there was nothing comparable to the scenes in London on 11 November 1918. We were in effect all so tired that the reaction of many was simply one of relief.

Mr Churchill's victory broadcast on the following day (7 May) came regretfully as something of an anticlimax since he told us what we now all knew. But we all wanted to hear it from his lips, in that well-remembered voice which had sounded defiance, encouragement and confidence to the world, but especially to Britain, during those five long, terrible, anguished years. We wanted to hear him say: 'The War in Europe is over,' and who will forget his closing words: 'Advance Britannia! Long live the cause of Freedom! God save the King.'

Hostilities ceased officially at one minute past midnight, that is to say at the first moment of 8 May, and for this reason V.E.-Day has always had an additional significance for me, for it happens to be Ruth's birthday.

On the morrow, however, there were soberer thoughts. In their broadcasts to their respective peoples both Mr Churchill and President Truman had warned that though the war in Europe had been won, the war in the Pacific still awaited victory. Though the Japanese forces had suffered crushing defeats by land and sea and air, they were still expected to put up a fiercely fanatical resistance in defence of their homeland against invasion. I learned subsequently that the United States Chiefs of Staff had estimated half a million Allied casualties alone in such an operation. Everyone in temporary government service was therefore required to sign on for a minimum of eighteen months when, it was said somewhat vaguely, 'the position would be reviewed'.

Though anxious and willing to remain as a temporary civil servant as long as I was wanted, I suddenly found myself at something of a loose end. P.W.E. was being cut down and reorganised to meet the new conditions of war. Many of its experts joined the British element of the Control Commission and the Allied Information Services in Europe. A small force of oriental experts remained but although I have always had a deep interest in the Orient, I could certainly not claim to have any expertise in this area.

Moreover the two organisations in liaison with which I had represented P.W.E. had disappeared. The E.A.C. really ceased to exist after the Unconditional Surrender of Germany – though it continued theoretically until replaced by the Conference of Foreign Ministers created by the Potsdam Conference. S.H.A.E.F. had similarly disintegrated from the same moment, when the British and American armies moved into their respective zones of occupation.

In looking back over some thirty years I believe that P.W.E. did its job with remarkable overall success. This was due to the combination of a brilliant and imaginative Director-General and a staff of which I have already written with the highest praise. I think, in retrospect, that our efforts to undermine the morale of the German people were not very effective until the tide of victory had turned and we were able to demonstrate conclusively that ultimate defeat was creeping nearer and nearer. Even then our most powerful weapon was epitomised in Bruce's basic instruction: 'Stick to the truth,' which is I am sure the secret of successful propaganda. All the same, it was proved to me that there was much to be said for old von Clausewitz' axiom that 'the best way of waging political warfare is to capture the enemy's capital'.

With the more clandestine P.W.E. activities of 'Black Propaganda' I had little or nothing to do, save that I knew about them. In so far as Germany was concerned, these were under the direction of Sefton (Tom) Delmer, who had been the correspondent of the *Daily Express* in Berlin before and after the Nazi Revolution. I had known him there and had been impressed, as I have told in *Knaves, Fools and Heroes*, by the fact that, contrary to most of his colleagues, Tom had adopted the technique of 'Know thine enemy'. He had infiltrated the Nazi Party to a remarkable degree and had acquired an intimate and unique knowledge of the characters and foibles of its leaders. This he and his staff now exploited to the full in an invaluable contribution to the work of P.W.E., and he has left a guarded account of his work in an autobiographical volume, *Black Boomerang*.

In our second objective, however, that of encouraging the enslaved peoples of the occupied countries, I am sure that our record of success was very high indeed. In the early days of Nazi victories, which almost justified the belief of the falterers in the invincibility of the Wehrmacht, those brave enough to listen to our broadcasts were first encouraged by them, then inspired and finally largely directed in their opposition to the enemy and in their confidence in an ultimate allied victory. Here Themistocles was proved justified in his appeal to the Ionians 'to damage the Barbarians' cause in battle, and bring confusion among them'.

Within our limits, we contributed our bit to the defeat of Hitler and the Nazi Reich, but I think that we all realised that the share of psychological warfare was but a small one. Just as intelligence must be the ancillary of policy, so psychological warfare must be the handmaiden of intelligence. I am glad to think, however, that Intelligence was both aware and fully appreciative of our efforts.

I have never ceased to be proud that I was permitted to belong to so hard-working, effective and dedicated a company, and, if temperament flared up (as it occasionally did), this was provoked more by professional competition than personal jealousy.

I was not left long in doubt as to my future. The decision had been taken at the highest level that the major Nazi war criminals should be tried before an International Military Tribunal with power to inflict the death sentence. It was necessary to prepare the British case in preparation for the prosecution and the Government set up for this purpose an interdepartmental body called the War Crimes Executive under the chairmanship of the then Attorney-General Sir David Maxwell-Fyfe (later Lord Chancellor and Earl of Kilmuir), which began its labours in June. David Maxwell-Fyfe was kind enough to invite me to join as an 'independent member', and thus began my connection with the Nuremberg Trials, of which I shall write in my third volume.

Meantime events began to move with increasing velocity, changing all our lives. On 15 June the National Government, which Mr Churchill had led with such skill and devotion since May 1940, resigned and Parliament was dissolved. Polling Day was on 5 July, but in order that the votes of the troops overseas might be counted, the results were delayed for three weeks. The Potsdam Conference, the last occasion on which the heads of the Three Great Powers would meet as allies, opened on 17 July, and the day previously President Truman received the first report that an atomic device had been exploded successfully. The results of the British elections announced on 26 July marked the decisive rejection of Mr Churchill and the Tory Party and placed Labour in office with an over-all majority for the first time in history. On the same day the Potsdam Ultimatum to Japan was issued calling on her to surrender unconditionally and on 6 August the first atom bomb was dropped on Hiroshima to be followed three days later by the second bomb on Nagasaki. Our world had been made and remade in eight short weeks.

On 10 August, the B.B.C. picked up a message put out by the Domei Agency from Tokyo that Japan had accepted unconditional surrender. It was unofficial and unconfirmed but it set rumours aflame. For five days nothing official was forthcoming – never did the news of victory seep out in such a fragmentary fashion as that of V.-E. and V.-J. day – and we longed for something definite. It came eventually in Mr Attlee's dry and unemotional voice, very different from Mr Churchill's rolling periods, but none the less impressive in its way. The greatest war the world had ever seen was over.

On this night of 14 August Bruce and I dined together. Little Hansteads had been abandoned at the end of July, when its usefulness had clearly been exhausted, and he had moved into the Ritz with me. It was a hot night and after dinner we sat out on the balcony of my sitting-room overlooking Piccadilly. Outside there was jubilation, though, again, it was muted. I do remember, however, seeing three naval officers of fairly senior rank solemnly dancing round a small fire which they had kindled on a traffic-island in the middle of the street. Every so often they would break off to fan the dying embers into fresh life by fanning them with their white-topped service caps, and then resume their terpsichorean ritual.

We sat talking over old episodes of the war; sometimes just sitting quietly and thinking about the future and what it held for us. We had been in some tight corners together. Bruce had been a fine chief and continued to be a good friend. During the past few days both of us had been invited to remain in the Foreign Office with our respective ranks and we had both declined on grounds of health. Bruce was a really sick man often in acute pain and owed it to himself and his friends to restore his health before anything else. He wanted to resume his literary career when he was well again. I had developed a 'tired heart' which had caused me to faint in my office on several occasions to the alarm of my secretaries, and this could only be cured by a period of rest. I was rising forty-three in age and I had no desire to remain in the civil service, much as I respected them, in time of peace, nor did I hanker after a professionally academic career. What I wanted more than anything else was to rejoin Ruth and resume our married life which had been so rudely interrupted, and Bruce had assigned me the job of winding up the affairs of our department in New York, whither I was to fly the following day.

At last shortly after midnight, there was a louder shouting in the streets and somebody called out, 'It's over at last. Attlee's spoken.' There were cheers and singing and Bruce went to ring up Bush House. Back came the duty-officer's reply: 'Yes, sir, Mr Attlee has just broadcast the official announcement of Japan's surrender.'

Even though we had known it for some days the sense of relief that it was 'official' was enormous. Then one began to think. A week before we had heard Sir John Anderson broadcast after the dropping of the first bomb, which precipitated us, all unknowing, into the benefits and perils of the Nuclear Age,

A new door has for the first time been prised open [he had said]. What lies on the other side remains to be seen. The possibilities for good or ill are infinite. There may, on the other hand, be a veritable treasure-house awaiting fruitful development in the interests of mankind. There might, on the other hand, be only the realisation of a maniac's dream of death, destruction and desolation. God grant that it may not prove to be so.

We could not know then that the peace of the world would remain intact for the next thirty years only by the very fear of John Anderson's apocalyptic vision. But he had said enough to 'give one seriously to think'. On any showing the Second World War had left behind it a far greater inheritance of chaos than had the First, and already one of our principal partners in victory was menacing our chances of effecting a lasting settlement. We, the British, were exhausted physically and mentally, financially imperilled, economically insecure and with a disintegrating Empire. Perhaps the blessings of the Nuclear Age would bring success and prosperity; perhaps not. At home a Socialist administration, virtually unskilled in the art of government and statesmanship, was faced not only with the inevitable problems of post-war reconstruction, which would in themselves prove overwhelmingly difficult, but also saddled with its self-imposed mission of pursuing with vigour that Social Revolution in England which had begun with Mr Lloyd George's 'People's Budget' of 1909. Though we were now spared the perils of war, the horrors of peace loomed all too darkly.

I thought of Ruth and the sort of life we should live together, and where. This gave me comfort for we had our love for one another. Moreover we were of an age to have enjoyed, though, alas, not always together, the old world now vanished beyond recall, and we had memories of our separate pleasures which would last for ever. These would supply the foundation for our joint happiness as we faced the new world. We could not tell what the future held for us, but whatever it was we could meet it together. And, despite the dangers of having standards of comparison, we could find a sort of brave encouragement and consolation in the wisdom of Daniel Webster: 'The past at least is secure.'

How we succeeded in finding comfort in past memories and happiness in future adventures, I shall tell in my third volume.

Index

INDEX

British Broadcasting Corporation, 91, 155, 169, 185, 186, 191, 202
Bromfield, Louis, 30
Brooke, Rupert, 46
Brooklyn Eagle, 27
Brooks, Sir Dallas, 170, 181
Browder, Earl, 56
Brown University, 90, 91
Browning, Robert, 46
Bruce, David, 175
Brüning, Heinrich, 55, 56, 166–8, 200
Bryan family, 52
Bryce, Lord, 67
Buchan, John, 16, 53, 123; *Memory Hold-the-door*, 13–14
Budapest, 44, 138
Bullitt, William, 61–2, 131
Bullock, Alan, 172
Burleigh, Lord, *see* Exeter, Marquess of
Bushey Park, 176
Butler, Harold, 147–8
Butler, Sir James: *Lord Lothian*, 65, 94
Butler, Sir Nevile, 115, 118
Butler, Nicholas Murray, 26
Butler, Rose, 115

Caccia, Harold, 67
Cadogan, Alec, 103
Cairo, University of, 33
Calais, 106
Calder, Ritchie, 173
Cambridge, 33, 75, 147
Cambridge, Mass., 23, 30–6
Campbell, Sir Gerald, 117, 121–8, 141, 147, 194
Campbell, Sir Ronald, 124
Canada, 12, 16, 134
Canberra, 86
Čapek, Karel, 182
Cardiff, 75
Casablanca Conference (1943), 199
Casey, Rt Hon. Lord, 85, 97; *Personal Experience*, 118
Cecil, Lord Robert, 17
Cemetery Ridge, 11

Central Illinois Railroad, 29
Chamberlain, Joseph, 139–40
Chamberlain, Neville, 62, 66, 70, 117, 130, 151, 152
Chancellorsville, 53
Channel Islands, 186
Chaplin, Charles, 140
Charles, River, 34, 36
Charles II, 51
Charleston, 17, 23, 49, 51
Charlottesville, 19, 23, 35, 52, 55, 63, 70, 84, 96–7, 114, 147, 192, 198
Charterhouse, 75
Chatham House, *see* Royal Institute of International Affairs
Chautemps, Camille, 161
Chequers, 107
Chesapeake Bay, 119
Chicago, 23, 29–30, 70, 77–8, 130
Chicago Daily News, 70
Chicago Tribune, 70, 78
Childs, Stephen, 87
China, 46
Choltitz, Gen., 186
Chungking, 85
Churchill, Sir Winston S., 18, 86, 95, 98, 104, 107, 111, 112, 113, 114, 116, 117–18, 119, 121–2, 126, 138, 140, 152–3, 162, 165, 169, 170, 201, 202, 203, 205; *Their Finest Hour*, 111–12
Ciechenowsky, Jan, 88
City of Benares, 109
Clark, Sir Kenneth, 19
Clausewitz, Gen. Carl von, 149, 156, 203
Clemenceau, Georges, 17, 130
Cleveland, Ohio, Council on Foreign Affairs, 80–1
'Cliveden Set', 42, 66
Cockburn, Claud, 41–2
Cockburn, Adm. Sir George, 41
Colbert, Claudette, 136
Cole, Wayne: *Charles Lindbergh*, 132
Coleraine, Lord, 183, 191
Colman, Ronald, 137